OECD Tax Policy Reviews: Colombia 2022

OECD
BETTER POLICIES FOR BETTER LIVES

Please cite this publication as:
OECD (2022), *OECD Tax Policy Reviews: Colombia 2022*, OECD Tax Policy Reviews, OECD Publishing, Paris, https://doi.org/10.1787/054722db-en.

ISBN 978-92-64-70671-2 (print)
ISBN 978-92-64-67813-2 (pdf)

OECD Tax Policy Reviews
ISSN 2707-7691 (print)
ISSN 2707-7705 (online)

Photo credits: Cover © David Antonio Lopez Moya/Shutterstock.

Corrigenda to publications may be found on line at: www.oecd.org/about/publishing/corrigenda.htm.

Foreword

This report on Colombia is part of the OECD Tax Policy Reviews series. OECD Tax Policy Reviews are intended to provide independent, comprehensive and comparative assessments of OECD member and non-member countries' tax systems or zoom in on a specific country tax policy topic. By benchmarking the tax systems of countries and identifying tailored tax policy reform options, the main objective of the Reviews is to enhance the design of existing tax policies and to support the adoption and implementation of tax reforms.

In 2021, the Tax Incentives Commission (TIC) identified the need for Colombia to develop a stand-alone Tax Expenditure (TE) report and to strengthen the measurement of the tax revenue foregone of TEs. Following up from the TIC report, Colombia requested OECD assistance in defining its TE benchmark and to provide technical support to improve the measurement of tax revenue forgone from TEs.

This OECD Tax Policy Review proposes a benchmark for the taxation of Income and Valued Added Taxes and seeks to identify the full list of TEs within the Colombian tax system. It provides an in-depth assessment of Colombia's TE reporting practices and makes specific recommendations as to how the measurement of TEs and the reporting of them can be improved. Finally, it provides item-by-item estimates on the revenue forgone from all the TEs within the corporate and personal income tax that can be estimated given the available data. The report was prepared in close collaboration with Colombia's *Dirección de Impuestos y Aduanas Nacionales* (DIAN) and *Ministerio de Hacienda y Crédito Público* (MHCP).

The review was written by Gioia de Melo and Yannic Rehm, with written inputs from and under the supervision of Bert Brys, from the OECD Centre for Tax Policy and Administration. The work benefited from productive meetings with tax officials from DIAN and MHCP, which were held remotely between October 2021 and June 2022. In particular, the authors would like to acknowledge the contributions of Catherine Fenwarth Benito-Revollo, Pastor Hamlet Sierra Reyes, Diana Marcela Parra Garzón, Jair Paolo Bedoya, Luis Adelmo Plaza, Sebastian Arcila Gomez, Ivon Maritza Albarracin, Daniela Gantiva Parada, Gloria Yori Parra, Alba Clemencia Avendaño Cruz, Estefania Jaimes Davila, Tomas Jaramillo Quintero, Nicolas Bernal (all DIAN) and Sammy Libos Zúñiga (MHCP). Financial support from the State Secretariat for Economic Affairs (SECO) of Switzerland is gratefully acknowledged. The OECD wishes to thank in particular Juan Pedro Schmid, Luisa-Fernanda Cardozo-Romero and Christian Braendli from SECO for their support and encouragement.

The authors would also like to thank colleagues from the OECD's Centre for Tax Policy and Administration, in particular David Bradbury, Stéphane Buydens, Mariona Mas Montserrat and Richard Clarke for their helpful input and feedback, as well as Natalie Lagorce, Carrie Tyler and Hazel Healy for their assistance with formatting and communications.

Table of contents

FIGURES

INFOGRAPHICS

TABLES

Executive Summary

Tax expenditures are tax provisions (i.e. exemptions, non-standard deductions, credits, reduced rates and deferrals) within the tax system that is in place that deviate from a benchmark tax system. The term tax "expenditure" (TE) arises from the fact that they are equivalent to public expenditure implemented through the tax system. When properly designed, TEs can stimulate economic growth and improve well-being. However, TEs often come at a significant tax revenue cost and may also raise distributional concerns and create distortions.

In 2021, the Tax Incentives Commission presented an in-depth review of tax incentives and tax expenditures within the Colombian tax system. The Commission concluded that there is a systemic over-use of TEs to correct for structural deficiencies in the tax system. It advised Colombia to focus on fundamental tax reform and break the undesirable spiral of continuously introducing poorly analysed tax expenditures. The Report also encouraged Colombia to define a "benchmark" tax system relative to which TEs are identified. According to the Commission, the absence of a well-defined benchmark tax system implied that some TEs remained unidentified while other tax concessions that were reported as a TE were in fact not a TE; this resulted in a biased estimate of the total revenue foregone of TEs that was reported by Colombia. The Commission also recommended that Colombia publish a standalone annual TE Report that would list all TEs and quantify the associated foregone tax revenues. In addition, the Commission noted that there was scope to improve the estimation methodology and the data that was used to measure tax revenue foregone. By allowing for fiscal transparency, the stand-alone TE report would enhance government accountability and support evidence-based decision making on the allocation of public resources.

Since the publication of the report of the Tax Incentives Commission, Colombia has made significant progress with respect to the measurement of the revenue foregone of TEs. Estimates of revenue forgone from TEs are presented in the Annex of the *Marco Fiscal de Mediano Plazo* (MFMP), an annual report published by the Ministry of Finance, which covers TEs from the Personal Income Tax (PIT), the Corporate Income Tax (CIT), the Value Added Tax (VAT), as well as fuel excise taxes and the carbon tax. In the last two years, the range of TEs that has been estimated has considerably increased.

Nevertheless, there remains significant scope to further improve the identification, measurement and reporting of TEs in Colombia. For instance, Colombia has not yet defined a benchmark tax system, and therefore has not been able to publish a coherent and complete list of all TEs within the tax system. The most recent edition of the MFMP provides aggregate estimates of revenue forgone, but it does not present revenue foregone of TEs on an item-by-item basis. Moreover, the revenue forgone arising from non-taxable income and from special CIT deductions (other than the deduction for investment in fixed assets) is not reported in the MFMP.

This Review provides further guidance on how to identify, measure and report TEs in Colombia. As such, this report provides useful input into future tax reform discussions and evaluations of the tax system in Colombia. It deepens the recommendations of the Colombian Tax Incentives Commission in 2021, and fills in the remaining gaps so that Colombia can start publishing a standalone TE report as soon as possible.

This Review provides estimates of the tax revenue forgone of CIT and PIT TEs on an item-by item basis. The OECD has estimated the revenue foregone of a wide range of TEs based upon two samples of depersonalized tax returns and exogenous information data that were provided by Colombia's Tax Administration (DIAN) for the purposes of this review. The OECD made a proposal for the formulas that can be applied to estimate the TEs for which data is available. These formulas have been applied by DIAN to all taxpayers that file a tax return, which have been merged with the corresponding exogenous information forms, if applicable. The revenue foregone estimates as well as the distributional analysis of a number of TEs calculated by DIAN have been included in this Review.

The Review defines an income tax benchmark for Colombia. The proposed "hybrid" income tax benchmark is based upon a theoretical concept of income that limits arbitrary decisions about what constitutes a TE, but is nonetheless adapted to include structural aspects of the Colombian tax system. Given the proposed TE benchmark, the review then seeks to identify all TEs within the CIT and PIT. In particular, the report lists 123 CIT TEs and 124 PIT TEs that have been identified in collaboration with Colombia's Tax Administration (DIAN) and its Ministry of Finance (MHCP).

The Review also presents a benchmark for the VAT in Colombia. The benchmark VAT base consists of final consumption plus gross fixed capital formation by private households, the government and non-profit organizations; the VAT is levied on a destination-basis. Under the VAT benchmark, the VAT paid on gross fixed capital formation by businesses is recoverable. This gives rise to a negative TE within the VAT, as this is currently not the case in Colombia. This negative VAT TE is likely large, but it has not been reported previously. The current exclusion of VAT on goods and services that are taxed under the "National Consumption Tax" also results in a VAT TE.

The Review makes several technical recommendations on how to improve the estimation methodology of VAT TEs in Colombia. In particular, the Review presents a methodology that would allow Colombia to differentiate its estimate for VAT non-compliance by economic sector in order to better disentangle TE revenue forgone from revenue losses due to tax evasion. Colombia could also start measuring the negative TE linked to the non-recoverability of VAT paid on investment in fixed assets. Significant scope exists to improve the measurement of revenue foregone from the VAT exemption within Free Trade Zones.

The Review describes the approach that DIAN currently follows to measure and report CIT and PIT TEs, and identifies areas for improvement. The key priority regarding the measurement of CIT and PIT TEs is to improve the granularity of the available data. Currently, CIT and PIT returns are not sufficiently detailed to identify revenue foregone of TEs on an item-by-item basis. In addition, the tax returns require taxpayers to file aggregated information that combines tax provisions that are TEs as well as provisions that are part of the benchmark, and are therefore not a TE. The tax returns will have to be changed such that these different types of tax provisions are filed separately.

The number of taxpayers that are required to submit exogenous information forms when they file their CIT return will have to increase, as long as more granular information is not available within the tax returns. In 2020, corporations that were required to submit these additional forms (i.e. with turnover above COP 100 million) constituted only 44% of all corporations. Reducing the COP 100 million turnover threshold would allow DIAN to report more representative item-by-item revenue forgone estimates. Exogenous information forms should also be redesigned to allow for more granularity. Only about half of all identified CIT TEs can be quantified based on the exogenous information that is currently available. DIAN is also encouraged to explore information that might be available in other government agencies and that could possibly be merged with tax returns data as well as to collect and use information for TE measurement purposes that can be provided by third parties, such as the financial sector.

The Review makes additional suggestions regarding the calculation of revenue forgone from CIT and PIT TEs. The Review recommends to move from the application of standard CIT rates to company-specific CIT rates (which might be lower or higher, depending on whether the company is subject to a special regime) to calculate tax revenue forgone. Furthermore, the Review recommends that DIAN report separately the interaction between reduced rates and tax base narrowing provisions that constitute a TE. To estimate revenue forgone from base narrowing TEs, DIAN is also encouraged to switch from applying an average marginal PIT rate (to the value of the TE) to applying the actual PIT rate schedule (to the sum of taxable income and the TE and then take the difference with the current tax liability) for each taxpayer.

The PIT return will have to be redesigned in order to estimate the revenue forgone from PIT TEs on an item-by-item basis. Less than 2% of the taxpayers that submit a tax return are required to submit supplementary tax forms that provide more detailed information on the tax provisions they claim. Therefore, the usefulness of exogenous information for the measurement of PIT TEs is severely limited. As a consequence, revenue forgone estimates from PIT TEs need to rely extensively on data from the tax returns and only 10% of PIT TEs can be estimated on an item-by-item basis with reasonable accuracy. In addition to ensuring that provisions that are viewed as TEs are not reported together with provisions that are considered part of the benchmark, DIAN should collect more disaggregated information within the tax returns that taxpayers are required to file. DIAN should explore additional sources of information to estimate certain TEs, such as information provided by pension funds on voluntary pension savings.

This Review concludes by suggesting a structure for a future standalone TE report and includes a set of clarifications that could be added in the report to avoid any misinterpretation of the results. The first chapter would define the benchmark for all taxes covered in the TE report, and describe the main assumptions underlying the revenue forgone methodology. The second chapter would summarise the changes that have been made since the prior edition of the report with respect to the definition of the benchmark, the methodology that is applied to measure revenue forgone and the data that is available as well as changes in tax policy. The third chapter would present a summary of the main revenue forgone estimates by type of tax and main types of TEs. The report would include a separate chapter for the TEs within the CIT, PIT and VAT, respectively. A separate chapter for TEs within other taxes could possibly also included. The full list of TEs would be included in an Annex of the report.

1 Income Tax Benchmark Proposal for Colombia

This chapter presents the proposed income tax benchmark for Colombia. The benchmark is based on a theoretical underpinning but adapted to the fundamental aspects of the current design of the Colombian tax system. The chapter stipulates the main rules and includes examples to help the reader better understand its implications.

Summary

This chapter presents the proposed income tax benchmark for Colombia. The benchmark is chosen such that it is aligned with key benchmark design principles including: the benchmark is well defined and transparent; it avoids discrimination across similar taxpayers and does not result in negative tax expenditures (TEs) whenever it is possible; the benchmark is consistent across tax provisions and taxes; it results in TEs that are "actionable" (i.e. they can be reformed); the benchmark is aligned with international obligations; and the chosen benchmark facilitates international comparability.

The income tax benchmark is chosen such that it increases transparency on the tax provisions that are deviating from the benchmark and their corresponding cost in terms of tax revenue forgone. It is based on a theoretical underpinning but adapted to the fundamental aspects of the current design of the Colombian tax system.

The chapter stipulates the main rules and definitions and includes examples and clarifications, which are presented in italics. This chapter could eventually be included in the TE report (without the examples included in italics) that DIAN plans to publish each year.

Annex C and Annex D provide a list of all TEs within the CIT and the PIT that have been identified in Colombia, based on the income tax benchmark proposal. These lists could serve as a template for the list of TEs that DIAN should aim at including in its annual TE report.

1.1 Introduction

Tax expenditures (TEs) are tax provisions within the tax system that is in place in a particular jurisdiction and year that deviate from a benchmark tax system. Put differently, TEs are tax provisions (i.e. non-standard deductions, credits, reduced rates, exemptions and deferrals) that are not included in the benchmark tax system. The identification of a TE thus depends on how the benchmark tax system is defined. The definition of the tax benchmark therefore constitutes the first step in TE analysis and reporting.

The benchmark tax system represents the standard taxation treatment that applies to similar taxpayers or types of activity. It should be defined such that it is aligned, as much as possible, with the following principles: the benchmark should be clear and easy to understand; avoid situations of discrimination across similar taxpayers; avoid negative TEs; be consistent across taxes; result in TEs that are "actionable" (i.e. that can be reformed, if such a reform would be desirable from a tax policy perspective) and aligned with international tax rules and agreements.

The choice of a tax benchmark unavoidably involves judgment and, therefore, may be contentious in some cases (Australian Government the Treasury, 2021[1]). These judgments are informed by long-standing features of a country's tax system as well as practice in TE publications in other jurisdictions.

The tax benchmark should not be interpreted as an indication of the way activities or taxpayers ought to be taxed. Instead, the benchmark is intended to bring transparency and coherence to the discussion and evaluation of the design of the tax system that is in place.

The proposed income tax benchmark for Colombia is defined on the basis of a theoretical concept of income that helps provide guidance and avoid as much as possible arbitrary decisions. However, the proposed benchmark is adapted to include structural aspects of the Colombian tax system. In other words, it is a hybrid approach as it considers a conceptual benchmark as the starting point but modifies it by taking into account fundamental features of Colombia's actual tax system. This approach ensures that the report covers a wide range of tax measures, including measures that may not be considered tax incentives or substitutes to direct program spending.

The proposed benchmark is a practical variant of a comprehensive income tax base, following the Schanz-Haig-Simons (SHS) definition of comprehensive income (Schanz, 1896[2]; Haig, 1921[3]; Simons, 1938[4]). SHS define income as the sum of consumption and the change in net wealth (stock of assets) in a given time period.[1] Consumption includes all expenditures except those incurred in earning or producing income. While the income tax benchmark overall follows the SHS definition of income, it also deviates in certain cases from this theoretical tax base. The major departures from a comprehensive income tax base are introduced and discussed below.

Major departures of the proposed income tax benchmark from a SHS comprehensive income tax base

The items that are listed below are characteristics of the proposed income tax benchmark, despite the fact that they imply a departure from a SHS comprehensive income tax base.[2]

- Income is taxable only when it is realized in exchange.
  - *Thus, the deferral of tax on unrealized capital gains under the tax system that is in place in Colombia is not regarded as a TE.*
- Nominal income rather than real current additions to purchasing power is taxable.
- There is a separate corporate income tax.
- The progressive personal income tax rate schedule and the exempt personal income tax bracket are included in the tax benchmark.
- Withholding taxes do not give rise to a TE insofar as they are a prepayment of the final tax liability that taxpayers need to pay.
- Imputed income on owner-occupied dwellings (i.e. the rental income that the owner-occupiers forego by living themselves in the house they own) is considered non-taxable income.
  - *This implies that the non-taxation of imputed housing income under the tax system does not give rise to a TE.*
  - *The fact that imputed housing is considered non-taxable also implies that the corresponding costs that households incur in earning that income are non-deductible. As a result, mortgage interest is non-deductible under the income tax benchmark. The deduction of mortgage interest payments (for owner-occupied property) from taxable income under the tax system in place constitutes a TE. The deduction of recurrent taxes on immovable property from taxable income constitutes a TE.*
- The benefits derived from non-market household services, such as those provided by a non-working spouse, are non-taxable income.
  - *The fact that this income is not taxed under the tax system that is in place therefore does not constitute a TE.*

A more detailed discussion of the income tax benchmark, and the implications for the definition of income TEs, is included in section 1.2 below. The proposed income benchmark description borrows heavily from the Australian and Canadian TE reports (Australian Government the Treasury, 2021[1]; Department of Finance Canada, 2021[5]).

1.2 The benchmark tax system for the personal and corporate income tax

The benchmark for the Personal Income Tax (PIT) and Corporate Income Tax (CIT), following the general approach described above, is further characterised as follows:

Unit of taxation

- For the CIT, the benchmark tax unit is the corporation (including the head entity of a consolidated group or a multiple entry consolidated group).
- Sole trader businesses, partnerships and trusts are not separate tax units. Income earned by these entities is taxable in the hands of the recipient.
- For the PIT, the benchmark tax unit is the individual.

Taxation period

- The fiscal year under the income tax benchmark is the calendar year.
- Taxable income is assessed on an accruals accounting basis – that is, recorded when the right to the income arises (even if it has not yet been received) and when costs are incurred (irrespective of when the payment is made).
- However, the taxation of income on a cash basis as a tax simplification measure, as it may apply to income under the PIT and/or as a tax simplification measure for small businesses, is also included in the income tax benchmark (i.e. not considered a TE).
- Capital gains are taxable only when they are realized in exchange.
- Under the benchmark, business and capital losses that are not deducted in the taxation period in which these losses arise can be carried over to subsequent taxation periods in recognition of the cyclical nature of business activity and investment.
  - *Loss carry-forward provisions are part of the tax benchmark and do not give rise to a TE. On the other hand, loss carry-backward provisions are not included in the benchmark and, to the extent that they would be allowed under the tax system in place, would give rise to a TE.*

Tax base

- The benchmark CIT base comprises all sources of income for the corporation, including profits from carrying out business activity and investment income including rental income, interest income, royalties, dividends and capital gains, as well as other sources of income including government cash transfers and donations.
  - *Any business income that is not fully included in the tax base gives rise to a TE. The differential tax treatment of non-profit organisations included within the special tax regime as well as the non-taxation of income received from contributions to Family Compensation Funds is viewed as a TE. Further, a reduction in the principal of a loan is viewed as taxable income. On the other hand, sources of finance that the business has issued or attracted (e.g. newly issued equity or debt) are not included as income insofar as the funding raised corresponds to a liability of the same value. See Annex C for provisions under the CIT that are considered TEs.*
- Current expenses incurred to earn taxable business income are deductible in the year they are incurred; this includes wages as well as corresponding payroll taxes and employer social security contributions and non-tax compulsory payments. The deduction of donations is not part of the benchmark (i.e. is viewed as a TE).

- Government royalties and resource taxes are not deductible for income tax purposes under the benchmark.
- The deductibility of interest payments from taxable corporate earnings is part of the income tax benchmark and, therefore, does not constitute a TE.
- A dividend participation exemption that takes into account that CIT has been paid on dividend income that is received and ensures that these dividends are therefore not taxed again under the CIT at the receiving company is included in the income tax benchmark.
- Depreciation deductions are made over the effective life of the asset, and balancing adjustments on disposal reconcile differences between the outstanding tax and economic value of the asset. Tax depreciation allowances that correspond to the economic depreciation of the asset are included in the benchmark; they therefore do not constitute a TE.[3]
  - *Any tax depreciation rate that exceeds the rates of economic depreciation constitutes a TE (e.g., immediate expensing, accelerated depreciation) and any tax depreciation that is slower than the economic depreciation of the asset constitutes a negative TE.*
- Similarly to other assets, businesses are allowed to depreciate natural resource assets over time according to the economic depreciation of the asset. If the exploration is successful, the same applies to intangible exploration expenses, which need to be capitalized and amortized gradually. To determine the decline in economic value, the standard treatment of the tax benchmark stipulates "cost depletion" which allows depreciation in accordance with the percentage of resources extracted from the property. Unsuccessful exploration can be expensed immediately.
  - *The deductions granted through the special exhaustion factor in hydrocarbon exploitation give rise to a TE.*
  - *The deduction rules that only apply to petroleum exploration carried out in private property or to concessions in force as of 28 October 1974, give rise to a TE as these rules include amortization rates unrelated to the percentage of the resource extracted.*
  - *The normal deductions for exhaustion that only apply to contracts in force as of 28 October 1974 as well as the deduction for depletion in the exploitation of mines or gases other than hydrocarbons and natural deposits for contracts in force as of 28 October 1974, give rise to a TE. As the taxpayer can choose a fixed percentage of the value of the product extracted or the actual cost (determined based on a technical estimate), the difference between the actual cost and the fixed percentage (if chosen) would be a TE.*
  - *Other rules regarding the amortization, depreciation and depletion of natural resources that only apply to contracts in force as of 28 October 1974 and that deviate from the benchmark treatment would also give rise to TEs.*[4]
- Taxpayers resident in Colombia are subject to tax on their worldwide income, while non-residents are taxable in Colombia on their income from Colombia sources only.
  - *This implies that the CIT exemption on dividends distributed by non-resident entities to a Colombian Holding Companies is a TE.*
  - *The capital gain tax exemption on income derived from the sale or transfer of the participation of a CHC in non-Colombian entities is a TE.*
  - *The capital gains exemption on income derived from the sale of shares or participations in a CHC is tax-exempt, except for the portion corresponding to the profits derived from activities carried out in Colombia, is a TE.*

- The benchmark PIT base comprises all sources of income for the individual, including income from employment, pension income, personal business income, partnership income and income from trusts, income from investment including dividends, rental income, royalties, interest and capital gains, as well as fringe benefits and government transfers and donations.
  - *The exemption on 25% of labour income is a TE. See Annex D for other provisions under the PIT that are considered TEs.*
- Expenses incurred to earn employment income such as expenses for commuting to work are not deductible – the deduction of these expenses from taxable personal income would constitute a TE – as the basic tax allowance within the PIT can be interpreted as providing a deduction to cover these costs.
  - *Skills and training-related expenses are not deductible from the tax benchmark.*
- Although the individual is the tax unit under the PIT, tax provisions that introduce some characteristics of family-based taxation to strengthen the equity of the tax system are part of the benchmark.
  - *This includes a deduction for dependents that is available in the tax system that is in place. Such a deduction would therefore not give rise to a TE. However, it is suggested that the revenue forgone associated with this provision is measured and reported in an Annex of the TE report.*
- Mandatory social security contributions are deductible payments from the income tax benchmark as the replacement income that these contributions will give rise to will be included as taxable personal income in the tax benchmark. Put differently, mandatory SSCs follow an exempt-exempt-tax (EET) treatment.
- While mandatory health contributions are deductible from the income tax benchmark, the health benefits received will not be included in the income tax benchmark insofar as they constitute a payment to cover the costs incurred.
- Instead, voluntary health and pension contributions follow a tax-tax-exempt benchmark. Voluntary contributions or payments do not constitute a tax-deductible expense under the income tax benchmark. The deduction of voluntary pension savings from the tax system that is in place would therefore constitute a TE. The return to these savings is not tax-exempt and, therefore, constitutes taxable investment income under the benchmark. The corresponding replacement income linked to the voluntary contributions made that will be received by the individual does not constitute taxable income under the income tax benchmark.
- Similarly to voluntary pension savings, the deferral of taxation on returns realised by investment funds is viewed as a TE. That is, the fact that returns are currently taxed only when distributed to investors is considered a TE.
- Any government transfer that represents replacement income is taxable under the benchmark. However, the compensation for damage or any wrong or injury suffered by a taxpayer constitutes non-taxable income.
  - *The non-taxation of maternity leave payments or the non-taxation of severance payments constitutes a TE.*
  - *The exemption of compensation for work-related accidents or illness does not constitute a TE.*
  - *The non-taxation of a disability benefit that would be received on a recurrent basis would constitute a TE as in that case it would be considered replacement income.*

  - *Various other examples listed in the Tax Incentives Commission Report such as the non-taxation of the excess of basic salary received by officers, non-commissioned officers, and professional soldiers of the military, executive-level personnel, patrolmen and agents of the National Police are TEs.*
  - *The exemption of the remuneration of officials of international organisations is a TE.*
- Gains from gambling are taxable.

Tax rate

- The benchmark CIT rate is the statutory general CIT rate in effect at any given time. As a result, any reduced rate constitutes a TE while a surtax gives rise to a negative TE.
  - *The surtax on banks gives rise to a negative TE.*
- The benchmark PIT rate and bracket structure is the standard rate schedule as it applies at any given time; "standard" refers to the tax rate schedule that is generally applicable to that particular type of income. The benchmark therefore allows for a schedular tax treatment.
  - *The zero-rate bracket that applies to labour, professional fees, capital, non-labour and pension income is included in the benchmark as it is universal in its application and seen as a fundamental aspect of the tax system and thereby not as a TE.*[5]
  - *The additional 12 000 UVT*[6] *exemption that applies to pension income is a TE.*
- For dividends and occasional gains, the benchmark includes the proportional tax rate under the tax system that is currently in place.
  - *The exemption of distributed dividends not exceeding 300 UVT is a TE.*
  - *If dividends are paid out of profits that were not taxed under the CIT, the tax system that is currently in place levies first a withholding tax rate that equals the CIT rate. This so-called "CIT recapture tax" constitutes a negative TE.*
  - *The non-taxation of dividends from mega-investments under the dividend withholding is a TE.*
  - *The difference between the 20% rate applied to occasional gains from lotteries and raffles and the 10% rate applied to other occasional capital gains represents a negative TE.*

Tax treatment of inflation

- Taxation of nominal income rather than real current additions to purchasing power is considered the benchmark.
  - *The non-taxation of the inflation component as part of capitalised income and as part of nominal interest income constitutes a TE.*

Preferential tax treatment for household savings

- Specific tax rules that apply to certain household saving vehicles are not part of the tax benchmark; as a result, they give rise to a TE.

Tax provisions within the CIT that correct for atypical taxes and tax treatments

- Taxes that are an integral part of the tax system currently in place, even if they are uncommon from an international perspective, are an integral part of the benchmark and do not constitute a TE.

Tax credits and deductions linked to the payment of these taxes that compensate for the weakness in the design of the tax system, despite a strong tax policy rationale, constitute a TE.

- *The business turnover tax (ICA) and the tax on financial transactions, which are uncommon from an international tax perspective, are part of the income tax benchmark. As a result, the corresponding ICA credit and deduction of the financial transaction tax are TEs within the CIT.*
- *The CIT credit to compensate for VAT paid on the acquisition, construction or formation and import of real productive fixed assets is a TE in the CIT. Also, the possibility to report a higher value of the assets (due to VAT paid) and to depreciate this value, gives rise to a TE. Instead, the unrecoverable VAT paid on fixed assets is a negative TE in the VAT.*

Tax provisions that aim at avoiding double taxation

- Measures that provide relief from double taxation are considered part of the benchmark income tax system. This includes double tax treaties and dividend participation exemptions.
  - *Although obligations that follow from the Andean Community (CAN) treaty are legally binding, these tax provisions could be viewed as tax incentives by installing a territorial-like tax system amongst CAN countries. The OECD suggests considering these provisions as part of the benchmark (i.e. not as a TE) given that they are tax treaties but still measure and report the associated revenue forgone in an Annex of the TE report in order to enhance transparency.*[7]

Tax base protection measures

- Tax base protection measures are included in the income tax benchmark.
  - *CFCs rules, transfer pricing rules and thin capitalization rules are part of the benchmark. Nonetheless, whenever tax provisions that are linked to these tax base protection rules would result in a more generous treatment than what would be the case under Colombia's standard worldwide taxation regime, these provisions would be viewed as a TE.*
- In the absence of a tax treaty that applies, the standard withholding taxes included in the Colombian domestic law that apply to that particular class of income constitute the benchmark tax rates. Exemptions or reductions relative to these basic rates will give rise to a TE.
  - *Reduced withholding rates for income from foreign portfolio capital investments, except for investments in public or private fixed income securities (25% if investor is domiciled in a low or zero taxation jurisdiction and 14% if the investor is not domiciled in a low or zero taxation jurisdiction) are a TE.*
- If a tax treaty exists, the benchmark rates of withholding tax for a class of income will be the 'basic rate', where the basic rate is the highest rate specified in the treaty for each withholding tax. Exemptions or reductions relative to the basic rates prescribed in a particular tax treaty will give rise to a TE.

Reductions to the CIT base or liability on account of payment of other taxes

- While it is a policy choice of the government to allow certain taxes to be deducted from the CIT base, the desire for transparency implies that these deductions are excluded from the income tax benchmark and are therefore considered a TE. The only exception would be employer social security contributions and payroll taxes paid by the employer as these taxes are part of wage costs whose incidence is assumed to primarily fall on workers and wage costs overall are deductible from taxable corporate profits. For example, the following deductions give raise to a TE:

- *The deduction of the compulsory compensation for exploiting non-renewable resources;*
- *The deduction of the carbon tax;*
- *The deduction of fuel excise tax/ duties.*

Additional tax benchmark design features

- Tax simplification measures that aim at reducing compliance costs for incorporated or unincorporated businesses are included in the income tax benchmark and, therefore, do not constitute a TE.
- However, tax simplification measures that would possibly result in a non-trivial tax advantage for the businesses or individuals involved would constitute a TE. For instance, a deduction of presumptive costs irrespective of the actual costs that the taxpayer has incurred would be considered a TE if the deduction is estimated to generally exceed effective costs.
  - *Taxpayers that provide professional services and hire a maximum of two employees for less than 90 continuous or discontinuous days can choose to either:*
    1. *have 25% of their income exempt; in this case, they are also obliged to observe the 40% net income ceiling, as is the case for employees. The difference between 25% of their income and the effective costs incurred, if positive, would constitute a TE.*
    2. *or deduct effective costs provided they meet the requirements listed in article 107 of the tax code. In this case, the total amount of deductions can exceed the 40% ceiling. This option does not give rise to a TE, as the deduction of business expenses is an integral part of the income tax benchmark.*
  - *Rather than deducting the actual labour costs, coffee growers have a deemed tax-deductible workforce cost equivalent to 40% of taxable income. The difference between the actual labour costs and the deemed deduction constitutes a TE.*

SIMPLE

- SIMPLE is a preferential regime and thereby gives rise to a TE.[8]

References

Australian Government the Treasury (2021), *Tax Benchmarks and Variations Statement 2020.* [1]

Department of Finance Canada (2021), *Report on Federal Tax Expenditures - Concepts, Estimates, Evaluations.* [5]

Haig, R. (1921), *The Concept of Income—Economic and Legal Aspects*, Columbia University Press. [3]

Schanz, G. (1896), "Der Einkommensbegriff und die Einkommensteuergesetze", *Finanzarchiv* 13, pp. 1-87. [2]

Simons, H. (1938), *Personal Income Taxation: the Definition of Income as a Problem of Fiscal Policy*, Chicago: University of Chicago Press. [4]

U.S. Department of the Treasury (2021), *Tax Expenditures.* [6]

Notes

1 Under a comprehensive income tax, income is taxed when it is accrued. Savings are made out of taxed earnings and the return on these savings (irrespective of whether the assets are owned directly or through a savings fund) is part of the benchmark and subject to income tax on an accrual basis. In return, the withdrawal of assets from such saving vehicles is fully exempted from tax; i.e. savings are taxed under a "taxed-taxed-exempt" regime.

2 This section is inspired by the U.S. TE report as well as the Australian and Canadian TE reports (Australian Government the Treasury, 2021[1]; Department of Finance Canada, 2021[5]; U.S. Department of the Treasury, 2021[6]).

3 Table A A.6 in Annex A compares tax depreciation rates in Colombia to economic depreciation rates estimated in the literature. Overall, these rates do not differ significantly. Hence, it could be argued that the standard depreciation rates in the Colombian tax system are aligned with the benchmark (i.e. do not give rise to a TE).

4 As provisions guaranteed in historical contracts cannot be changed, these TEs are likely non-actionable.

5 Even if the exempt bracket is viewed as part of the benchmark, the threshold in Colombia is particularly high compared to other countries. It is hence suggested that the revenue forgone associated with this provision is measured and reported in an Annex of the TE report.

6 *Unidad de Valor Tributario* (UVT) refers to the Tax Value Unit. In 2020, 1 UVT = COP 35 607.

7 Exempt income from the Andean Community treaty includes: income from capital gains obtained on the sale of assets located in another CAN member country, income from the exploitation of natural resources in another member country, income from royalties on intangible assets in a member country, income from interest and other financial returns whose payment is recorded and imputed in another member country. Dividends and participations are only taxable by the member country where the company that distributes them is domiciled.

8 The OECD recommends listing this regime as a TE in the report separately from the CIT and PIT TEs as the regime covers a wider range of taxes. Measuring revenue forgone from SIMPLE may be challenging due to the lack of information on benchmark revenues. However, the mere acknowledgement that the regime provides preferential treatment for small and medium businesses is considered informative and contributes to enhancing transparency.

2 Identifying and Measuring Tax Expenditures in the Value-Added Tax

This chapter defines the value-added tax (VAT) benchmark. The chapter then zooms in on the measurement of VAT TEs; first, by providing a high-level description of the method Colombia currently applies to estimate revenue forgone and second, by making a number of technical recommendations on how the methodology can be improved and complemented with further analysis. It pays particular attention to how revenue forgone from the VAT exemption to Free Trade Zones could be measured.

Summary

This chapter starts by defining the value-added tax (VAT) benchmark, which allows for identifying VAT Tax Expenditures (TEs) in a coherent manner. The chapter then zooms in on the measurement of VAT TEs; first, by providing a high-level description of the method DIAN currently applies to estimate revenue forgone and second, by focusing on specific characteristics of the applied methodology. The chapter also makes a number of technical recommendations on how DIAN's methodology can be improved and complemented with further analysis. These recommendations refine the existing approach by making sure it is aligned with the suggested VAT benchmark and increase the transparency about revenue forgone and complement the top-down model with VAT return data when it comes to specific provisions that cannot be modelled in a macroeconomic framework.

General assessment of the methodology

- DIAN's top-down model (based on national accounts statistics rather than tax return data) to quantify VAT TEs is aligned with international practise and captures correctly the functioning of the VAT system and the channels through which deviations from the benchmark result in VAT revenue forgone.
- DIAN's current (implicitly defined) VAT benchmark is not fully aligned with the OECD's VAT benchmark proposal. In particular, the DIAN TE benchmark assumes that no sector (except for the hydrocarbon sector) can recover VAT paid on gross fixed capital formation (GFCF). In contrast, under the OECD's VAT benchmark, businesses are entitled to a credit for the input VAT paid on investment in capital assets. The current DIAN method therefore ignores the tax revenue impact of the non-recoverability of VAT paid on GFCF when estimating item-by-item tax revenue forgone. As a result, DIAN does not measure the negative TE and, thereby, overestimates the VAT revenue forgone as it does not take into account the additional VAT revenue collected by not providing businesses a refund for the VAT paid on capital assets.
- The VAT revenue forgone that is calculated using DIAN's top-down model is adjusted by the compliance gap to ensure that revenue lost due to non-compliance is not wrongly assigned to the revenue forgone from the TEs. However, relying on an economy-wide compliance gap to estimate product-level TEs, is problematic. DIAN's current approach overestimates the tax revenue forgone for goods and services produced by sectors with a non-compliance rate exceeding the average non-compliance rate; the opposite holds for the tax revenue foregone in sectors that are highly compliant.
- The methodology DIAN applies to measure revenue forgone from the Free Trade Zone (FTZ) exemption is incorrect as it compares the input VAT that the FTZ user would have paid in the absence of the exemption to the actual VAT the FTZ user collects when it sells goods and services to the national territory. Furthermore, as explained below, in the OECD's view revenue forgone from the FTZ exemption only arises as a result of the interaction between the FTZ exemption and VAT exclusions.
- A wide range of VAT TEs are neither listed nor measured by DIAN, including the exclusion of food and beverages consumed in restaurants, bars and other shops that are taxed under the National Consumption Tax. These TEs should be measured for transparency purposes but also because revenue forgone from TEs not captured by the DIAN model (and for which potential revenue is not adjusted) leads to an overestimation of the compliance gap and consequently to an underestimation of the TEs the model does measure.

Recommendations regarding VAT revenue forgone measurement

- To improve the preciseness of DIAN's VAT model, the OECD suggests breaking down the compliance gap. To do so, DIAN needs to estimate potential revenue by sector, which cannot be done within the current demand-side framework. DIAN could use a supply-side approach in line with the International Monetary Fund (IMF) VAT GAP methodology (Hutton, 2017[1]). Potential revenue by sector (calculated based on national accounts data) will then be compared to actual revenue from sector-coded tax returns to obtain sector-level compliance gaps. The item-by-item revenue forgone estimates could still be calculated using a demand-side framework but would be adjusted by the corresponding sectoral compliance gaps.
- The following recommendations were made regarding the treatment of VAT paid on gross fixed capital formation (GFCF):
  - The suggested benchmark tax system would allow businesses to recover the VAT paid on total GFCF and, as a result, DIAN would start measuring the negative TE due to the fact that currently VAT paid on investment in fixed assets is not recoverable for businesses.
  - In order to increase the transparency of the VAT TE figures, the report suggests splitting the overall TE estimate into separate items, namely: 1) the total (net) revenue forgone; 2) the revenue forgone resulting from the positive TE (this measure is currently reported by DIAN); and 3) the negative TE arising from the non-recoverability of VAT paid on GFCF.
  - To measure the negative TE from non-recoverable VAT paid on GFCF, a proposal was made on how to determine the value of GFCF made by both incorporated and unincorporated businesses.
- Revenue forgone from the FTZ VAT exemption arises only in two cases: 1) excluded goods are sold from the national territory to FTZ businesses (the domestic business gets an input VAT refund that it would not get if the FTZ exemption did not exist); 2) FTZ businesses sell excluded goods and services to the domestic economy without paying any input VAT (if the FTZ exemption did not exist, these businesses would have had to pay input VAT without being able to recover it). The chapter suggests two alternative approaches to estimate revenue forgone from the interaction of these exclusions with the FTZ exemption. Which of these approaches DIAN will prefer to measure TEs will depend on the available data and the resources that are available to make the TE estimate as precise as possible. The chapter also discusses how this estimation could be integrated into the VAT model or, otherwise, if the estimation is carried out separately, how the compliance gap should be adjusted.
- In addition to defining a VAT benchmark, the chapter recommends listing all VAT TEs within the TE report, including the tax provisions that are currently not measured by DIAN. As a result of exchanges between the MOF, DIAN and the OECD in the context of the elaboration of this review, DIAN included an estimate of the revenue forgone from the VAT exclusion of food and beverages consumed in restaurants and bars in the latest edition of its MFMP for the first time (Minhacienda, 2022[2]). Annex E provides a list of all TEs within the VAT that have been identified in Colombia, based on the VAT benchmark proposal. The list could serve as a template for the list of TEs that DIAN should aim at including in its annual TE report.
- If DIAN were to follow the suggestions made by the OECD, it will have to gradually develop its VAT model from a purely top-down approach based on national accounts statistics to a hybrid approach that combines the use of macroeconomic statistics and VAT return data. Actual VAT returns could enhance the estimation of revenue forgone, in particular for TEs that are currently not within the scope of the DIAN top-down model such as the FTZ exemption. In addition, VAT returns could be used to check the robustness of the estimates obtained on the basis of national

accounts data. The report identifies those TEs (such as the designation of VAT-free days) that have to be estimated using data sources other than the national accounts. Finally, the report lists VAT TEs that are currently quantified by DIAN whose measurement could be improved using alternative data sources.

2.1 The benchmark tax system for the value-added tax

This section defines the VAT benchmark and provides in italics examples of provisions that would be considered (or not) a tax expenditure (TE) based on the criteria chosen. The structure follows closely the approach followed by the Canadian TE Report (Department of Finance Canada, 2021[3]).

Tax base

- The benchmark VAT base comprises domestic final consumption plus gross fixed capital formation (GFCF) by private households, the government and non-profit organizations. While VAT paid on inputs and gross fixed capital formation by businesses is recoverable, the fact that certain entities, such as the general government and non-profit organizations, cannot recover the VAT they paid on their consumption and GFCF is an integral part of the VAT benchmark and, therefore, does not give rise to a TE.[1]
    - *The non-recoverability of VAT paid by businesses on GFCF in Colombia is a negative TE.*
    - *The VAT exclusion of goods and services that are taxed under the "National Consumption Tax" is a VAT TE. For example, the VAT exclusion of food and beverages consumed in restaurants and bars that are taxed at a rate of 8% under the National Consumption Tax is a VAT TE.*[2]
    - *The VAT exclusion applied to financial services is a TE.*
    - *If housekeeping services in Colombia are generally provided by salaried workers (who are required to pay SSCs and are subject to PIT on their income earned) rather than self-employed workers (who earn personal business income and work for several households), then the VAT exclusion on these services would not be viewed as a TE.*
    - *VAT applied to a different base other than final consumption gives rise to a TE (e.g. the VAT levied within the construction sector*[3]*).*
- The tax applies on a "destination basis", that is, the tax is levied in the jurisdiction where consumption takes place, following the taxation rules set out in the OECD/G20 International VAT/GST Guidelines (OECD, 2017[4]). Hence, the VAT is applied to goods and services imported into Colombia, but not to goods and services exported from Colombia. As a result, the VAT exemption applied to exports is not considered a TE.
    - *The exemption of services that are provided in the country and are used exclusively abroad by companies or people without business or activities in Colombia is not considered a TE.*
    - *Tax exemptions for tourism-related goods and services whose consumption takes place within Colombia, either by tax-resident or non-residents, are a TE. However, goods that are purchased by non-residents in Colombia but that are consumed outside of Colombia are not included in the VAT benchmark; the refundability of the VAT paid at the border in relation to these purchases is therefore not a TE.*
    - *The VAT exemption for tourist services provided to individuals who are not resident for tax purposes in Colombia and that are consumed within the Colombian territory, originated in*

packages sold by operating agencies or hotels registered in the national tourism registry is a TE.

- The non-taxation of sales of goods and services by unincorporated businesses which, among other requirements, report turnover below the VAT registration threshold, is viewed as a simplification measure and thereby not as a TE.
- Under the proposed VAT benchmark, a sale/ purchase that gives rise to VAT should occur via a market transaction and involve transactions that are legal. That is, the proposed benchmark seeks to identify only actionable TEs.
  - *The non-taxation of imputed rents (i.e. the notional value of home occupancy by homeowners) on owner-occupied housing is not a TE.*
  - *The non-taxation of goods and services households produce for their own consumption (e.g. food and agricultural products) is not a TE.*
  - *The non-taxation of illegal consumption is not considered a TE as it is consumption beyond the control of national authorities.*
  - *The non-taxation of services provided by the government for free such as education and health is not considered a TE.*
  - *Exclusions applied to services provided by the private sector that are similar in nature to services provided by the general government for free are considered TEs. Identifying the revenue forgone from VAT exemptions on the private provision of services such as education and health is policy-relevant as these exemptions are well known to be poorly targeted and generally benefit mostly high-income deciles.*
  - *The non-taxation of public services provided for free to citizens but bought by the government from private businesses (e.g. outsourcing of sewage services and waste collection) is not considered a TE.*[4]

Unit of taxation

- VAT is imposed using a multi-stage system under which tax is collected by businesses on their sales of goods and services at all stages of the production and marketing chain. At each stage of production, businesses can claim tax credits to recover the VAT paid on their business inputs, so that the VAT effectively applies only to the value-added at each stage. The only tax that is not refunded is the tax collected at the last stage of the multi-stage process.
  - *The non-taxation of fuel under the VAT at the last stage of the multi-stage process (when fuel is sold to the final consumer) is a TE.*

Tax rate

- The benchmark rate is the standard VAT rate in effect at any given time.
  - *Exemptions, exclusions and reduced rates give rise to a TE.*

2.2 The DIAN VAT model

Colombia applies a top-down approach to estimate revenue forgone from VAT TEs. A top-down approach aims to measure the difference between estimated potential revenue under full compliance and revenue under the benchmark by means of macroeconomic statistical data. In contrast, a bottom-up approach would start from tax return data at the firm level. Making use of national accounts product-level supply and use tables (see Table 2.1 and Table 2.2), the model allows the tax administration to estimate the potential revenue for any set of real or hypothetical VAT rates.

In the framework deployed by DIAN, it takes three steps to obtain revenue forgone from VAT TEs. First, all exemptions, reduced rates and exclusions are maintained to estimate the tax revenue under the current tax regime, assuming full compliance (i.e. potential revenue). That is, VAT is levied on all final consumption as recorded in national accounts statistics. To obtain the global (i.e. economy-wide) compliance or evasion gap, DIAN then compares the result to the actual VAT revenue that has been collected. Third, DIAN re-estimates tax revenue in the model under the benchmark tax system without exclusions, reduced rates and exemptions (i.e. benchmark revenue). The difference between revenue under the benchmark tax system and potential revenue under the current tax system, corrected for the non-compliance rate, equals revenue forgone. To obtain item-by-item estimates, DIAN only modifies a single tax rate or provision at a time, changing it from the current to the benchmark rate.[5]

DIAN follows a demand-side approach, which implies that the product-by-industry use table is the key data source for DIAN's VAT model. Supply and use tables are standard elements of the System of National Accounts (United Nations, 2009[5]). In Colombia, the national statistical agency (DANE) compiles the tables, which are released with a one-year lag. DIAN therefore works with supply and use tables from the previous year, but it adjusts the data to reflect the growth of the economy. In its columns, use tables present intermediate consumption and final uses (Table 2.1 and Table 2.2). Final demand, in turn, consists of the final consumption of households and the government, gross fixed capital formation, and exports. In the rows, the uses are broken down into the products demanded in the economy. In the case of Colombia, 396 products are available in the use table. By using additional data sources, DIAN further breaks down the table into 471 products to reflect the complete list of products subject to preferential VAT rates.

Besides the use table, the second ingredient necessary to estimate potential revenue in DIAN's model is a vector of VAT rates by product, identifying whether the goods or services are taxed at the standard VAT rate, a reduced rate, a zero rate or are excluded. DIAN then applies the VAT rate vector to all domestic uses in the economy including final consumption, intermediate consumption, and gross fixed capital formation (Table 2.1 and Table 2.2).

The fact that VAT paid on intermediate consumption can be recovered is an integral part of any VAT system, which aims at taxing domestic final consumption. Hence, VAT paid by businesses on inputs as recorded in the intermediate consumption columns of the use table needs to be deducted from potential revenue. The VAT refund matrix breaks down VAT paid on inputs into recoverable and non-recoverable VAT.

Exclusions are fundamentally different from reduced rates or exemptions. They break with the logic of the VAT system because businesses cannot recover input VAT paid on the production of excluded goods and services. To account for the impact of exclusions, DIAN estimates the share of excluded goods and services among the output of each sector in the supply table. These shares are then applied to each sector column in the intermediate demand matrix. For example, if 10% of a sector's outputs are excluded goods and services, the model assumes that VAT paid on 10% of each of the sector's inputs cannot be recovered. Implicitly, DIAN assumes that sectors producing excluded and non-excluded products use a uniform fraction of each of their inputs to produce the excluded output.

Table 2.1 Structure of the key macroeconomic data used by DIAN (Supply Table)

	Industries				Imports	Total
Products	Agricult., forestry, etc.	Manufact. of paper	...	Services		
Agriculture, forestry, etc.	Output by product by industry				Imports by product	Total supply by product
Paper and paper products						
...						
Services						
Total	Total output by Industry				Total imports	Total supply

Note: Stylized table for illustrative purposes.

Table 2.2. Structure of the key macroeconomic data used by DIAN (Use Table)

	Industries				**Final uses**			**Total**
Products	Agricult., forestry, etc.	Manufact. of paper	...	Services	Final consumpti on	Gross capital formation	Exports	
Agriculture, forestry, etc.	Intermediate consumption by product and industry				Final uses by product and by category			Total use by product
Paper and paper products								
...								
Services								
Value added	Value added by component and industry							VA
Total	Total output by industry				Total final uses by category			

Note: Stylized table for illustrative purposes.

Exports are exempt from VAT, both under the current tax system and the benchmark. It implies that, once exported, excluded goods and services become exempt and businesses can recover input VAT. To adjust potential revenue, DIAN estimates the export share for each excluded good or service produced in the domestic economy in the supply table. This allows DIAN to remove the recoverable input VAT paid on the production of these products from potential revenue. In effect, exports reduce the share of excluded output in each sector that DIAN has computed in the previous step.

Subsequently, DIAN removes from potential revenue the recoverable VAT paid on gross fixed capital formation in the hydrocarbon sector. Only businesses in the hydrocarbon sector can currently reclaim VAT paid on gross fixed capital formation in Colombia (article 485-2 of the TC). In the model, DIAN reduces potential revenue to account for that provision, but it subtracts the same amount (taking into account only the hydrocarbon sector) from potential revenue in both the current and benchmark scenario. The value of recoverable VAT paid on investment in the hydrocarbon sector comes from an external data source and is not determined within the model.

Removing the VAT exclusion on non-market services (e.g., public education or public health care provision) is not actionable because no transaction takes place and because the user does not pay for the service. Hence, when computing VAT revenue under the benchmark scenario, the standard rate is not applied to these services that are provided for free. For sectors that are partly market and partly non-market, DIAN deploys non-market shares it obtains from other data sources.

Finally, potential revenue is adjusted to take into account the revenue forgone linked to other TEs or tax provisions that reduce revenue and are not being captured by the model (e.g. the VAT exemption for FTZ users, VAT-free days).

Table 2.3. Illustration of the current DIAN VAT model

	+ VAT paid on total domestic uses	- VAT paid on inputs	+ Non-recoverable input VAT paid on production of excluded goods	- Recoverable VAT paid on business GFCF
Potential revenue: Current tax system	• Multiply the vector of current VAT rates by the final consumption, intermediate consumption and the GFCF columns in the use table.	• Multiply the vector of current VAT rates by the intermediate consumption column in the use table.	• Estimate the share of excluded goods and services among each sector's output in the supply table. • Calculate export share by sector and reduce the rate obtained in the previous step to account for the recoverability of input VAT when excluded products are exported. • Multiply shares by input VAT paid in the use table to obtain input VAT that cannot be recovered.	• Estimate VAT paid on GFCF by the hydrocarbon sector outside of the framework.
Benchmark scenario: Removal of one TE	• Change one exemption, exclusion or reduced rate to the standard rate within the vector of VAT rates and re-estimate potential revenue	• Change one exemption, exclusion or reduced rate to the standard rate within the vector of VAT rates and re-estimate potential revenue.	• Remove exclusion of the product if exclusion is not allowed under the benchmark and re-calculate shares. • Apply new shares to the use table and re-estimate non-recoverable VAT.	• No change.

Note: Excludes adjustments regarding evasion and other adjustments.

2.3 General assessment

DIAN's approach to quantifying VAT TEs is aligned with international practise. Canada, for instance, draws on national accounts and supply and use tables to estimate revenue forgone from its GST system. (Department of Finance Canada, 2021[3]).An equivalent conceptual approach can also be found in the CASE reports that calculate VAT Gaps for countries in the European Union (Poniatowski et al., 2019[6]). DIAN's top-down model correctly captures how the VAT functions in practice and through which channels TEs determine VAT revenue forgone. As with any top-down model, the accuracy of the results ultimately depends on the quality of national accounts (i.e. the granular supply and use tables), which are the key data source for the exercise.

It should be noted that the OECD has learnt how the model operates based on technical notes as well as discussions with the DIAN experts. However, without complete access to the model (including the data tables, the tax vector, and the coding), it was not possible to verify DIAN's actual implementation of the generally sound approach.

The OECD suggests Colombia to evaluate the possibility of applying a supply-side model in line with the IMF VAT Gap methodology (Box 2.1) to break down the compliance gap by sector and thereby improve this adjustment. The alternative supply-side model could then also be applied to compute revenue forgone on an item-by-item basis, but should in theory deliver similar results. The OECD's suggestion to contemplate switching to the supply-side model therefore does not imply that DIAN's model is unfit for its current purposes. The main contribution would be to obtain sectoral compliance gap estimates. The following sections explain these and other potential technical improvements of the VAT TE measurement in detail.

DIAN could gradually develop its VAT model from a purely top-down to a hybrid approach that combines the use of national accounts and VAT return data. As DIAN explores and integrates VAT return data into its TE analysis – for instance in order to break down the compliance gap and update its methodology regarding the FTZ exemption – it should be mindful of the large potential this type of data has to improve TE analysis more broadly. For example, in the future, VAT returns could be more broadly used to determine revenue forgone from certain TEs that are not included in the VAT model such as revenue forgone from the FTZ exemption. It could also use VAT returns data to check the robustness of some national accounts estimates. For instance, comparing the export share by sector in supply/use tables to the exports by business in VAT returns to check if the average obtained from macroeconomic data is sufficiently precise and to evaluate how much variation there is within each sector. DIAN might also want to check for inaccuracies in the excluded output shares by sector from the national accounts by comparing these shares to similar data from VAT returns by sector. Using VAT return data is also of paramount importance to assess non-compliance in more depth, for example by comparing individual business's net VAT collection with the average of businesses of similar size, location and type of sector.

2.4 Potential improvements discussed with DIAN

Several potential improvements have been discussed with DIAN, which would refine the existing approach, make sure it is aligned with the suggested VAT benchmark, increase the transparency regarding revenue forgone or complement the top-down model with VAT return data when it comes to specific provisions that cannot be modelled in a macroeconomic framework.

Treatment of VAT paid on gross fixed capital formation

Under current rules, businesses in Colombia cannot reclaim the VAT paid on investment goods. The only exception is gross fixed capital formation (GFCF) in the hydrocarbon sector. Currently, DIAN estimates item-by-item TEs based on the assumption that no sector (other than the hydrocarbon sector) can recover VAT paid on gross fixed capital formation, both in the benchmark and the current tax system. Such a treatment removes the revenue impact of the non-recoverability of VAT paid on GFCF (negative TE) from the estimation of item-by-item revenue forgone. As a result, revenue forgone is overestimated. In fact, non-standard rates and the non-recoverability of VAT paid on investment are two TEs operating on the same item, but with opposite signs. That is, while revenue is lost due to lower rates (or other types of positive TEs), the non-recoverable investment VAT increases government revenue (negative TE).

The OECD made three suggestions on how to improve item-by-item transparency but also the measurement of revenue forgone linked to the investment provisions in the Colombian VAT system:

1. As already mentioned in the benchmark section, following international practise, the suggested benchmark tax system allows businesses to recover the VAT paid on total gross fixed capital formation in all sectors.
2. It would be advisable to differentiate between the revenue impact of reduced rates, exemptions and exclusions, and the non-recoverable VAT levied on investment when reporting revenue forgone by item. Presenting only the impact of the non-standard rates (as it is done in Colombia currently) overestimates total revenue forgone. On the other hand, only presenting the net (i.e. combined) impact of both the non-standard rate and the non-recoverable VAT levied on investment would not be fully transparent either. In that case, the reader of the TE report might wrongly assume that reduced rates,

exemptions and exclusions have a small or even positive (for goods primarily demanded for investment purposes) impact on tax revenue.

DIAN could therefore present for each product, a decomposition of both TEs. The report could include three columns, with one denoting the total (net) revenue forgone. The other two would present revenue forgone resulting from the positive TE (what is currently reported) and from the non-recoverability of VAT paid on gross fixed capital formation (Table 2.4). As long as the VAT paid on GFCF remains non-recoverable, net revenue forgone of VAT TEs applied to a product can be negative, even after taking into account the revenue forgone of exclusions, exemptions, and reduced rates. In particular, revenue forgone might be negative for products that are mainly used as investment goods.

Table 2.4. How to present revenue forgone linked to the VAT paid on GFCF

Product	Revenue forgone		
	Total	**Exclusion/exemption/ reduced rate* (I)**	**Non-recoverability of VAT paid on GFCF (II)**
Machinery	-2 360	7 140	-9 500
Coffee	675	770	-95

Note: Values included for illustrative purposes but do not reflect actual estimates.
* Revenue impact of rate variation if rules on investment VAT remain unchanged.

3. Once reported separately, the negative TE from non-recoverable VAT on gross fixed capital formation needs to be measured correctly. Its measurement has to take into account that all businesses can reclaim VAT paid on investment under the suggested benchmark, both corporations and unincorporated businesses (which are included in the GFCF of the household sector in national accounts). On the other hand, private households and the government cannot reclaim VAT paid on investment under the suggested benchmark.

   To obtain the correct estimate, the demand for GFCF in the use table needs to be split, for each product row, into the share coming from the government, households, and the corporate sector – and only the VAT paid by the corporate sector should be considered recoverable in the benchmark scenario. On the product level, this type of data is usually not available. However, total GFCF is typically broken down into broad asset categories (e.g., dwellings, machinery and equipment etc.) and by institutional sector in national accounts. Furthermore, unincorporated businesses, are part of the household sector in national accounts but can recover VAT paid on investment under the suggested benchmark (as they are not treated differently than incorporated businesses), representing an additional complication.

   In the absence of a split between GFCF by private households and unincorporated businesses, DIAN could assign all housing investment within the household sector to private households. Specifically, when subtracting recoverable VAT under the benchmark scenario, it would first remove the investment in dwellings by the household sector from the total GFCF recorded in the construction row of the use table. Other GFCF within the household sector could be assigned to unincorporated businesses that can recover VAT paid on investment. A similar exercise needs to be performed for government investment. However, GFCF by the government is not concentrated on one asset. Therefore, the asset categories in the national accounts must be matched to the products in the use table for all GFCF assets purchased by the government. Ideally, DIAN can obtain a precise correspondence table between the two classifications (product rows in the use table and asset categories integrated the national accounts) from the statistical office. In the absence of such a table, the OECD proposed a mapping that would use the available information to the best extent possible.

Breaking down the global compliance gap

Currently, DIAN calculates an economy-wide VAT compliance gap, represented by the ratio of actual VAT revenue to the modelled potential revenue under the current tax system. Subsequently, revenue forgone is adjusted by the compliance gap (or evasion rate) to ensure that revenue lost due to non-compliance is not wrongly assigned to the revenue forgone of VAT TEs. Without any correction, absolute revenue forgone would be overestimated for each item because part of the difference between potential VAT revenue and the benchmark revenue is caused by non-compliance.

Relying on a global compliance gap to estimate product-level TEs is problematic, however. The current approach overestimates revenue forgone for goods and services produced in sectors for which non-compliance exceeds the global average while the reverse applies to goods and services from highly compliant sectors.

To break down the compliance gap, DIAN needs to estimate potential revenue by sector, which it cannot do within its current demand-side framework. To obtain sector-level compliance gaps, potential revenue by sector (using the supply-side approach) needs to be compared to actual revenue from sector-coded tax returns that DIAN has access to.

The IMF VAT GAP model offers a framework to decompose total revenue losses into sector-level compliance and policy gaps (Hutton, 2017[1]). DIAN could leverage the IMF approach to break down its economy-wide compliance gap by sector. Then, these more granular compliance gaps can be applied to revenue-forgone estimates for the different products. However, DIAN would need to re-estimate potential revenue by sector using the IMF model because, unlike DIAN, the IMF follows a supply-side approach. The national accounts identities suggest that, in theory, the demand-side approach applied by DIAN and the supply-side approach applied by the IMF should deliver the same result for revenue forgone by product.

An obvious question would be whether it makes sense for Colombia to switch entirely to a supply-side approach – not only to estimate sectoral compliance gaps but also to estimate the revenue forgone by product. Since the IMF model needs to be introduced in any case to obtain potential revenue for the compliance gap, it would be straightforward to apply the benchmark rate instead of the current rate – and also calculate revenue forgone. However, the supply-side approach requires more data tables (e.g., granular data on exports, imports and investment by product and sector). If approximations are necessary, the supply-side approach will likely deliver less precise results.

Two options are available to DIAN:

1. **Switch completely to a supply-side approach.** DIAN can switch to estimating revenue forgone by product based on the supply table ("supply-side approach") if reliable data sources are available and then correct revenue forgone by sectoral compliance gaps obtained by the IMF methodology.
2. **Use the supply-side approach only to calculate sectoral compliance gaps.** DIAN can continue estimating revenue forgone by product based on the use table ("demand-side approach"), but then correct revenue forgone by sectoral compliance gaps obtained by implementing the IMF methodology. It may be worth calculating revenue foregone by item based on both the supply table and the use table and comparing the results to assess the accuracy of the two options.[6]

If DIAN decides to break down the compliance gap by sector, it could apply the IMF VAT Gap methodology as expounded in Box 2.1. Some adjustments would be necessary, however, to align the framework with how the VAT system works in Colombia.

DIAN can follow the five steps outlined in Box 2.1 to compute potential revenue by sector under the current tax rate regime. When estimating compliance gaps, DIAN should assume VAT on investment is not recoverable (except for the hydrocarbon sector) as it currently does.[7]

Further adjustments that DIAN currently applies and that aim at aligning the national accounts with the way that the VAT functions in practice (e.g., excluding consumption by residents abroad) should also be maintained. This applies to how DIAN deals with the non-recoverability of input VAT paid on excluded products. In the supply-side approach, it would continue to estimate the share of excluded products among each sector's output (e^s) and disallow the sector to recover VAT paid on the same share of its inputs.

The methodology outlined in Box 2.1 also discusses how actual revenue from VAT returns can be calculated to ensure it is consistent with how potential revenue is estimated from the supply and use tables. For example, tax payments need to be reallocated from the year of payment to the year the taxable transaction took place. One additional difficulty concerns the fact that some businesses do not actually transfer money to the government when they are liable to pay VAT but rather reduce the (non-refundable) excess credits they have accumulated over past periods. DIAN could check total net assessments (as defined in Box 2.1) against net collections for earlier years to evaluate the magnitude of the difference and the importance of accumulated excess credits. It is also crucial for DIAN to verify with the statistical agency how businesses operating in multiple industries are assigned to individual sectors, and whether this is broadly in line with how the same is done in VAT returns.

The last step explains how DIAN could apply the compliance gap by sector to the revenue forgone by product if it decides to maintain the demand-side approach to quantify the VAT TEs. For each product, the compliance gap would be equal to the weighted average of compliance gaps found in the industries that produce the product. In detailed supply and use tables, usually only one sector produces a certain good. In that case, no weighted average would be necessary because DIAN would simply make use of that sector's compliance gap.[8]

Box 2.1. The IMF VAT Gap methodology

The International Monetary Fund has developed a top-down framework to estimate revenue gaps in the VAT (Hutton, 2017). It allows tax administrations to quantify and decompose revenue losses by industry sector. For each sector, the total gap is broken down into compliance and policy gaps. The compliance gap contrasts actual tax receipts with how much VAT a country could collect under the current rate regime in the absence of tax evasion. The policy gap assesses the revenue loss from non-standard VAT rates and exclusions. The two key data sources are detailed national accounts tables and by-sector information on actual VAT collections.

Even though the policy gap (i.e. VAT rates below the standard rate and exclusions) is similar to revenue forgone in TE analysis, the two concepts are not identical. For example, in the standard configuration, the policy gap assumes full compliance (i.e. does not deduct the rectangle in the upper right corner of Figure 2.1). In contrast, revenue forgone estimates are adjusted for non-compliance by assuming tax compliance would not change when moving to the benchmark tax system (i.e. deducts the rectangle in the upper right corner of Figure 2.1).Furthermore, the IMF reports policy gaps on the industry level whereas revenue forgone is typically presented by product. These discrepancies originate from the different goals of the two undertakings. The IMF VAT GAP framework aims at identifying high and low-compliance sectors, as well as those industries that strongly benefit from the current set of reduced rates and exclusions. In contrast, TE reports quantify the revenue forgone from individual product-level tax provisions that deviate from a benchmark tax system.

Infographic 2.1. Breakdown of policy and compliance gaps

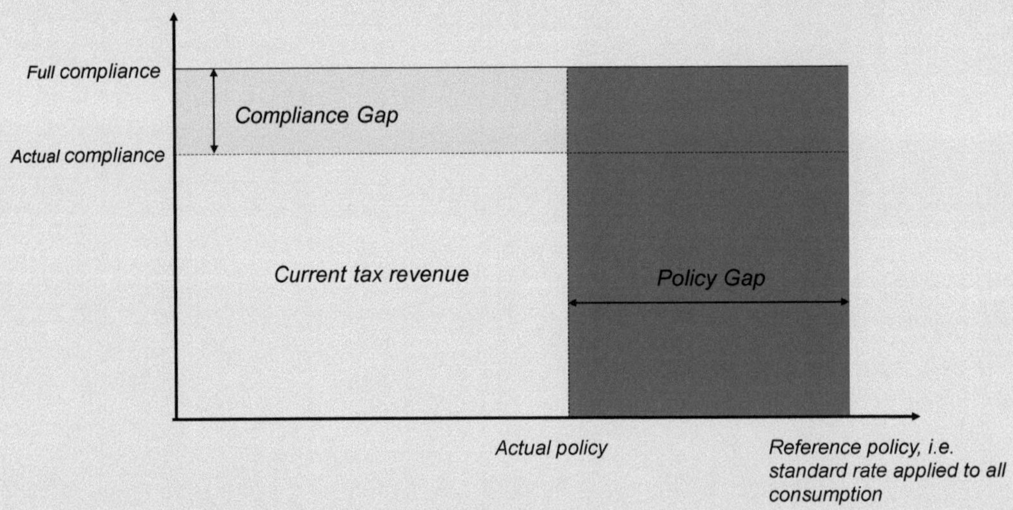

Source: Adapted from (Hutton, 2017[1]).

The IMF follows a supply-side approach when estimating potential revenue. In national accounts, the supply table records output from domestic production. It constitutes the starting point of the IMF's revenue estimate. Broadly speaking, the IMF models VAT as a tax on value-added minus exports plus imports. First, the model applies the respective VAT rates to domestic output. Then, potential revenue is corrected to account for: (i) the recoverability of VAT paid on inputs and investment, (ii) the inclusion of imports in the VAT base and (iii) the VAT exemption of exports.

The following steps and data sources are required to estimate potential VAT revenue (PR) by sector (s) in the IMF VAT GAP framework:

- The model starts from the **VAT levied on the output of each sector** (O^s) in the supply table. The vector of actual VAT rates by product (p) is multiplied by each sector column in the supply table. In each column, the sum of goods and services (in the rows) delivers the sector total.

$$PR_O^s = \sum_p O_p^s * Rate_p$$

- As part of any VAT system, businesses can recover **VAT paid on inputs** (N^S). Hence, the potential revenue represented by the intermediate consumption columns in the use table multiplied by the tax vector needs to be **subtracted**. In each column, the sum of goods and services (in the rows) delivers the sector total. The same applies to VAT paid on **capital formation** $(GFCF^S)$.
  - If a product-by-industry investment matrix is unavailable, the second-best option would be to check whether the use table records capital formation as a row at the very bottom. If not, capital formation by sector could be approximated based on the consumption of fixed capital recorded as part of total output at the bottom of the use table. If neither of these sources is available, value-added by sector could proxy the share of total capital formation assigned to each sector.
  - To account for the non-recoverability of input and investment VAT paid on the production of excluded goods and services, one estimates the share of excluded products among each sector's output (e^s) and disallow the sector to recover VAT paid on the same share of its inputs.

$$PR_N^s = \sum_p (N_p^s + GFCF_p^s) * Rate_p * (1 - e^s)$$

- **Imports** (M^s) are subject to VAT but not part of the domestic output as recorded in the supply table. Hence, the potential revenue represented by each sector column (s) in the import use table multiplied by the tax vector by product (p) needs to be **added**. In each column, the sum of goods and services (in the rows) delivers the sector total. If the statistical office does not compile an import use table by product and sector, the *UN Handbook on Supply and Use Tables and Input-Output Tables* (United Nations, 2018[7]), in particular chapter 8, could provide guidance on how DIAN could proceed.

$$PR_M^s = \sum_p M_p^s * Rate_p$$

- **Exports** (X^s) are not subject to VAT but part of the domestic output as recorded in the supply table. Hence, the potential revenue represented by the sector-by-product export matrix multiplied by the tax vector needs to be **subtracted**. For each sector column, the sum of goods and services (in the rows) delivers the sector total.
- Unfortunately, such a matrix is often not available. In that case, export shares by sector can be applied to total sector output by product in the supply table

$$PR_X^s = \sum_p X_p^s * Rate_p$$

- Potential revenue by sector is a function of the four components.

$$PR^S = PR_O^s - PR_N^s + PR_M^s - PR_X^s$$

To obtain the policy gap by sector, potential revenue is computed twice. First, the tax vector carries the set of current VAT rates (CR). Then, it consists of the standard VAT rate (SR) for each product, removing reduced rates, exemptions and exclusions. The ratio between the two measures defines the policy gap.

$$Policy\ Gap^s = \frac{PR_{SR}^s - PR_{CR}^s}{PR_{CR}^s}$$

The compliance gap requires information on the actual tax revenue by sector. Choosing the right measure for actual revenue is not straightforward, however. To be aligned with the national accounts, revenue should be assigned to the tax period rather than the period in which the tax is transferred to the government. Otherwise, delays in payment or the time schedule of refund would affect the compliance gap. The natural approach would be to work with the net VAT self-assessed by businesses as recorded in their annual VAT returns. However, not all declared VAT will eventually be collected – and some businesses will be allowed to recover less VAT than initially declared.

The IMF recommends using "accrued collections", a measure that combines actual tax payments for debits and assessments for VAT credits. As a first step, VAT payments received from each business in a sector are reallocated to the tax period. Thereby, the measure avoids relying on self-assessed tax liabilities. However, businesses regularly use credits from earlier periods to reduce the VAT burden in the current tax period. Merely reallocating actual tax receipts would hence lead to a biased compliance gap. For example, a zero VAT liability in a given tax period does not necessarily mean that no VAT should be assigned to that period. The business could have accumulated excess credits that it used up in the tax period. Reductions in excess credit therefore need to be counted as VAT liabilities, which requires data on the stock of excess tax credits by businesses.

Once potential revenue (PR) and actual revenue (AR) are available at the sector level, the ratio between the two defined the compliance gap.

$$Compliance\ Gap^s = \frac{PR_{CR}^s - AR^s}{PR_{CR}^s}$$

The supply framework warrants one important adjustment to potential revenue. The output of the wholesale and retail sector is not recorded as a regular column in the supply table, but is only available in the form of trade margins. At the same time, the commercial sector collects net VAT, which will appear in the sector-coded tax returns. Without adjustment, the compliance gap of sectors would be overestimated because the national accounts record VAT levied on trade in the sector producing the product. In tax returns, on the other hand, parts of the value-added would appear in the wholesale and retail sector. To make the national accounts and tax return data consistent, customs data can be used to reallocate imports to the agent of import (e.g., a trading business), rather than the final destination. If a full import use table is available, one can assign the entire final consumption column to the wholesale and trade sector. If available, business surveys allow performing the same adjustment for exports. The statutory rate for the wholesale and retail sector can be computed as a weighted average of the tax rates applicable to all (product-level) trade margins in the supply table.

Source: Based on (Hutton, 2017[11]).

Revenue forgone from Free Trade Zones

Businesses located in Free Trade Zones (FTZs) enjoy a VAT exemption on purchases from abroad and on inputs they buy from the national territory. However, FTZ businesses are obliged to charge VAT if they sell goods and services back to the domestic economy following a special tax base calculation.

Currently, DIAN estimates revenue forgone from FTZs outside the VAT model, focusing only on the TE that arises from the exemption of goods and services sold by domestic businesses to FTZ users (disregarding the import exemption). To calculate revenue under the benchmark, DIAN takes the effective average VAT rate on imports to the entire Colombian economy and applies it to the total value of goods and services sold to businesses in FTZs. The effective rate aims at taking into account that some goods and services are excluded or taxed at reduced rates. Finally, DIAN subtracts the VAT actually collected by FTZ businesses from this "benchmark" revenue to determine the TE.

This procedure is incorrect as it compares the input VAT the FTZ user would have paid in the absence of the exemption to the actual VAT the FTZ user currently collects when it sells goods and services that are not excluded to the national territory. The latter value does not only include the value of the inputs involved in the production but also the value added by FTZ users in the production of these goods and services and hence is not comparable. Furthermore, the latter value corresponds to a tax liability that arises in any case – whether FTZs exist or not. Just like domestic businesses, FTZ businesses are obliged to declare and charge VAT on sales to the national territory. It is hence unclear why such a figure would not also be part of the benchmark revenue collected in the absence of FTZs. As re-sales from FTZs to the national economy are subject to VAT and VAT is levied on final consumption occurring in FTZs, all revenue forgone linked to the FTZ VAT exemption originates from the existence of other TEs, in particular exclusions. In the absence of exclusions, VAT revenue forgone from the FTZ exemption would be zero.

Revenue forgone from the FTZ VAT exemption arises only in two cases:

- Excluded goods and services are sold from the national territory to FTZ businesses;
- FTZ businesses sell excluded goods and services to the domestic economy.

In the first case, when a domestic business sells a VAT excluded good to a FTZ user, the FTZ turns the VAT exclusion applied to the good into a VAT exemption. The FTZ user does not pay any VAT on its purchase but the domestic business (selling the good to the FTZ user) can now (because of the exemption rather than the exclusion) recover the VAT it had paid on the inputs purchased to produce the VAT excluded good. In the absence of FTZs (or if one domestic business sells the excluded good to another domestic business), the domestic business would not be allowed to receive a refund for the input VAT paid on the production of excluded goods. Hence, because of the FTZ exemption, the government loses revenue (it now has to refund the domestic business the input VAT). Therefore, in the first case, the FTZ exemptions result in a positive TE.[9]

In the second case, when a FTZ business sells a VAT excluded good or service to a domestic company, the FTZ business did not pay VAT on the inputs it used to produce the excluded good in the first place (because all inputs it purchases from the national territory or from abroad are VAT exempt). However, without the FTZ VAT exemption, the same business would have paid VAT on all the inputs it has purchased and, because it used these inputs to produce excluded goods and services, the business would not have been allowed to receive a refund for the input VAT it paid. Again, because of the FTZ exemption, the government loses revenue (it does not collect the unrecoverable input VAT it normally collects when businesses produce excluded goods). Therefore, in the second case, the FTZ exemption results in another positive TE.[10]

Whether revenue forgone from these two types of cases is large or not depends on the type of goods FTZ users buy from the national territory and the goods and services FTZ users sell to the domestic territory. If most inputs are excluded goods or if most outputs benefit from a VAT exclusion, the revenue forgone might be significant. However, even in the case in which this revenue forgone was small, this would not imply that economic distortions caused by FTZs would be negligible. A TE can shift the burden between taxpayers, induce behavioural responses, or increase incentives for tax fraud, but these effects are not reflected in revenue forgone estimates.

To estimate VAT revenue forgone from FTZs, DIAN should first define a benchmark, which removes the VAT exemption on FTZs but keeps in place all other TEs (exclusions, reduced rates, exemptions). Such an approach would allow DIAN to isolate VAT revenue forgone linked to FTZs from other VAT TEs.

Quantifying revenue forgone from FTZs requires determining the relative weight of excluded goods and services among the output of businesses involved in sales between FTZs and the domestic territory. The OECD presented two options to DIAN:

1. DIAN can rely primarily on data from tax returns. In light of the type of information available in VAT returns, different strategies need to be used for each of the two scenarios that give rise to revenue forgone.
    a) Revenue forgone from the recoverability of input VAT when domestic businesses sell excluded goods to FTZ users: Unfortunately, VAT returns currently only ask domestic businesses to specify total sales to FTZs.[11] It hence does not seem possible to determine the share of excluded goods and services among the sales made by domestic businesses to FTZ users (Table 2.5). However, domestic businesses need to declare the sales of excluded goods and services to domestic users in their VAT returns.[12] DIAN could therefore assume that sales of excluded goods and services to FTZ users mirror the overall share of excluded goods among domestic businesses' sales as implicitly available in their tax returns. [13] Once DIAN has found, for each domestic business, a proxy for the share of excluded goods among non-FTZ-related sales, other information available in the VAT return would allow DIAN to estimate the size of the excess recoverable input VAT linked to the fact that sales to FTZs are treated similarly to exports and are thereby VAT exempted. For each domestic business, the VAT returns include a breakdown of exempt, reduced rate, and excluded inputs, which enables DIAN to calculate the total input VAT paid by each domestic business. Finally, DIAN would multiply the excluded-goods-to-FTZ-users output share (e.g. 2% of the business' output are excluded goods sold to TZs) and the total input VAT paid. The result approximates the amount of input VAT that was recoverable by the domestic business because of the FTZ VAT exemption.

For each domestic business i with sales to FTZ users:

$$Revenue\ forgone_i \approx \frac{Excluded\ sales\ to\ nonFTZ_i}{Sales\ to\ nonFTZ_i} * \frac{Sales\ to\ FTZ_i}{Sales_i} * Input\ VAT_i$$

$Input\ VAT_i$ is obtained from tax returns.

   b) Revenue forgone from the non-payment of input VAT when FTZ businesses sell excluded goods and services to domestic users: For FTZ businesses, the amount of excluded goods sold to the domestic economy can be obtained from the import VAT declarations (Form 500), which ask businesses to specify the imported products.[14] However, for FTZ businesses, information on the breakdown of inputs purchased is missing (Table 2.5). This is because FTZ businesses do not submit the standard VAT declaration but only declare as imports their sales to the domestic territory (they do not pay VAT on their inputs). Hence, DIAN would have to find a proxy for the amount and composition of inputs (both purchased from the national territory and abroad) used by FTZ businesses to produce excluded goods sold to the national territory. One option would be to first determine the sector of each FTZ business[15] and then draw upon the supply and use tables to estimate the ratio of input VAT to output for the respective sector. Estimating total input VAT per sector would require multiplying the sector column in the use table and the current-rate VAT vector. Subsequently, DIAN would apply that ratio to the total sales of excluded goods by the FTZ business to the national territory. DIAN could then estimate the VAT that FTZ businesses would have paid (and would not have been able to recover) if they had produced the same excluded goods in the domestic territory and sold them to the domestic market.

For each FTZ business i in sector s with sales to domestic users:

$$Revenue\ forgone_i \approx Excluded\ sales\ to\ domestic\ users_i * \frac{Input\ VAT_s}{Output_s}$$

$Input\ VAT_s$ requires multiplying the sector column in the use table and the current-rate VAT vector. The output of the sector $Output_s$ is estimated from the supply table.

Table 2.5. Missing data linked to sales involving Free Trade Zone businesses

		Breakdown of inputs	
		Available	Not available
Share of excluded sales	Available		**FTZ to domestic users**
	Not available	**Domestic to FTZ users**	

2. If detailed VAT returns cannot be used in the way that was suggested above, DIAN can combine a more limited use of VAT returns with drawing upon information about production structures recorded in the supply and use tables. Such an approach would only require DIAN to determine from VAT returns (i) the sector of businesses and (ii-a) total sales *to* FTZs (for domestic businesses) or (ii-b) *from* FTZs to the domestic territory (for FTZ businesses). Based on this information, DIAN could then assume that transactions involving FTZs mirror the average activity of businesses in the respective sector, as recorded in supply and use tables. For example, if the supply table states that 10% of a sector's output consists of excluded goods and services, the same share would be applied to FTZ-related sales. Furthermore, the approach assumes (as in 1b) that the composition of inputs used for sales involving FTZs is sufficiently similar to the average composition of inputs in the sector. Based on the supply and use tables, DIAN would estimate the average value of inputs necessary to produce one unit of each sector's output. Finally, combining for each business (i) total sales to or from FTZs, (ii) the sector, (iii) the average share of excluded goods and services among the output of the sector (from the supply table), (iv) the average size and composition of inputs per unit of the sector's output (from the use table) and (v) the vector of current VAT rates, DIAN could proxy the revenue forgone (i.e., recoverable input VAT) linked to the FTZ VAT exemption. The difference with the first option is that this approach does not require DIAN to estimate the share of excluded goods for each business.

For each domestic business i in sector s with sales to FTZ users:

$$Revenue\ forgone_i \approx Sales\ to\ FTZ\ users_i * e_s * \frac{Input\ VAT_s}{Output_s}$$

For each FTZ business i in sector s with sales to domestic users:

$$Revenue\ forgone_i \approx Sales\ to\ domestic\ users_i * e_s * \frac{Input\ VAT_s}{Output_s}$$

$Input\ VAT_s$ requires multiplying the sector column in the use table and the current-rate VAT vector. The output of the sector $Output_s$ is estimated from the supply table.

The share of excluded goods among total output of sector s (e_s) can be obtained from the supply table as well (and is readily available from the VAT model).

DIAN can choose to integrate the measurement of the FTZ VAT exemption into its existing VAT model. In the model, the impact of the FTZ exemption applied to excluded goods would be similar to the export of excluded goods (exclusions turning into exemptions), which are already reflected in the model. The model would remain unchanged when calculating revenue forgone from other TEs. Both for the benchmark and for potential revenue, the share of output going to or coming from FTZs is set to zero. However, revenue forgone of other TEs would be affected because the compliance gap estimate will be impacted by the FTZ revenue forgone adjustment.

Contrary to common practice, DIAN should modify potential revenue rather than benchmark revenue when quantifying the FTZ exemption.[16] To calculate revenue forgone from the FTZ VAT exemption within the model, the share of excluded output of each sector can be used to approximate the share of excluded output sold to FTZ users or sold by FTZ businesses to domestic companies (as in option 2). Alternatively, more precise estimations can be derived from VAT returns covering FTZ-related sales (following the suggestions in option 1). For each sector, excluded output produced in FTZs and sold to domestic users or produced in the domestic economy and sold to FTZ users should be aggregated and divided by total sector output. For example, DIAN may determine that 1% of the output of sector 1 are excluded goods sold between domestic companies and FTZ users. Incorporating these shares into the model would increase recoverable input VAT (as excluded goods become exempt through the FTZ exemption) in each sector, which would reduce government revenue. Consider the following example: Without FTZs, 10% of output in sector 1 would be excluded goods. In such a scenario, the model assumes that 10% of input VAT paid by businesses in sector 1 cannot be recovered (and that 90% of the input VAT paid can be recovered). Let's assume that that 50% of the output in sector 1 is sold to FTZ businesses. This would imply that 50% of the excluded goods sold by businesses in sector 1 are VAT exempt. As a result, only 5% of the input VAT paid cannot be recovered and 95% of the input VAT paid can be recovered. As a result, the potential revenue is reduced by reducing the shares of excluded output (because FTZs turn exclusions into exemptions) and by increasing the share of recoverable VAT by sector.

To calculate the compliance gap, actual VAT revenue would be compared to potential revenue in the presence of FTZs. The fact that FTZs reduce potential revenue is thereby already taken into account. As a result, the compliance gap is not inflated and there is no need to adjust it further.

If DIAN does not integrate FTZs into the model, it needs to adjust potential revenue (i.e. subtract the revenue forgone from FTZs) when it estimates the compliance gap in the model. Otherwise, when comparing actual revenue to potential revenue, the model would wrongly assign the revenue forgone from FTZs as VAT non-compliance. The result would be an inflated estimate of the compliance gap, which in turn would bias downward all TEs.

To a varying degree, the suggested approaches rely on the assumption that transactions between FTZs and the national territory are comparable to other business transactions in terms of the share of excluded goods and services sold, either on the level of the business or at the sector level. This may not be correct as the VAT exemption can incentivize FTZ businesses to specialize in the production of excluded goods and services – and domestic businesses to route excluded goods and services through FTZ businesses before re-selling them to the domestic market. DIAN should attempt to evaluate the extent to which such behaviour is actually taking place. Domestic businesses and FTZ businesses may be asked to provide more detailed information to DIAN, which would serve different causes, including improving the accuracy of the measurement of VAT TEs.

2.5 Impact of tax expenditures that are currently not reported

Table 2.6 lists tax provisions whose revenue foregone are currently not measured. Any VAT TE that is not measured within the DIAN model (or that is outside the model and for which potential revenue is not adjusted) leads to an overestimation of the compliance gap. In order to avoid this bias, these TEs should be measured – if not by using the DIAN VAT model, then through other means – such that the potential VAT revenue can be adjusted accordingly when computing the VAT compliance gap. Priority should be given to the largest VAT TEs; TEs that are expected to have low revenue foregone or for which the estimation would be time consuming and complicated can be given lower priority. Even if revenue forgone cannot be measured, the TE report should list these TEs in order to increase transparency. If revenue forgone can only be determined with a high degree of uncertainty, an estimate may be included to provide an order of magnitude, but in this case, the report should indicate that the revenue foregone estimate is highly uncertain. Table 2.6 includes preliminary recommendations about the VAT TEs that are currently not reported and that could be measured with priority, based on the size of the expected revenue forgone and based on data availability other than information included in the national accounts.

The information included in Table 2.6 is based on a comparison of the full list of VAT exclusions, exemptions and reduced rates with the information that is included in the *Marco Fiscal de Mediano Plazo (MFMP)* (Minhacienda, 2021[8]). As the MFMP does not report revenue forgone on a product-by-product basis but rather lists TEs within groups, it is not straightforward to determine whether a TE is currently measured or not by DIAN. The list provided below is therefore tentative. Annex E provides a list of all TEs within the VAT that have been identified in Colombia, based on the VAT benchmark proposal. The list could serve as a template for the list of TEs that DIAN should aim at including in its annual TE report.

The consumption of food and beverages in restaurants and bars is excluded from VAT and, instead, is taxed under the National Consumption Tax at a rate of 8%. The National Consumption Tax itself would be included in the benchmark tax system. As a result of exchanges between the MOF, DIAN and the OECD in the context of the elaboration of this Review, DIAN has included an estimate of the revenue forgone from the VAT exclusion of food and beverages in restaurants and bars in the latest edition of its MFMP for the first time (Minhacienda, 2022[2]). DIAN is advised to continue estimating the revenue forgone from this exclusion and to continue highlighting that the consumption is taxed under the National Consumption Tax.[17] In addition, DIAN could provide information in the report on the revenue generated by the National Consumption Tax that is applied to food and beverages consumed in restaurants and bars. In the future, measuring revenue forgone from this exclusion would ideally apply a sector-specific VAT compliance gap for bars, restaurants and other businesses that sell food. While such an estimation might be challenging, it would add significant value and would therefore be worthwhile to be undertaken.

Finally, DIAN could include a separate section on VAT measures introduced during the pandemic. Table 2.7 presents transitory VAT relief and recovery measures introduced during the pandemic. The expected revenue foregone of these measures should be deducted from potential revenue that is determined using the DIAN VAT model and the revenue forgone of these measures could be reported separately.

Table 2.6. Permanent VAT TEs currently not reported in the Marco Fiscal de Mediano Plazo (MFMP)

Not listed as a TE nor revenue forgone measured	Potentially large revenue forgone	Data for measuring revenue forgone outside the model likely available
Exclusions		
Food and beverages served in restaurants, cafeterias, ice cream shops, fruit shops, bakeries or take away, alcoholic beverages consumed in bars and discotheques taxed under National Consumption Tax	√[1]	
Import of goods subject to postal traffic under USD 200	√	√
Goods and services sold or imported to overseas archipelago department of San Andrés and Providencia		
Imports of food for human and animal consumption from neighboring countries to Vichada, Guajira, Guainía and Vaupés		
Sale of goods for human and animal consumption, clothes, medicines for human and veterinary use, hygiene articles and building materials in Guainía, Guaviare, Vaupés and Vichada Departments and Amazonas only if they are used within the corresponding department borders		
Sales of bicycles, motorcycles, motocross and spare parts in Amazonas, Guainía, Guaviare, Vaupés and Vichada		
Products that are purchased or introduced to the department of Amazonas within the framework of the Colombian-Peruvian agreement and the agreement with the Federative Republic of Brazil.		
Supply of airplane fuel for national air transport services (passenger and cargo) from and to Guainía, Amazonas, Vaupés, San Andrés y Providencia, Arauca and Vichada		
Bicycles, electric bicycles, electric scooters, skates, skateboards, electric skateboards, scooters, and electric scooters, up to 50 UVT (USD 470 approx.)[2]	√	√
Desktop or laptop computers whose value does not exceed 50 UVT (USD 465 approx.)[2]	√	√
Smart mobile devices (tablets and cell phones) whose value does not exceed 22 UVT (USD 210 approx.)[2]	√	√
The sale or import of machinery and equipment for the development of projects or activities that are registered in the National Registry for the Reduction of Greenhouse Gas Emissions	√	√
Imports of machinery and equipment for recycling, waste disposal and treatment and water treatment		
Imports for diplomatic missions use		
Objects with artistic, cultural and historical interest purchased by museums part of the National Museum Network and public entities		
Exemptions		
Tourist services provided to residents abroad that are used in Colombian territory, originating from packages sold by operating agencies or hotels registered in the national tourism registry	√	√
Tourist packages sold by hotels registered in the national tourism registry to operating agencies, provided that the tourist services have to be used in the national territory by residents abroad	√	√
VAT free days (clothing, appliances, toys, sports items, school supplies, goods and supplies destined to the agricultural sector)[2]	√	√
Solar panels		
Complete passenger public transport motor vehicles and individually purchased motorized chassis and bodywork to form a new complete public passenger transport motor vehicle.		
Reduced rates		
Passenger air tickets, related services and the administrative fee associated with their marketing	√	√

Note 1. DIAN has included an estimate for the first time in the MFMP 2022 (Minhacienda, 2022[2]).
Note 2. DIAN already corrects potential revenue from the VAT model considering these TEs. However, the revenue forgone from these TEs is not published separately.

Table 2.7. Transitory VAT relief and recovery measures introduced during the pandemic

Not listed as a TE nor revenue forgone measured	Potentially large revenue forgone	Data for measuring revenue forgone outside the model likely available
Exclusions		
Artisan crafts (Law 2068 of 2021)		
Restaurants under franchise agreements (Law 2068 of 2021)	√	√
Exemptions		
Hotel and tourism services (Law 2068 of 2021)	√[1]	√
Mobile phone plans (voice calls and Internet) up to two UVTs during 4 months (Decree 540 of 2020)		
Import of cars for the transport of passengers or cargo until 31 December 2021 (Decree 789 of 2020)	√	√
Import and sale of supplies indispensable for the prevention and the provision of the medical services against COVID-19 (Decree 438 of 2020; Decree 551 of 2021)		
Reduced rates		
Flight tickets up to December 2022[2]	√	√
National air fuel Jet A1 and/or air fuel 100/130		
Refunds		
VAT paid by some sports organizations during some athletic events in 2021 and 2022		

Note 1. DIAN has included an estimate for the first time in the MFMP 2022 (Minhacienda, 2022[2]).
Note 2. DIAN already corrects potential revenue from the VAT model considering these TEs. However, the revenue forgone from these TEs is not published separately.

2.6 Suggested steps to estimate VAT revenue forgone

The analysis and recommendations presented in the previous sections leads to the following steps to estimate revenue forgone on an item-by-item basis:

1. Estimate revenue forgone from FTZs and other TEs that are not part of the top-down model (see previous sections).
2. Calculate potential revenue under the current tax system within the top-down model, and correct it for the amount obtained in the previous step (ideally by sector).
3. Access and compile actual by-sector VAT revenue from tax return data. Estimate the compliance gap by contrasting actual revenue with the model-based potential revenue (ideally by sector).
4. Estimate revenue forgone from product-level provisions within the top-down model and correct the amount by the compliance gap.

2.7 Additional potential improvements regarding VAT revenue forgone measurement

Finally, DIAN may also want to evaluate the benefits of using tax return data and other sources of information to check the robustness of the estimates that are derived from the VAT model.

In addition, there are some TEs currently measured in the VAT model that possibly could be measured more precisely using other data sources. For example:

- The exemption on internet connection and access services from fixed networks of residential subscribers in socioeconomic levels 1 and 2. It may be worth exploring whether telecom companies can provide DIAN with the value of this consumption.
- Revenue forgone from the VAT exclusion on financial services is likely not well captured in the national accounts data. This is an area in which, robustness checks using additional data could improve the measurement significantly. It may also be worth acknowledging in DIAN's TE report that the current estimates of this TE may not be very reliable.

References

Asociación Nacional de Empresarios de Colombia (2019), *Estudio de Impacto Jurídico, Económico Y Fiscal De Las Zonas Francas.* [9]

Department of Finance Canada (2021), *Report on Federal Tax Expenditures - Concepts, Estimates, Evaluations.* [3]

Hutton, E. (2017), "The Revenue Administration–Gap Analysis Program: Model and Methodology for Value-Added Tax Gap Estimation", *IMF Technical Notes and Manuals* 4. [1]

Minhacienda (2022), *Marco Fiscal de Mediano Plazo 2022.* [2]

Minhacienda (2021), *Marco Fiscal de Mediano Plazo 2021.* [8]

OECD (2017), *International VAT/GST Guidelines.* [4]

Poniatowski, G. et al. (2019), *Study and Reports on the VAT Gap in the EU-28 Member States: 2019 Final Report*, CASE-Center for Social and Economic Research. [6]

United Nations (2018), *Handbook on Supply and Use Tables and Input-Output Tables with Extensions and Applications.* [7]

United Nations (2009), *System of National Accounts 2008.* [5]

Notes

[1] Private households, the government and non-profit organizations cannot recover input VAT under the multi-stage VAT system. Hence, for VAT purposes, their investment activity is similar to final consumption. State-owned companies are treated for benchmark purposes as private companies.

[2] This report follows the terminology used in Colombia with VAT exclusions referring to VAT exemptions in the OECD terminology and exemptions referring to zero-rated goods or services.

[3] In this case the tax is levied exclusively over the service fees obtained by the constructor. When fees are not agreed upon, the tax will trigger on the profit of the builder. The only input VAT that can be credited is input VAT directly associated with the provision of the service. VAT paid over costs and expenses necessary for the construction of the building are non-creditable.

[4] Even if this case may be debatable, charging VAT on these services would be impractical and would not lead to an increase in revenue. For this reason, the report recommends not listing or measuring it as a TE.

[5] Colombia currently applies an additional 3% downward adjustment to the resulting estimate.

[6] Note that revenue-forgone estimates require less granular data than the estimation of compliance gaps by sector. For example, a product-by-sector split of investment is necessary to obtain potential revenue by sector but not to obtain potential revenue by product.

[7] The proposed changes to measuring investment VAT outlined above only refer to the calculation of *benchmark* revenue within the model.

[8] Similar to the economy-wide compliance gap, the calculation assumes that the same compliance gap applies regardless of whether the output is used (i) as an intermediate input or (ii) goes to final demand.

[9] See Scenario 3 in Annex B for a graphical representation.

[10] See Scenario 4 in Annex B for a graphical representation.

[11] See box 33 in the Form 300 (Declaración del Impuesto sobre las Ventas – IVA).

[12] See box 39 in the Form 300 (Declaración del Impuesto sobre las Ventas – IVA).

[13] If DIAN can reconstruct these data points from alternative sources like the Export Declarations (Form 600) submitted by domestic businesses or the "Formulario de Movimiento de Mercancías", these breakdowns should be preferred over the approximations presented here.

[14] Note that it is not necessary to determine whether the FTZ business used inputs from the national territory or from abroad. It is sufficient to know or approximate the total value of excluded goods sold from FTZ businesses to domestic users.

[15] The sector of each business can be obtained based on its tax identification number. There also exist studies that have already assigned all FTZ businesses to sectors (Asociación Nacional de Empresarios de Colombia, 2019[9]).

[16] Benchmark revenue could be viewed as equivalent to the potential revenue scenario DIAN has estimated so far.

[17] The National Consumption Tax was not levied during this year as part of the temporary COVID relief measures.

3 Measuring and Reporting Corporate Income Tax Expenditures

This chapter presents the approach that Colombia currently follows to measure and report CIT TEs, and identifies areas for improvement including (i) the measurement of CIT revenue forgone, (ii) the presentation of CIT revenue forgone in the TE report, (iii) the extension of the TE report with a distributional analysis of CIT TEs and (iv) the additional data sources that can be used to quantify revenue forgone. The chapter also includes item-by-item CIT revenue forgone estimates for 2020 and distributional analysis of a few TEs estimated by DIAN following the assistance provided by the OECD.

Summary

This chapter presents the approach that DIAN currently follows to measure and report CIT TEs, and identifies areas for improvement. The chapter presents recommendations in a number of areas, including (i) the measurement of CIT revenue forgone, (ii) the presentation of CIT revenue forgone in the TE report, (iii) the extension of the TE report with a distributional analysis of CIT TEs and (iv) the additional data sources that can be used to quantify revenue forgone. The chapter also includes item-by-item CIT revenue forgone estimates for 2020 carried out by DIAN based on exogenous information merged to business tax returns for all corporations that are required to submit this information.

General assessment of the DIAN TE methodology

- The two most recent editions of the *Marco Fiscal de Mediano Plazo (*MFMP) – the annual report published by the Ministry of Finance, which includes an annex with TE results (Minhacienda, 2022[1]; Minhacienda, 2021[2]) – have introduced a number of improvements in the measurement of CIT TEs, following the guidance provided by the Tax Incentives Commission (OECD, DIAN and Minhacienda, 2021[3]). For example, while tax revenue forgone from reduced rates was previously only estimated for Free Trade Zones, it is now estimated also for other special regimes (ZOMAC, ZESE, hotels, publishers, state owned companies, non-profit organisations, co-operatives, and perennial crops). Furthermore, in line with the recommendation of the Tax Incentives Commission, the report includes the number of firms that are subject to each special regime.
- In order to measure CIT TEs, DIAN currently uses information from corporate tax returns. As only aggregated information needs to be provided in the tax return, DIAN can only quantify and report a number of aggregate CIT TEs in the TE appendix of the *MFMP*. Furthermore, the aggregated information that needs to be filed combines both items that are considered TEs and items that are not TEs, following the CIT TE benchmark that has been presented in this report. For example, the cell with information on exempt income in the tax return combines exempt income that qualifies as a TE but also income that is not a TE (under the TE benchmark that is proposed), such as income that is exempt under CAN treaty rules. The same applies to tax credits that constitute a TE in general with the exception of tax credits from taxes paid abroad; all of these tax credits are aggregated in the tax return that is filed by each business. This aggregation makes it difficult to even produce accurate *aggregate* TE estimates. In order for DIAN to calculate and report tax revenue forgone on an item-by-item basis, more disaggregated tax return data is required. This data could possibly be complemented with data from other sources.
- In light of these limitations, DIAN made available to the OECD some additional information that businesses need to provide. This information, which DIAN refers to as “exogenous information”, can be merged with tax returns to estimate item-by-item tax revenue forgone. While these forms allow for the estimation of a selection of CIT TEs, the use of this additional source of information remains limited as it does not cover the entire business population because only companies with turnover above COP 100 million are required to submit these forms. Furthermore, our analysis shows that only about half of all identified CIT TEs can be quantified based on the exogenous information that is currently available.
- To quantify revenue forgone, DIAN currently multiplies the *standard* CIT rate with the amount of exempt income that is recorded in the tax return. Such an approach, even if standard practice, biases the item-by-item revenue forgone estimates because it is very common for companies to simultaneously benefit from base narrowing TEs (non-taxable income, exempt income, non-

standard deductions) and a reduced CIT rate. In practice, if a base-narrowing TE is abolished, the reduction in revenue forgone will be much lower than that estimated applying the standard rate as many companies benefit from reduced rates.

OECD recommendations to improve the measurement and reporting of CIT revenue forgone

Going forward, the methodology that is applied could be further refined, and the presentation of the revenue foregone could be further developed. DIAN should also start collecting more disaggregated information, both within the tax returns that businesses need to file as well as within the exogenous information that businesses need to provide. This will allow increasing the accuracy of the CIT revenue foregone estimates and increase transparency. This analysis, and the corresponding recommendations, are developed in detail in the following sections.

- Section 3.2 presents the tax equations that can be applied to measure revenue forgone from different TEs on an item-by-item basis. The analysis also recommends DIAN to switch from applying the standard CIT rate to applying the company-specific CIT rate (which might be lower or higher, depending on other TEs in place) to calculate tax revenue forgone.
- Section 3.3 includes the item-by-item revenue forgone estimates carried out by DIAN based on data from all taxpayers that submit exogenous information forms, following OECD recommendations. The section also makes recommendation with respect to the types of tables with information on CIT revenue forgone that could be included in the TE report. In order to increase transparency, we recommend to report the interaction between reduced rates and tax base narrowing provisions that constitute a TE as part of the table that summarizes revenue forgone from CIT TEs. In addition, DIAN could include in its TE report a table that presents the total revenue forgone of each special tax regime (i.e. the impact of the reduced CIT rate and all other TEs that businesses within that special tax regime benefit from). Finally, the section refers to Annex C which seeks to provide a comprehensive list of all 123 CIT TEs that have been identified.
- Section 3.4 provides examples of how DIAN could leverage the tax microdata by including a distributional analysis of the TEs that businesses benefit from.
- Section 3.5 presents recommendations on how to improve the amount and quality of data that is needed to measure TEs. The tax forms that corporations need to file will have to be revised in order for DIAN to be able to calculate aggregate TE estimates. The section also argues that more and better data will have to be collected. Finally, the section includes a list of CIT TEs for which the data collection should be prioritized based on the expected magnitude of the revenue forgone.

3.1 Current CIT TE measurement, reporting and data availability

The publication of a report that provides information on the revenue foregone of TEs has been required by law in Colombia since 2002. Revenue forgone estimates are presented in the Appendix of the *Marco Fiscal de Mediano Plazo* (MFMP), an annual report published by the Ministry of Finance (Minhacienda, 2022[1]). The current MFMP includes the revenue forgone of CIT TEs by sector of activity and covers all entities that (i) submit a tax return and (ii) are considered taxpayers.[1] The MFMP only reports revenue forgone from a selection of CIT TEs, namely aggregate estimates of: exempt income, tax credits, some reduced rates and the special deduction for investment in fixed assets. Revenue forgone arising from non-taxable income and from special deductions (other than the deduction for investment in fixed assets) is not reported.

The two most recent editions of the MFMP have introduced a number of improvements in the measurement of CIT TEs, following the guidance provided by the Tax Incentives Commission (OECD, DIAN and Minhacienda, 2021[3]). For example, while tax revenue forgone from reduced rates was previously only estimated for Free Trade Zones (FTZs), DIAN now estimates it also for other special regimes (ZOMAC, ZESE, hotels, publishers, state-owned companies, non-profit organisations, co-operatives and perennial crops). Furthermore, the MFMP report now provides an estimate of the revenue forgone from a selection of other TEs that FTZs businesses benefit from; i.e. apart from the reduced rate, revenue forgone from tax credits and exempt income is also reported separately for FTZs.[2]

The information that businesses file within the CIT returns is the unique information source that is used by DIAN to estimate tax revenue foregone of CIT TEs. However, the information recorded in CIT returns is aggregated and can therefore only be used to estimate revenue forgone from certain aggregate TE categories. Revenue forgone from exempt income and tax credits is currently reported in an aggregate way covering all tax provisions that fall within that category. Currently, DIAN cannot provide item-by-item CIT TE estimates because different TEs are grouped together and recorded in a very limited number of cells within the tax return.

The estimation of tax revenue forgone using current CIT returns will remain complex under the proposed TE benchmark. The cells in the CIT return that need to be filled in typically include items that are TEs and items that are not considered TEs under the proposed CIT TE benchmark. For example, the cell with information on exempt income in the tax return combines information on exempt income that qualifies as a TE but also income that is not a TE, such as income that is exempt under CAN treaty rules. The same applies to tax credits, that constitute a TE in general, but tax credits from taxes paid abroad are not viewed as a TE; these different tax credits are however aggregated in the tax return that is filed by each business. This aggregation will bias the calculation of aggregate TE estimates. In order for DIAN to calculate and report tax revenue forgone on an item-by-item basis, more disaggregated tax return data is required.

Under the current rules in Colombia, businesses with annual turnover exceeding COP 100 million are required to file supplementary tax forms. These data sources are called *exogenous information* and could enable DIAN to quantify revenue forgone on an item-by-item basis from several TEs once they are merged with CIT tax returns. However, the information available from these data sources remains incomplete. For example, companies with turnover above COP 100 million only represent around 44% of the legal entities that submit a CIT return. Hence, estimating revenue forgone by means of exogenous information leads to an underestimation or, put differently, provides a lower bound of the actual revenue forgone. According to DIAN's estimates, 70% of total exempt income and 85% of total tax credits are claimed by firms whose turnover exceeds the threshold. Hence, in the case of CIT TEs, relying on exogenous information to measure revenue forgone on an item-by-item basis constitutes a reasonable strategy, given the data limitations, as TEs are mostly claimed by large corporations. Nevertheless, this approach does lead to an underestimation of total revenue forgone and does not substitute the need for more detailed CIT tax returns that would allow for the estimation of foregone tax revenues on an item-by-item basis based on the full taxpayer population.

To quantify revenue forgone from exempt income, DIAN currently multiplies the *standard* CIT rate with the size of the amount of exempt income recorded in the tax return DIAN.[3] Such an approach biases the revenue forgone estimates because it is very common for companies to simultaneously benefit from base narrowing TEs and a reduced CIT rate. Revenue forgone from reduced rates is calculated by multiplying the company's current taxable income (which can be lower than the benchmark income due to other TEs) with the difference in CIT rates. For example, the taxable income of a FTZ business would be multiplied by 15% (30% standard rate minus 20% rate in FTZs) to obtain the revenue forgone linked to the reduced CIT rate.

3.2. Measuring revenue forgone

Tax revenue forgone of a TE refers to the direct ex-post revenue loss associated with a tax provision that is not included within the benchmark tax system, holding other factors constant. Put differently, the tax revenue foregone from a TE is calculated by determining the sum of the tax liability the taxpayers would face in the absence of the particular TE, net of the sum of the tax liability the taxpayers actually face in the presence of the TE.

This section provides recommendations on how to measure revenue forgone from different types of CIT TEs. It describes how revenue forgone can be measured and provides a set of equations to implement the item-by-item measurement of the different types of CIT TEs, such as non-standard deductions, exempt income, non-taxable income, reduced rates, deferrals, and tax credits.

Non-standard deductions, exempt and non-taxable income

The OECD recommends that revenue forgone from base narrowing TEs (i.e. non-standard deductions, exempt and non-taxable income) is measured using the CIT rate that each company is subject to. That is, (i) the standard CIT rate, (ii) the reduced rate if the company benefits from a special regime or (iii) a higher rate for companies in the financial sector. Such an approach is preferred over DIAN's current approach, which multiplies the tax base narrowing amount that is claimed with the *standard* CIT rate regardless of whether the company pays the standard rate or not. Even though the standard CIT rate is the benchmark rate, multiplying the base narrowing amount with the standard rate biases the revenue foregone estimate upwards (in the case of reduced rates) and provides a wrong indication of the actual revenue foregone that can be attributed to the base narrowing provision. In fact, the DIAN approach combines the effect of two TEs: the base narrowing provision and the impact of the reduced CIT rate.[4]

Revenue forgone across the total number of firms n from a provision p that grants exempt income $Exempt\ income_{p,i}$ is equal to:

$$Revenue\ forgone_p = \sum_{i=1}^{n} (Exempt\ income_{p,i}) * Rate_i$$

Where $Rate_i$ stands for the CIT rate business i is subject to. The same formula applies to non-standard deductions or special deductions and non-taxable income.[5]

The revenue forgone from enhanced deductions is equal to the additional deduction exceeding the standard deduction that is included in the benchmark, multiplied by the company's CIT rate. If the benchmark stipulates full deductibility of the costs incurred (e.g. for the cost linked to salary payments), the additional deduction would be calculated by multiplying the deductible item (e.g. the salary payment to first-job employees under the age of 28) with the difference between the allowed deduction under the enhanced deduction (e.g. 120%) and the standard benchmark deduction (e.g. 100%). Revenue forgone from a provision p that grants an enhanced deduction for amount $Enhanced\ deduction_{p,i}$ then equals:

$$Revenue\ forgone_p = \sum_{i=1}^{n} (Enhanced\ deduction_{p,i}) * (DD_{p,enhanced} - DD_{p,benchmark}) * Rate_i$$

Where $DD_{p,enhanced}$ stands for the currently allowed deduction (in percentage) and $DD_{p,benchmark}$ for the permitted deduction under the benchmark (in percentage).[6]

Reduced rates

Revenue forgone from reduced rates can be split into two separate components:

1. The first component multiplies the difference between the standard rate and the reduced rate with taxable income, in line with the approach that DIAN currently follows. In this calculation, taxable income corresponds to the actual taxable income of each business that has been reduced by all other base narrowing TEs that the business can claim (e.g. deductions, exemptions, or non-taxable income). The first category therefore attempts to isolate the revenue forgone from the reduced rate by abstracting from the interaction between the reduced rate and other TEs.

   The following formula illustrates the proposal in the case of FTZ businesses; the same formula applies to other special regimes (mega-investments, stability contracts, hotels, etc.). The revenue forgone from the reduced rate $Rate_i$ of 20% applicable to k FTZ businesses with current $Taxable\ income_{\ i}$ would be equal to:

$$Revenue\ forgone_{FTZ} = \sum_{i=1}^{k} (Taxable\ income_i) * (Rate_{benchmark} - Rate_i)$$

2. The second component reflects the interaction between reduced rates and the TEs that narrow the tax base (i.e., non-standard deductions, exempt income, and non-taxable income). This amount is equal to the revenue forgone that could (potentially) be recovered if Colombia would decide to abolish both types of TEs (i.e. the reduced rate as well as the base narrowing TEs). The revenue forgone from the interaction is obtained by multiplying the total value of the special deductions, exempt income and non-taxable income for each firm i with the difference between the standard CIT rate and the reduced rate, and then summing the result for all companies subject to the reduced rate.[7]

   The revenue forgone from the interaction for k FTZ businesses subject to a reduced rate $Rate_i$ of 20% would be equal to:

$$Revenue\ forgone_{Interaction,FTZ} = \sum_{i=1}^{k} \Big(\sum Deductions + \sum Exempt\ income + \sum Non - taxable\ income + \sum Enhanced\ deduction * (DD_{enhanced} - DD_{benchmark}) \Big)_i * (Rate_{benchmark} - Rate_i)$$

The presentation of the TEs into these 2 components would allow DIAN to (i) isolate the revenue forgone from different type of base-narrowing TEs and the reduced CIT rate; and (ii) demonstrate how the different types of TEs reinforce each other and thereby result in additional revenue forgone. Nonetheless, it should be noted that breaking down the revenue forgone in such a way is merely a matter of displaying total revenue forgone in a more transparent manner.

Overall, this break down of total revenue foregone into three separate components (i.e., the TE corresponding to tax base narrowing discussed in the previous subsection, the reduced tax rate and their interaction discussed in this subsection) would increase transparency; the sum of these three components would be equal to the difference between (benchmark tax base x benchmark tax rate) and (current tax base x current tax rate).

Deferrals

While accelerated tax depreciation allowances do not alter the total amount of the depreciation allowances that can be deducted over the life of an economic asset, they do change the moment in time, and therefore the tax value, when these depreciation allowances can be claimed. Measured on a cash-flow basis, the revenue foregone of accelerated tax depreciation in a given year equals the revenue forgone due to the *additional* depreciation allowances that can be deducted in the year, relative to the amount that would be deductible under the tax benchmark, which are tax depreciation allowances that match the economic depreciation of the asset.[8]

Revenue forgone calculated on a cash flow basis is defined by the cost of a TE to the government in a given year.[9] Accelerated tax depreciation results in positive tax revenue forgone initially, followed by periods during which revenue receipts are higher than they would have been under tax depreciation that equals the economic deprecation of the asset (because a higher percentage of the asset's value has already been deducted). Ultimately, the total depreciated value is equal to the cost of the asset. Under the proposed TE benchmark, tax depreciation allowances match the economic depreciation of the asset over the asset's useful economic life. Because of the impact on tax revenue in different time periods, the cash flow-based estimate of accelerated tax depreciation is not only the result of the accelerated depreciation of investments made in the current year, but the revenue forgone in any given year is also impacted by the accelerated deductions claimed with respect to investments dating from previous time periods (Department of Finance Canada, 2012[4]). For that reason, the net cash-flow fiscal cost in a given year could be positive or negative depending on past, current and projected investments (Department of Finance Canada, 2021[5]; Villela, Lemgruber and Jorratt, 2010[6]). Due to this period-specific impact of tax deferrals, detailed information about investment patterns over time would be required to correctly determine the size of the TE.

The cash flow revenue forgone estimated in the current period could be defined as follows:

$$Revenue\ forgone_{p,t} = \sum_{i=1}^{n} (Effective\ depreciation_{p,t,i} - Economic\ depreciation_{p,t,i}) * Rate_{t,i}$$

Where $Effective\ depreciation_{p,t,i}$ stands for the allowed amount of depreciation for all assets that fall under the accelerated depreciation provision p that were depreciated by business i in year t. Some of these assets may have been purchased in t while other may have been purchased in previous years. The economic depreciation term refers to the value that would have been depreciated for asset p in firm i if the depreciation schedule had followed the economic depreciation rates (i.e. the benchmark).

The Canadian TE report (Department of Finance Canada, 2012[4]) identifies five key methodological steps to measure revenue forgone from accelerated tax depreciation:

1. Determine the useful life[10] for each type of investment subject to accelerated depreciation. If the asset cannot be matched to a particular asset type, use a weighted average of the most similar asset types. For example, clean energy generation equipment may include a broad variety of assets with potentially different benchmark depreciation rates.
2. Create, for every taxpayer, a separate time series on an asset-by-asset basis including all assets that benefit from accelerated tax depreciation as reported in the CIT return.
3. Recalculate claims and balances under the useful life (i.e. economic) depreciation rates (counterfactual).
4. Estimate the total current-year revenue forgone by comparing actual tax depreciation in the year to the depreciation allowances under the TE benchmark (i.e. the counterfactual).
5. Break down the total revenue forgone by separating the impact of current and prior year's investments.

Tax credits

The revenue forgone from tax credits is equal to the total amount claimed by companies that either (i) reduces the final tax liability or (ii) is refunded. Not all tax credits are viewed as a TE – for example, the foreign tax credit for taxes paid abroad by resident taxpayers earning foreign source income is not viewed as a TE under the proposed benchmark. DIAN is therefore advised to list revenue forgone from tax credits on an item-by-item basis in addition to providing an estimate of total revenue forgone.

3.3. Revenue forgone estimates and reporting recommendations

Revenue forgone estimates

This section provides item-by-item revenue forgone estimates for Colombia in 2020. The OECD produced preliminary estimates based on a representative sample of CIT tax returns that was merged with exogenous information. The coding has been shared with DIAN so that the proposed methodology could be applied to all taxpayers. This report includes the results of the calculations made by DIAN, following the OECD's recommendations, and based on the methodology described in the previous section.

The figures included in Table A and Table B were calculated by DIAN based on exogenous information that was merged to tax returns. As only 44% of corporations in Colombia are required to file these supplementary forms, the estimates represent a lower bound of the revenue forgone associated with a specific TE.

The totals in the tables also represent a lower bound estimate because a large fraction of TEs cannot be measured on an item-by-item basis due to a lack of data. For this reason, the revenue forgone linked to the "other" category is likely large. For example, revenue forgone from other exempt income (including some non-TE components such as exempt income from Andean Community tax treaties) was equal to COP thousand million 3 961 in 2020. If Colombia were to follow the recommendations made in section 3.5, the design of future tax returns would ensure that TEs and tax provisions that are part of the TE benchmark are not included together in a single box. Consequently, the table is not comparable to figures reported in the MFMP (2022). A tentative full list of CIT TEs is included in Annex C.

Table 3.1. Item-by-item CIT revenue forgone in 2020 for provisions with available data (Table A)

Tax expenditure	Revenue forgone (2020)	
	COP thousand million	% of GDP
Exempt income	**1 332**	**0.13%**
Income derived from the sale of renewable electricity (15 years, Art 91, Law 2010 of 2019)	*0*	
Income from certain waterway transport services (art 91, Law 2010 of 2019)	*5*	
Income from investment in higher agricultural productivity (10 years, art 91, Law 2010 of 2019)	*2*	
Income from investment in sawmills and related invest. in the lumber industry (art 91, Law 2010 of 2019)	*3*	
Income from the sale of property for public interest projects (art 91, Law 2010 of 2019)	*204*	
Income generated in creative industries (orange economy, 7 years, art 91, Law 2010 of 2019)	*11*	
Income received by authors, translators and copyright holders of certain books (art 28, Law 98 of 1993)	*3*	
Income received by hotels constructed between 2002-2017 (30 years, art 18, Law 788 of 2002)	*10*	
Income received by hotels renovated between 2002-2017 (30 years, art 18, Law 788 of 2002)	*1*	
Income received by non-profit organisations (art 146, Law 1819 of 2019)	*478*	
Profit on the first sale of low income housing (VIS) and financial returns generated in the first 5 years from VIS loans (art. 235-2, TC)	*616*	
Other	*n/a*	
Non-taxable income	**1 301**	**0.13%**
Compensation for eradication or renewal of crops, or control of pests (Art 70, Law 223 of 1995)	*1*	
Contributions by National Television Commission to regional stations (Art 40, Law 488 of 1998)	*69*	

Distribution of gains from shares from companies listed in the Colombian Stock Exchange (Art 37, Law 1819 of 2016)	*272*	
Donations to projects approved by the Multilateral Fund of the Montreal Protocol (Art. 32, Law 488 of 1998)	*0*	
Funds for scientific, technological, or innovative projects (Art 37, Law 1450 of 2011)	*544*	
Incentives for rural capitalization (Art 20, Law 788 of 2002)	*1*	
Income distributed to employee shareholders (up to 10% of profits, Art 44., Law 789 of 2002)	*0*	
Income from derivatives with Colombian stock exchange-listed company as underlying (Art. 37, Law 1430 of 2000)	*16*	
Income from Forest Incentive Certificates (Lit c Art 8, Law 139 of 1994)	*7*	
Income from the expropriation of property for public use (Art 67, Law 388 of 1997)	*11*	
Income provided from resources managed by Fogafín and Fogacoop (Art 11, Law 788 of 2002)	*0*	
Inflationary component if capitalized (Art 10, Decree 2686 of 1999)	*1*	
Profits from sale of shares registered in a Colombian Stock Exchange (Art 9, Law 633 of 2000)	*125*	
Profits from the liquidation of a limited liability company (Art 43, Decree 2053 of 1974)	*0*	
Public funding for urban mass transport network (Art 29, Law 488 of 1998)	*240*	
Seed capital provided by the State (Art 16, Ley 1429 de 2014)	*7*	
State contributions to cover obligations of public entities in liquidation (Art 77, Law 633 of 2000)	*0*	
Subsidies paid by the government in the Agro Ingreso Seguro program (Art. 58, Law 1111 of 2006)	*7*	
Other	*n/a*	
Non-standard deductions	**6 105**	**0.61%**
30% deduction for investment in fixed assets (Art 68, Law 863 of 2003)	*831*	
50% of the financial transaction tax (Art. 86, Law 2010 of 2019)	*1 031*	
130% of the salaries paid to workers hired as apprentices or in training (Art. 189, Law 115 of 1994)	*56*	
200 % of the salaries paid to female workers who are victims of proven violence (Art. 23, Law 1257 of 2008)	*1*	
200 % of the salaries paid to widows and orphans of members of the Armed Forces killed in combat, kidnapped, or missing (Art. 127, Law 6 of 1992)	*24*	
200% of salaries paid to workers with a proven disability of no less than 25% (Art. 31, Law 361 of 1997)	*19*	
Carbon tax (Par 2, Art. 222, Law 1819 of 2016)	*91*	
Contributions made by corporations to education institutions (Art. 87, Law 2010 of 2019)	*57*	
Donations for educational programs (Art 87, Law 2010 of 2019)	*38*	
Donations to libraries (Art. 75, Law 1819 of 2016)	*1*	
Gifts to customers, suppliers, and employees (Art. 63, Law 1819 of 2016)	*341*	
Investments in detention centers (Art. 98, Law 633 of 2000)	*0*	
Maintenance of assets declared as in cultural interest (Art. 14, Law 1185 of 2008)	*4*	
Mutual investment fund contributions (Art. 7, Law 75 of 1986)	*15*	
Scholarships for employees (Art. 87, Law 2010 of 2019)	*3*	
Taxes, fees, and contributions (art 86, Law 2010 of 2019)	*3 593*	
Other	*n/a*	
Tax credits	**4 075**	**0.41%**
25% of donations to certain non-profits (art 105, Law 1819 of 2016)	*177*	
25% of donations to higher education and science (art 174, Law 1955 of 2019)	*1*	
25% of environmental investment (art 103, Law 1819 of 2016)	*41*	
25% of research & development investment (art 171, Law 1955 of 2019)	*223*	
40% of investments by public service companies providing aqueduct and sewerage services (Art. 104, Law 788 of 2002)	*4*	
50% of local turnover tax ICA (art 86 Law 2010 of 2019)	*2 298*	
Donations to foundations defending and protecting human rights (Art. 37, Law 488 of 1988)	*2*	
Donations to sports and recreational or cultural organizations (Art. 37, Law 488 of 1998)	*1*	
Input VAT paid on fixed capital assets (art 95, Law 2010 of 2019)	*1 328*	
Other	*n/a*	
Reduced rates*	**1 332**	**0.13%**
Reduced rate on taxable income	***1 032***	***0.10%***

Free Trade Zones [20%] (art 101, Law 1819 of 2016)	*340*	
Stability contracts [**] (Law 963 of 2005)	*174*	
Hotels, theme parks, ecotourism parks, agro-tourism, nautical docks, old age tourism [9%] (art 41, Law 2068 of 2020)	*5*	
ZESE first 5 years [0%] (art 268, Law 1995 of 2019)	*206*	
Micro and small ZOMAC [0%] (art 237, Law 1819 of 2016)	*178*	
Medium and large ZOMAC [50% of the standard rate] (art 237, Law 1819 of 2016)		
*Non-profit organisations [20%]*** (art 146, Law 1819 of 2019)*	*16*	
Publication industry (9%) (art 100, Law 1819 of 2016)	*18*	
State-owned alcohol production and gambling [9%] (art 100, Law 1819 of 2016)	*16*	
Perennial crops [9%] (art 100, Law 1819 of 2016)	*6*	
Cooperatives [20%] (art. 19-4, Colombian tax code, art. 142 Law 1819 of 2016)	*71*	
*Mega-investments [27% or 9%] (art 75, Law 2010 of 2019)*** **	*n/a*	
Other	*n/a*	
Interaction between reduced rates and other TEs	***300***	***0.03%***
Free Trade Zones [20%] (art 101, Law 1819 of 2016)	*34*	
Stability contracts [**]	*20*	
Hotels, theme parks, ecotourism parks, agro-tourism, nautical docks, old age tourism [9%] (art 41, Law 2068 of 2020)	*3*	
ZESE first 5 years [0%] (art 268, Law 1995 of 2019)	*9*	
*Micro and small ZOMAC [0%] (art 237, Law 1819 of 2016)*******	*2*	
*Medium and large ZOMAC [50% of the standard rate] (art 237, Law 1819 of 2016)*******		
*Non-profit organisations [20%]*** (art 146, Law 1819 of 2019)*	*194*	
Publication industry [9%] (art 100, Law 1819 of 2016)	*1*	
State-owned alcohol production and gambling [9%] (art 100, Law 1819 of 2016)	*5*	
Perennial crops [9%] (art 100, Law 1819 of 2016)	*1*	
Cooperatives [20%] (art. 19-4, Colombian tax code, art. 142 Law 1819 of 2016)	*30*	
*Mega-investments [27% or 9%] (art 75, Law 2010 of 2019)*** **	*n/a*	
Other	*n/a*	
Increased rates	**-475**	**0.05%**
Increased rate on taxable income	***-346***	***0.03%***
Financial institutions [32%+4%] (Law 2155 of 2021)	*-346*	
Interaction between increased rates and other TEs	***-129***	***0.01%***
Financial institutions [32%+4%] (Law 2155 of 2021)	*-129*	

Note: Estimates based on 2020 tax records from the population of taxpayers and supplementary taxpayer data. Values in thousand million Colombian pesos. Item-by-item TEs are estimated based on supplementary taxpayer data from exogenous information forms and thereby do not cover all taxpayers that benefit from these TEs (with the exception of reduced rates). It is suggested that the new TE report includes an "Other" row where TEs which are currently measured using tax return data but not disaggregated on an item-by-item basis can be reported. The estimates reported in this table were calculated by DIAN. OECD provided an initial coding proposal based on a sample of 815 business tax returns merged to exogenous information forms but was not involved in the final calculations.

* The reduced rates row includes estimates from revenue forgone arising from the two components mentioned in section 3.2, namely the revenue forgone resulting from applying a reduced rate to actual taxable income and the revenue forgone resulting from the interaction between reduced rates and base narrowing TEs.

** Each stability contract can grant a different CIT rate.

*** Surpluses not invested or allocated in the development of the non-profit organisation's "worthy purpose" are subject to a 20% CIT rate.

**** No company qualified to benefit from the mega-investment regime in 2020. The same applied to the Free Trade Zone regime in Cucutá taxed at a rate of 15%.

***** The applicable rates have changed since 2022. See Annex C for more details.

Source: DIAN.

Table 3.2. Revenue forgone in 2020 from tax expenditures granted to companies that benefit from a reduced rate (Table B)

Revenue forgone by type of special regime and type of tax expenditure	Revenue forgone (2020) COP thousand million
Free Trade Zones [20%] (art 101, Law 1819 of 2016)	**486**
Exempt income	*0*
Non-taxable income	*1*
Non-standard deductions	*60*
Tax credits	*50*
Reduced rate [on taxable income and interaction between reduced rates and other TEs]	*375*
Stability contracts* (Law 963 of 2005)	**1,822**
Exempt income	*0*
Non-taxable income	*140*
Non-standard deductions	*945*
Tax credits	*542*
Reduced rate [on taxable income and interaction between reduced rates and other TEs]	*195*
Hotels, theme parks, ecotourism parks, agro-tourism, nautical docks, old age tourism [9%] (art 41, Law 2068 of 2020)	**9**
Exempt income	*0*
Non-taxable income	*0*
Non-standard deductions	*1*
Tax credits	*0*
Reduced rate [on taxable income and interaction between reduced rates and other TEs]	*7*
ZESE first 5 years [0%] (art 268, Law 1995 of 2019)	**221**
Exempt income	*1*
Non-taxable income	*0*
Non-standard deductions	*0*
Tax credits	*5*
Reduced rate [on taxable income and interaction between reduced rates and other TEs]	*215*
Micro and small ZOMAC [0%] & Medium and large ZOMAC [50% of the standard rate] (art 237, Law 1819 of 2016)****	**187**
Exempt income	*0*
Non-taxable income	*0*
Non-standard deductions	*0*
Tax credits	*5*
Reduced rate [on taxable income and interaction between reduced rates and other TEs]	*181*
Non-profit organisations [20%] (art 146, Law 1819 of 2019)**	**539**
Exempt income	*280*
Non-taxable income	*1*
Non-standard deductions	*43*
Tax credits	*4*
Reduced rate [on taxable income and interaction between reduced rates and other TEs]	*211*
Publication industry [9%] (art 100, Law 1819 of 2016)	**20**
Exempt income	*0*
Non-taxable income	*0*
Non-standard deductions	*0*
Tax credits	*1*
Reduced rate [on taxable income and interaction between reduced rates and other TEs]	*19*
State-owned alcohol production and gambling [9%] (art 100, Law 1819 of 2016)	**26**

Exempt income	*0*
Non-taxable income	*0*
Non-standard deductions	*2*
Tax credits	*2*
Reduced rate [on taxable income and interaction between reduced rates and other TEs]	*22*
Perennial crops [9%] (art 100, Law 1819 of 2016)	**8**
Exempt income	*0*
Non-taxable income	*0*
Non-standard deductions	*0*
Tax credits	*1*
Reduced rate [on taxable income and interaction between reduced rates and other TEs]	*7*
Cooperatives [20%] (art. 19-4, Colombian tax code, art. 142 Law 1819 of 2016)	**164**
Exempt income	*10*
Non-taxable income	*0*
Non-standard deductions	*41*
Tax credits	*12*
Reduced rate [on taxable income and interaction between reduced rates and other TEs]	*101*
Mega-investments [27% or 9%] (art 75, Law 2010 of 2019)*	**n/a**
Financial institutions [32%+4%] (Law 2155 of 2021)	**1,231**
Exempt income	*329*
Non-taxable income	*119*
Non-standard deductions	*716*
Tax credits	*542*
Increased rate [on taxable income and interaction between reduced rates and other TEs]	*-475*

Note: Estimates based on 2020 tax records from the population of taxpayers merged with supplementary taxpayer data. Values in thousand million Colombian pesos. Item-by-item TEs are estimated based on supplementary taxpayer data from exogenous information forms and thereby do not cover all taxpayers that benefit from these TEs. The estimates reported in this table were calculated by DIAN. OECD provided an initial coding proposal based on a depersonalised sample of 815 business tax returns merged to exogenous information forms but was not involved in the final calculations.
The reduced/increased rate row includes the two components described previously, that is (i) the revenue forgone resulting of applying the difference in tax rates to taxable income and (ii) the interaction between reduced rates and base narrowing TEs
* Each stability contract can grant a different CIT rate.
** Surpluses not invested or allocated in the development of the non-profit organisation's "worthy purpose" are subject to a 20% CIT rate.
*** No company qualified to benefit from the mega-investment regime in 2020. The same applied to the Free Trade Zone regime in Cucutá taxed at a 15% rate.
**** The applicable rates have changed since 2020. See Annex C for more details.
Source: DIAN.

Reporting recommendations

This section also provides recommendations on how to report CIT revenue forgone in the TE report:

- Whenever possible, DIAN should report revenue forgone instead of the aggregate value of tax exemptions, non-taxable income, deductions, or tax credits. Because businesses can pay a CIT rate that is higher or lower than the standard rate (due to surtaxes or special regimes), revenue forgone cannot be easily inferred from the aggregate size of TEs.
- The main CIT revenue forgone table (Table A) lists subtotals by type of TE (tax credits, deductions, etc.) and, where data is available, includes rows with item-by-item estimates.
- For each type of TE, the table also contains a row that records the revenue forgone that cannot be measured on an item-by-item basis ("Other"). Currently, no estimate can be provided in these rows because the aggregate boxes in the tax return (for example, total exempt income) include both TE and non-TE components.

- Over time, DIAN could add more information in the table by adding the revenue forgone in previous years. This will indicate how the revenue foregone has changed over time.
- In the TE report, values would be expressed both in thousand million pesos and as a percentage of GDP.
- A total of all measured CIT TEs could be included; this total should however be interpreted with caution given the difficulties of summing different TEs. If the total is provided, the report should explicitly mention that the revenue forgone concept does not take into account the interaction between the CIT TEs, and that some TEs are not included in the total because of lack of data. In line with the recommendations made in the preceding section, rows that report revenue forgone from the TEs that cannot be disaggregated within a category (Other), would have to be calculated using the company-specific CIT rate rather than the standard CIT rate.
- In addition, DIAN could include an additional table (Table B) that reports total revenue forgone from TEs for firms that are subject to special regimes. Even if all revenue forgone linked to companies under special regimes was included in Table A, Table B would summarize all the revenue forgone that is measured only considering companies that benefit from special regimes. Hence, it would be possible to identify revenue forgone from base narrowing TEs aside from the interaction component. Table B would therefore complement the data in Table A.
- The 2022 edition of the MFMP includes a column that records the number of firms that benefit from a reduced rate and are subject to each special regime (FTZ, stability contracts, etc.), in line with the recommendation of the Tax Incentives Commission (OECD, DIAN and Minhacienda, 2021[3]). In the future, the number of firms subject to each special regime could be included in Table B.

Item-by-item discussion

In addition to the tables that provide an overview of revenue forgone from individual CIT TEs (Table A) and revenue forgone linked to companies subject to special regimes (Table B), the TE report could include item-specific tables for each TE measured on an item-by-item basis. These tables would explain why a specific provision is considered a TE, provide a brief description of the data source and estimation method used to calculate the revenue forgone from that particular TE as well as include information about the reliability of the revenue forgone estimate. The table would indicate if the estimate is based on tax return data or exogenous information.

The item-by-item discussion would also provide additional context to guide the interpretation of the revenue forgone figure. For example, when discussing the revenue forgone of a particular TE, it should be mentioned whether the TE corrects for a distortion that is created by another TE. For example, the discussion of revenue forgone from the CIT credit granted for investment in fixed assets should refer to the fact that, in contrast to the proposed benchmark, businesses in Colombia cannot recover the VAT paid on investment (negative VAT TE). Table 3.3 provides an illustrative example.

More specifically, the item-by-item table should include the following elements:[11]

- (i) TE identifier; (ii) Name of the TE; (iii) Revenue forgone in the current year and in the five preceding years; (iv) Tax type; (v) TE type; (vi) Year of implementation; (vii) Year of expiration; (viii) Legal reference; (ix) Reliability of the estimate; (x) Data source used to estimate revenue forgone; (xi) Estimation method; (xii) Paragraph that states why the provision deviates from the benchmark and provides more detail about the TE.

Table 3.3. Suggested presentation of item-by-item CIT revenue forgone

NT17 Profits from the sale of shares registered in a Colombian stock exchange

Year	2015	2016	2017	2018	2019	2020
Revenue forgone (COP thousand million)	.	.	.	.	.	125

Tax:	*Corporate income tax*	*Legal reference:*	*Art 9, Law 633 of 2000*
Tax expenditure type:	*Non-taxable income*	*Estimate reliability:*	*Medium-High*
Implementation:	*2000*	*Data source:*	*Exogenous data (Companies with turnover > 100 m.)*
Expiration:	*n/a*	*Estimation method:*	*Microsimulation applying the respective corporate tax rate paid by business*

Note**. Reason why this measure is not part of benchmark tax system:** Income from the sale of shares registered in a Colombian stock exchange is exempt from taxation under the corporate income tax if the sale does not exceed 10% of the outstanding shares and if the shares are owned by the same real beneficiary. Under the benchmark, the corporate income tax base comprises all sources of income, including profits from carrying out business activity and investment income, rental income, interest income, royalties, dividends, and capital gains, as well as other sources of income such as government cash transfers and donations.

Full list of TEs in appendix tables

Finally, a comprehensive list of TEs such as the one included in the appendix of this report (Annex C) could be included in the appendix to the TE report.[12] Ideally, this list should provide information about the legal reference and a brief explanation of the extent to which the tax provision deviates from the benchmark. This list would include all TEs, and not just those that were measured on an item-by-item basis.

3.4. Distributional analysis

For certain tax provisions, the detailed tax microdata will allow DIAN to move beyond aggregate revenue forgone estimates and also provide information on the types of firms (e.g. by size or profitability) that benefit the most from specific TEs. The section includes a set of graphs estimated by DIAN upon OECD recommendations and is included for illustrative purposes only.

Figure 3.1 shows the percentage of companies claiming four selected TEs within five broad annual turnover groups. Figure 3.2 presents the distribution of total revenue forgone across the same groups. Both figures also include the share of corporations in each turnover group. Note that this type of analysis is currently only possible for businesses with annual turnover above COP 100 million because no exogenous information is available for smaller firms. This restriction implies that the bottom deciles of firms (in terms of turnover) cannot be represented in the graphs. Total revenue forgone therefore corresponds to total revenue forgone *among* firms with turnover above COP 100 million. As an alternative to Figure 3.1 and Figure 3.2 DIAN could present the firms across turnover deciles but keep the first deciles blank to signal that no exogenous information is available for these firms. Once exogenous information is collected for more firms, DIAN could present the share of companies claiming TEs by turnover decile across the entire distribution.[13]

These figures need to be interpreted with caution. TEs seem to be regressive but some (e.g. the ICA tax credit and the VAT tax credit) were introduced to neutralize distortive structural design flaws in Colombia's tax system. Indeed, some of the current preferential tax treatments are necessary design features that seek to correct, albeit indirectly, for the tax distortions generated by the tax system's structural design flaws. As the Tax Incentives Commission pointed out, reforming TEs will need to be part of a broader fundamental and progressive reform of the tax system that not only abolishes these TEs but at the same time addresses the structural design weaknesses within the Colombian tax system (OECD, DIAN and Minhacienda, 2021[3]) .

Figure 3.1. Share of businesses claiming the TE within selected annual turnover groups (2020)

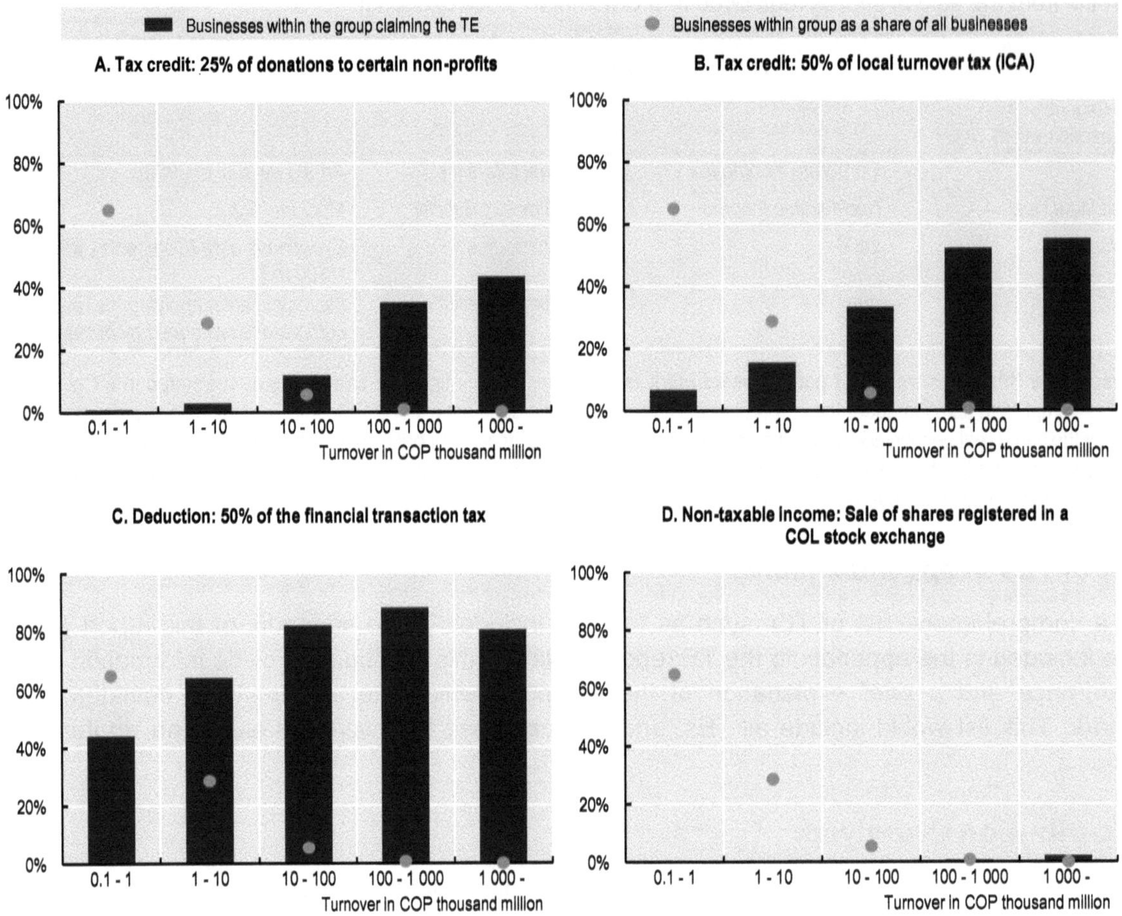

Note: Based on the full taxpayer population that submitted exogenous information forms in 2020. Only includes businesses with annual turnover above COP 100 million (0.1 COP thousand million).
Source: DIAN.

Figure 3.2. Distribution of revenue forgone across selected annual turnover groups (2020)

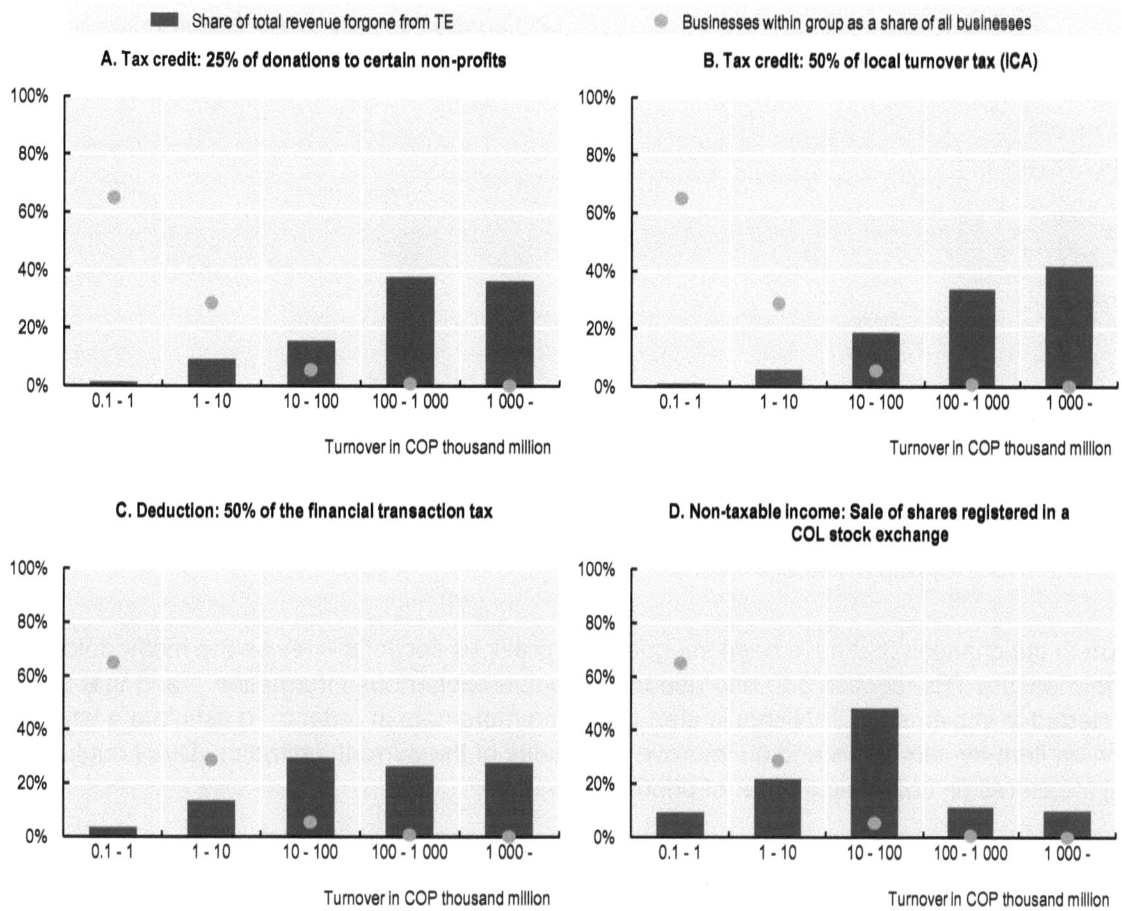

Note: Based on the full taxpayer population that submitted exogenous information forms in 2020.Only includes businesses with annual turnover above COP 100 million (0.1 COP thousand million).
Source: DIAN.

3.5. Strengthening the TE measurement through more and better data

The use of the exogenous data constitutes a significant step forward because it allows DIAN to estimate the revenue forgone of a selection of TEs on an item-by-item basis compared to the analysis that is currently included in the MFMP. However, the available information remains incomplete; not all companies are required to submit the information, which results in an underestimation of revenue forgone, and only about half of the identified CIT TEs can be measured based on the data that is currently available (Table 3.4). Furthermore, the information reported in the exogenous information forms can occasionally be not aligned with what is reported in tax returns. For this reason, the use of exogenous data should always be complemented with tax returns data and should not be seen as a substitute for improving the granularity of CIT tax returns.

Table 3.4. Data availability to measure CIT revenue forgone on an item-by-item basis

Category	CIT TEs currently measurable on an item-by-item basis / All identified CIT TEs
Exempt income	11/16
Non-taxable income	18/24
Non-standard deductions	16/26
Deferrals	0/9
Tax credits	9/16
*Reduced rates **	11/21
Increased rates	1/1
Other	0/10
Total	**66/123**

Note: Based on comparing Table A with the list of identified TEs in Annex C.TEs classified as measurable on an item-by-item basis refer to TEs available in exogenous information forms.

* No company qualified to benefit from the mega-investment regime in 2020. The same applied to the Free Trade Zone regime in Cucutá taxed at a 15% rate. Two other reduced rate regimes were introduced in 2020 and 2021, respectively: First sale of land, real estate or real estate units that are new constructions (9%) [Law 2068 of 2020] and International maritime transportation services provided by vessels or naval artefacts registered in the Colombian registry (2%) [Law 2133 of 2021].

In addition to the changes that have been suggested in previous sections – revise the methodology that is applied to measure TEs (section 3.2) and use the available exogenous information – and that DIAN has already started to implement, DIAN should start collecting more data in order to (i) estimate a larger share of TEs on an item-by-item basis and (ii) improve the quality of the current estimates. DIAN could take the following measures (in decreasing order of priority):

1. **Ensure that aggregate revenue forgone estimates can be obtained from CIT tax returns**. Ensuring that TEs are reported separately from non-TEs in the tax return would allow DIAN to obtain aggregate revenue forgone estimates by type of TE (e.g. exempt income, non-taxable income, non-standard deductions, etc.). This should be the first priority.[14]
2. **Increase the number of taxpayers that are required to submit exogenous information**. Lower the annual turnover threshold that requires companies to submit exogenous information (COP 100 million).
3. **Redesign the CIT return and the exogenous information forms**. Improve the available information by revising the tax return and exogenous information forms. The revision could include:
   - *Disaggregate tax credits by type of credit, following the example of other countries such as Chile, the United Kingdom, and the United States.*
   - *Report the use of the individual enhanced deductions in separate cells in form F-2516. Currently, cells L355, L356 and L358 of this form include more than one type of enhanced deduction which hinders DIAN from calculating revenue forgone on an item-by-item basis. For example, the 120% deduction of the total salary payments made to first-job employees under 28 years old is reported in the same cell together with four other enhanced deductions.*[15]
   - *Explore whether accelerated depreciation and amortization related to natural resources could be measured based on the stock of remaining asset values over time, which might be available from form F -2516 (boxes AE40, AD40).*
   - *Some provisions in the Colombian tax system combine enhanced deductions with special deductions or immediate expensing. For example, a 165% deduction is allowed for investments in or donations to Colombian film projects. If the company made a donation, the total amount should be considered a TE (165%) as donations are not deductible under the proposed*

benchmark. If the company instead carried out an investment, then the provision combines an enhanced deduction with immediate expensing. In the second case, to measure the deferral associated with immediate expensing, DIAN would need to use the respective economic depreciation rate as the benchmark. If one tax provision is linked to several different benchmarks depending on how it is used, revenue forgone could only be calculated if the tax returns ask taxpayers to specify, which benefit they claim; i.e. companies would have to report separately whether the deduction is a donation or an investment.

4. **Explore additional sources of information**. Review sources of exogenous information that might be available in other government agencies and entities and that could possibly be merged with tax returns data; identify sources of information that third parties, such as the financial sector, could be asked to report to DIAN.

Priority should be given to TEs that are highly distortive, at risk of being abused or for which the expected revenue forgone is large. The following TEs could be given priority:

- Sale of shares in a non-resident entity by a CHC. Income derived from the sale or transfer of a Colombian Holding Company (CHC)'s stake in entities that are not resident in Colombia are exempt from income tax (Law 2010 of 2019).
- Sale of shares in a CHC. The income derived from the sale or transfer of the shares or participations in a Colombian Holding Company (CHC) are exempt except for the value corresponding to the profits obtained from activities carried out in Colombia (Law 2010 of 2019).
- Investments in the exploration of mining and hydrocarbon. Certificates of investment given by the ministry of finance to new investments in the exploration of mining and hydrocarbon (Law 1819 of 2016).
- Mutual investment fund contributions: Deduction of the contributions to mutual investment funds (Law 75 of 1986).
- Real estate valuation (Law 74 of 1994).
- Salaries paid to first-job employees who are under twenty-eight years of age (120%). Deduction of 120% of the employer's salary payments for employees who are under twenty-eight (28) years of age as part their first job (Law 2010 of 2019).
- Deduction of royalties paid for the exploitation of non-renewable natural resources (Art. 107 of the Tax Code).

References

Australian Government the Treasury (2021), *Tax Benchmarks and Variations Statement 2020.* [7]

Department of Finance Canada (2021), *Report on Federal Tax Expenditures - Concepts, Estimates, Evaluations.* [5]

Department of Finance Canada (2012), *Tax Expenditures and Evaluations 2012.* [4]

IMF-OECD (2020), "Chile : Technical Assistance Report—Assessment of Tax Expenditures and Corrective Taxe", *Country Report No. 2020/305.* [8]

Minhacienda (2022), *Marco Fiscal de Mediano Plazo 2022.* [1]

Minhacienda (2021), *Marco Fiscal de Mediano Plazo 2021.* [2]

OECD, DIAN and Minhacienda (2021), *Tax Expenditures Report by the Tax Experts Commission*. [3]

Villela, L., A. Lemgruber and M. Jorratt (2010), "Tax Expenditure Budgets - Concepts and Challenges for Implementation", *IDB Working Paper Series* IDB-WP-131. [6]

Notes

[1] Non-profit entities whose income is exempt are not considered taxpayers as long as they use their income in the subsequent period to continue developing their main activity. Following OECD guidance, the revenue forgone linked to the special regime (20%) that applies to *taxable* income of non-profit organisations has been included in the most recent edition of the MFMP (Minhacienda, 2022[1]).

[2] Since previous editions of the MFMP, DIAN reports the revenue forgone from a special deduction on the investment in fixed assets and revenue forgone from the reduced rate applicable to companies that have signed a stability contract.

[3] Section 3.2 recommends to apply the company-specific CIT rate instead while reporting the remainder revenue forgone as a second component of reduced rates.

[4] Note, however, that even though the suggested method attempts to isolate the revenue forgone of each provision, it remains a static calculation and not an estimate of the revenue gain, which would take into account behavioural responses.

[5] The additional revenue forgone from the interaction between reduced rates and these TEs (i.e. revenue forgone that could only potentially be recovered if both reduced rates and the other TEs were to be repealed) would be isolated and reported for each reduced rate regime as separate item (see Table 3.1 and second component in the reduced rates section for a detailed discussion of the interaction).

[6] Note that some provisions in the Colombian tax system combine enhanced deductions with special deductions or immediate expensing. For example, a 165% deduction is allowed for investments in or donations to Colombian film projects. If the company made a donation, the total amount should be considered a TE (165%) as donations are not deductible under the proposed benchmark. If the company instead carried out an investment, then the provision combines an enhanced deduction with immediate expensing. In the second case, to measure the deferral associated with immediate expensing, DIAN would need to use the respective economic depreciation rate as the benchmark. If one tax provision is linked to several different benchmarks depending on how it is used, revenue forgone could only be calculated if the tax returns ask taxpayers to specify, which benefit they claim; i.e. companies would have to report separately whether the deduction is a donation or an investment.

[7] Currently DIAN applies the *standard* CIT rate to calculate revenue forgone from exempt income. Hence, the interaction between this type of TE and the reduced rate is included in the revenue forgone of exempt income.

[8] Under the proposed benchmark tax depreciation allowances reflect estimates of economic depreciation.

[9] Alternatively, the net present value method takes into account the impact of transactions that take place in the current fiscal period on the current as well as on future fiscal periods (IMF-OECD, 2020[8]). As it accounts for the time value of money, it is a more complex method that requires making assumptions about future cash flows and the discount rate.

[10] The useful life of an asset implicitly defines its economic depreciation rate, which would be equal to the benchmark depreciation rate as per the proposed benchmark in the first chapter.

[11] The structure and content of these table follow the reporting practices of the Australian TE report (Australian Government the Treasury, 2021[7]).

[12] This list was the result of a detailed analysis carried out jointly by DIAN, the MOF and the OECD.

[13] The OECD provided DIAN with the necessary coding to carry out the distributional analysis, which DIAN applied to the universe of taxpayers that submit exogenous information forms.

[14] If some item-by-item estimates are available, DIAN could then calculate the residual between the aggregate category (e.g. total revenue forgone from non-taxable income) and the sum of individual TEs, and include a value in the row "other" in Table A.

[15] Other enhanced deductions reported in the same cell include: Salaries, social benefits and other labour payments, paid to widows and orphans of members of the Armed Forces killed in combat, kidnapped or missing (200%); salaries and social contributions paid to handicapped workers (200%); salaries paid to old age workers who do not receive an old-age pension (120%) and salaries and social contributions of workers hired as apprentices in addition to those foreseen legally (130%).

4 Measuring and Reporting Personal Income Tax Expenditures

This chapter presents the approach that Colombia currently follows to measure and report Personal Income Tax (PIT) Expenditures, and identifies areas for improvement. It presents the equations that can be applied to measure revenue forgone from different PIT TEs on an item-by-item basis and discusses strategies to obtain more granular data. The chapter also includes the item-by-item revenue forgone estimates calculated by DIAN following the OECD's proposed methodology and presents a distributional analysis of a number of PIT TEs.

Summary

This chapter presents the approach that DIAN currently follows to measure and report Personal Income Tax Expenditures, and identifies areas for improvement.

General assessment of the DIAN TE methodology

- Following the guidance provided by the Tax Incentives Commission (OECD, DIAN and Minhacienda, 2021[1]), the two most recent editions of the *Marco Fiscal de Mediano Plazo* (MFMP) have introduced a number of improvements to the measurement of PIT TEs. For instance, the 2022 edition of the MFMP has started to include information on an item-by-item basis – although in terms of the amounts that are declared rather than the corresponding revenue forgone – for a selected number of PIT TEs, including the pension income exemption, the exemption of voluntary pension contributions and the mortgage interest deduction.
- The aggregate estimates available in the MFMP draw on information from individual tax returns. Similar to the CIT TEs, data from specific cells in the tax return combines information on tax provisions that are viewed as a TE as well as provisions that are part of the benchmark (and are therefore not a TE).
- To calculate revenue forgone, DIAN applies the average marginal tax rate based on the information available at the time of the publication of the MFMP report. This approach yields biased estimates for a number of reasons and can be improved.
- Less than 2% of the taxpayers that submit a tax return are required to submit supplementary tax forms that provide more detailed information on the tax provisions they claim. Individual taxpayers are required to submit these so-called "exogenous information forms" if their gross income exceeds COP 500 million (approximately USD 132 000) and if, in addition, the sum of their gross capital and non-labour income exceeds COP 100 million. These limitations severely limit the usefulness of exogenous information for the measurement of PIT TEs.

Recommendations to improve the measurement and reporting of PIT revenue forgone

A first priority would be to ensure that provisions that are viewed as TEs are not reported together with provisions that are considered part of the benchmark in the PIT tax return. DIAN should also start collecting more disaggregated information within the tax returns that taxpayers need to file. This will allow DIAN to estimate more PIT TEs on an item-by-item basis, increase the accuracy of the PIT revenue foregone estimates and increase transparency. Furthermore, more taxpayers should be required to provide additional exogenous information.

Going forward, the methodology that is applied to estimate revenue foregone could be further refined, with the goal of using the available PIT micro data more efficiently. DIAN could also improve the way it reports PIT TEs. This analysis, and the corresponding recommendations, are developed in detail in the following sections.

- Section 4.2 presents the tax equations that can be applied to measure revenue forgone from different PIT TEs on an item-by-item basis. The analysis also recommends DIAN to switch from applying an average marginal PIT rate to applying the actual PIT rate schedule to the taxable income (with and without the TE) of each taxpayer and then take the difference to estimate revenue forgone. Applying an average marginal PIT rate is only recommended when only aggregate TE data is available.
- Section 4.3 includes the revenue forgone estimates calculated by DIAN following the OECD's recommendations based on PIT returns data from all taxpayers. This Section also makes

recommendations with respect to the types of tables with information on PIT revenue forgone that could be included in the TE report. Finally, the Section refers to Annex D, which provides a comprehensive list of all 124 PIT TEs that have been identified in collaboration with DIAN and the Ministry of Finance. Section 4.4 provides examples on how to use tax returns to perform distributional TE analysis by analysing the distribution of claimants and revenue forgone on an item-by-item basis for a number of TEs.

- Section 4.5 discusses strategies DIAN could pursue to obtain more granular data. Recommendations include (i) redesigning the PIT return, (ii) increasing the number of taxpayers that are required to submit exogenous information, (iii) using additional data that allows for breaking down information in cells in the tax return that record both TEs and non TEs, or multiple TEs and (iv) exploring additional sources of information. Section 4.6 discusses additional analysis DIAN could conduct using tax returns such as bunching analysis to assess taxpayers' behaviour. Section 4.7 discusses SIMPLE and whether some TEs within this preferential regime could be reported.

4.1 Current PIT TE measurement, reporting and data availability

The *Marco Fiscal de Mediano Plazo* (MFMP) includes very limited information on the revenue foregone of TEs within the PIT (Minhacienda, 2022[2]). Up to 2021, the tables in the MFMP only included an aggregate estimate of all exempt income items and tax credits. The MFMP report published in 2022 includes more information; it reports the revenue foregone of all deductions although this includes not only non-standard deductions but also deductions that are part of the benchmark (and that are therefore not a TE). The revenue foregone of non-taxable income does not feature in the report. DIAN presents PIT revenue forgone estimates in summary tables that include also the revenue forgone from CIT TEs. The report then reports total exempt income and total deductions rather than the corresponding forgone tax revenue. The 2022 edition of the MFMP also includes item-by-item estimates (in terms of aggregate take-up rather than revenue forgone) for a selected number of TEs, including the pension income exemption, the exemption of voluntary pension contributions and the mortgage interest deduction.

The estimates available in the MFMP draw on information from individual tax returns. Similar to the concerns that were raised with respect to the CIT TEs, the aggregated data that is filed within the PIT returns combines tax provisions that are TEs as well as provisions that are part of the benchmark. As a result, DIAN's current revenue foregone estimate of exempt income is biased upwards by income that is not taxed under the TE benchmark, such as income that is exempt as a result of double taxation treaties.[1] Similarly, by treating all deductions as TEs, the MFMP overestimates the PIT TEs as many of these deductions are included in the benchmark tax system, and they are therefore not a TE.[2]

Because tax returns data is only available with a time lag, DIAN produces estimates for two consecutive years based on the same data source. For example, the revenue forgone estimates for 2021 and 2020 that are published in the 2022 edition of the MFMP both draw upon tax returns from 2020.

To calculate revenue forgone, DIAN applies an average marginal tax rate based on the information available at the time of the publication of the MFMP report. For example, the MFMP 2022 estimated an average marginal tax rate of 7.4% on the basis of tax returns data from 2020. Section 4.2 discusses the use of the average marginal tax rate and makes recommendations for an alternative approach that would yield more accurate estimates of the TEs' revenue foregone.

Similarly to the CIT, supplementary "exogenous information" is available to calculate the revenue foregone of PIT TEs. However, less than 2% of the taxpayers that submit a tax return are obliged to submit these supplementary tax forms. Individual taxpayers are required to submit exogenous information forms if their gross income exceeds COP 500 million (approximately USD 132 000) and if, in addition, the sum of their gross capital and non-labour income exceeds COP 100 million. Taxpayers who receive capital or non-labour income are also required to submit exogenous information if they are unincorporated businesses that employ workers and therefore withhold income tax on behalf of their employees and/ or are VAT registered. In light of the limited scope of the exogenous information, Section 4.2 includes recommendations on how to optimise the use of the tax returns data for the measurement of the revenue foregone of PIT TEs. Section 4.3 presents recommendations on how to improve the reporting on PIT TEs and Section 4.4 discusses how more data could be collected, either from tax returns or from additional information sources, in order to improve the accuracy of the TE estimates.

4.2. Measuring revenue forgone

Exempt income, non-taxable income and non-standard deductions

Unlike CIT TEs, and as a result of the progressive PIT rate schedule, the removal of a PIT TE that would increase taxable income could push a taxpayer into a higher tax bracket, which implies that the increase in taxable income would be taxed at a higher marginal PIT rate than the statutory PIT rate that applied when the TE was in place.

As micro data for each taxpayer is available, DIAN can estimate tax revenue forgone by applying the *actual* PIT rate schedule (Table 4.1) to the *actual* taxable income of each individual in each fiscal year. Instead, DIAN currently applies an average marginal tax rate, which is the average effective marginal rate across all taxpayers. This method, however, results in biased estimates as it disregards that a reduction in exempt income, non-taxable income and non-standard deductions (as a result of the withdrawal of a TE) can have an impact on the taxpayer's marginal PIT rate. Furthermore, the average marginal tax rate that DIAN applies may be different from the average marginal rate that applies to taxpayers who benefit from a particular TE. As a result, DIAN currently underestimates the tax revenue forgone from regressive TEs, which are claimed by taxpayers with high taxable income and who therefore face a higher marginal PIT rate.

Table 4.1. Personal Income Tax Schedule in Colombia in UVT (2020)

Income	0- 1 090	1 090- 1 700	1 700- 4 100	4 100- 8 670	8 670- 18 970	18 970- 31 000	31 000-
Marginal rate	0%	19%	28%	33%	35%	37%	39%
Tax liability	0	(x - 1 090) * 19%	(x- 1 700) * 28% + 116	(x - 4 100) * 33% + 788	(x - 8 670) * 35% + 2 296	(x- 18 970) * 37% + 5 901	(x - 31 000) * 39% + 10 352

Note: 1 UVT = COP 35 607 (2020).
*Applies to: labour income, income from professional services, capital income, non-labour income and pension income. However, pension income additionally benefits from an exemption of up to 12 000 UVT.
Source: DIAN

To implement the suggested approach, DIAN should first calculate, for each taxpayer, the PIT liability when the exempt income, non-taxable income or non-standard deduction is added to taxable income. Then, it should take the difference between the re-calculated tax liability and the current tax liability that the taxpayer faces when applying the PIT schedule to the actual taxable income that has been declared. Finally, the revenue forgone would be aggregated across individuals.

For a provision p that grants $Exempt\ income_p$ and the $Tax\ liability(Taxable\ income)$ defined by the general PIT schedule (see Table 4.1), revenue forgone generated by n taxpayers would be estimated as follows:[3]

$$Revenue\ forgone_p = \sum_{i=1}^{n}\big(Tax\ liability\ (Taxable\ income_i + Exempt\ income_{i,p}) - Tax\ liability(Taxable\ income_i)\big)$$

Dividend income and occasional gains

As discussed in Chapter 1, the proposed benchmark rate for dividend income and occasional gains is the proportional rate currently in place (10%). As a consequence, TEs that narrow the tax base linked to dividend income and occasional gains should be measured by taking into account the 10% benchmark rate. Tax revenue forgone from the exemption for dividend income up to 300 UVT (art 35, Law 2010 of 2019) would be measured as follows:

Let $Exempt\ income_{d,i}$ represent exempt dividend income from individual i up to 300 UVT, then revenue forgone from this item is calculated as follows:

$$Revenue\ forgone_d = \sum_{i=1}^{n}\big(Exempt\ income_{d,i}) * 10\%\big)$$

TEs that require a specific estimation methodology

The estimation of revenue foregone of a number of TEs would require a different estimation methodology than the method that has been introduced above:

- **Pension income exempt up to 12 000 UVT (art 96, Law 223 of 1995).** Under the proposed income benchmark, the zero-rate bracket of the general PIT rate schedule (1 090 UVT) is included within the benchmark. However, pension income benefits from an additional exemption (12 000 UVT). The excess allowance claimed above the standard allowance is a TE. To compute revenue forgone, this excess allowance should be added to the pensioner's taxable income and the general PIT rate schedule should then be applied. Finally, the difference between this amount and the current tax liability of the pensioner, summed over all pensioners, then yields revenue foregone from this TE.
- **Voluntary contributions to private pension funds and AFC housing savings (art 15-16, Law 1819 of 2016).** In the 2020 tax return, voluntary contributions to private pension funds and AFC housing savings are reported separately from other exempt income, as part of DIAN's strategy to increase transparency. However, as these contributions can be reported in four different boxes (one for each type of income), there is a risk that taxpayers declare the same amount several times. However, DIAN's analysis shows that this type of over-reporting is not very common and that more than 96% of taxpayers only record a contribution in one of the four cells. Furthermore, it is not clear whether taxpayers who report values in multiple boxes mistakenly included contributions multiple times or whether they attempted to split their actual contribution among several boxes. In the future, DIAN could estimate revenue forgone based on the sum of all four cells, while making sure it does not exceed the maximum 3 800 UVT and noting in the report that revenue forgone may be somewhat overestimated. In the future, DIAN is encouraged to revise the tax return and only include one (instead of four) cell in the tax return (see recommendation in Section 4.5) so that the contribution can be declared independently of the type of income the taxpayer earns. The same

methodology and suggestion applies to the deduction of mortgage interest (art 89, Law 2010 of 2019) which is also reported in four cells (i.e. one cell per type of income).

It is currently only possible to estimate jointly revenue forgone from the exemption of both voluntary contributions to private pension funds and AFC housing savings. Despite of being incomplete, the available "exogenous information" from the supplementary tax form (1022) could be used to obtain an indication of the respective size of these TEs. The exogenous information suggests that between half and two thirds of the revenue forgone is due to voluntary pension contributions. However, it should be noted that the aggregate revenue forgone calculated from the supplementary data form does not match with the aggregate calculated from individual tax returns because fewer taxpayers need to submit the additional form.

Additional measurement tools to deal with low data availability in PIT returns

Unfortunately, the structure of the tax returns with several provisions being grouped into one box implies that the approach described above cannot be implemented for many items in the short term. In many cases, the information that is grouped within a single entry point within the tax return combines deductions (exempt or non-taxable income) that are considered TEs with deductions that are not viewed as a TE (e.g. mandatory contributions to RAIS, exempt income from CAN treaties). In some of these instances, the revenue foregone could be estimated indirectly, as is the case for the following PIT provisions:

- **Voluntary contributions to the individual savings schemes (Law 1819 of 2016) and inflationary component (art 27, Law 75 of 1986).** Under the proposed benchmark, the non-taxation of mandatory contributions to pension schemes is not viewed as a TE. However, the PIT tax return includes non-taxable income cells in which taxpayers record both the mandatory social security contributions, which are not a TE, together with other non-taxable income that is considered a TE including voluntary pension contributions and the inflationary component. DIAN could simulate the amount of compulsory pension contributions that taxpayers were required to make and deduct this amount of the total amount that has been declared. The difference would then equal non-taxable income that is viewed as a TE. Once this amount is determined, the revenue foregone can be calculated using the formula that was presented above.
- **25% of labour income (art 104, Law 1607 of 2012).** The 25% labour income deduction is considered a TE because it applies in addition to the zero-rate bracket. Even though the value of this exemption is not recorded separately in the tax return, it can be simulated based on other information on labour income that is declared in the tax return. DIAN may wish to include a separate cell for this tax provision in the tax return in order to estimate the corresponding TE in an accurate manner, in particular as the revenue forgone associated to it is high as Table 4.3 shows.[4]

Suggested methodology to integrate sources that cannot be merged with tax returns

DIAN could use aggregate data from other sources (beyond the information from tax returns) in order to increase the number of TEs for which the revenue foregone can be estimated even though aggregate information is expected to yield less accurate estimates. In some instances, data on the aggregate usage of a TE may be available from a data source that cannot be merged with the data from the tax returns. In this case, DIAN could possibly revert back to using an average marginal tax rate approach. This approach is used in the Chilean TE report for the exemption of returns from voluntary pension savings (SII, 2021[3]). However, rather than using the approach as described above, DIAN could refine its use by targeting it more closely to groups of taxpayers, depending on whether they use or not a particular TE. For example, DIAN could first estimate the average marginal tax rate that applies to taxpayers who make voluntary pension contributions to then, estimate the corresponding TE if no other data sources are available.

Table 4.2 demonstrates that calculating the average based on a subpopulation that is more aligned with the target group of a TE can yield significantly different average marginal rate estimates.

Table 4.2. Average Marginal Personal Income Tax Rates (AMTR) in Colombia for selected groups

Group	Average Marginal Personal Income Tax Rate
All taxpayers	*8.8%*
Taxpayers with pension income	*4.0%*
Taxpayers with positive gross income	*9.1%*
Taxpayers with capital income	*9.7%*
Taxpayers with income from professional services	*11.5%*
Taxpayers claiming mortgage interest deduction	*15.9%*
Taxpayers with voluntary contributions to private pension funds or AFC housing savings	*19.3%*
Taxpayers with taxable income above exempt income threshold	*22.0%*

Note: Based on a sample of 110 695 income tax records from 2020 provided by DIAN. Calculations need to be repeated using the full census of tax records. Only includes taxpayers who file a tax return.
Source: OECD based on data provided by DIAN.

Tax credits

Similar to the CIT, the revenue forgone from PIT tax credits is equal to the total amount claimed by the individual that either (i) reduces the final tax liability or (ii) is refunded. Not all tax credits are viewed as a TE – for example, the tax credit for taxes paid abroad by national taxpayers who receive income from foreign sources would be part of the proposed benchmark. DIAN is therefore advised to break down revenue forgone from tax credits on an item-by-item basis in addition to providing an estimate of total revenue forgone.

4.3. Revenue forgone estimates and reporting recommendations

Revenue forgone estimates

This Section presents item-by-item revenue forgone estimates for 2020. The OECD calculated preliminary estimates based on a representative sample of PIT tax returns that was merged with exogenous information on mandatory contributions reported by employers. The coding was shared with DIAN so that the proposed methodology could be applied to the taxpayer population. This Review includes the results of these calculations made by DIAN based on the OECD's suggestions and following the methodology described in the previous section.

Table 4.3 reports revenue forgone from PIT TEs for the limited number of items for which this analysis was feasible given the high degree of aggregation of the information that needs to be filed within the tax returns. It cannot be compared to the estimates included in the MFMP 2022 as Table 4.3 disregards boxes in which TEs and non-TEs are reported together unless a credible approach to disentangle the two components has been identified.

Table 4.3. Item-by-item PIT revenue forgone in 2020 for provisions with available data

Tax expenditure	Revenue forgone (2020)	
	COP thousand million	% of GDP
Exempt income	**13 551**	**1.4%**
*25% of labour income (art 104, Law 1607 of 2012)**	*7 187*	
Additional exempt bracket granted to pension income (art 96, Law 223 of 1995)	*5 001*	
Voluntary contributions to private pension funds and AFC housing savings (art 15-16, Law 1819 of 2016)	*1 330*	
Dividend income up to 300 UVT (art 35, Law 2010 of 2019)	*34*	
Other	*n/a*	
Non-taxable income	**1 887**	**0.2%**
Voluntary contributions to the mandatory individual savings scheme (labour income)	*467*	
Voluntary contributions to the mandatory individual savings scheme (professional services)	*38*	
*Voluntary contributions to the mandatory individual savings scheme (capital income) & inflationary component***	*222*	
*Voluntary contributions to the mandatory individual savings scheme (non-labour income) & inflationary component***	*740*	
Payments by employer for food (art 84, Law 788 of 2002)	*18*	
*Non-taxable occasional gains****	*402*	
Other	*n/a*	
Non-standard deductions	**1 969**	**0.2%**
Mortgage interest deduction (art 89, Law 2010 of 2019)	*656*	
50% of the financial transaction tax, interest on educational loans, contribution to severance for self-employed (art 86 & 89, Law 2010 of 2019)	*1 313*	
Other	*n/a*	
Tax credits	**67**	**0.0%**
Investment in research & development and donations (art 171, Law 1955 of 2019)	*42*	
Input VAT paid on fixed capital assets and 50% of local turnover tax (art 86 & 95, Law 2010 of 2019)	*24*	
Other	*n/a*	

Note: The table lists all item-by-item TEs that can be estimated based on the data that is currently available from Personal Income Tax returns merged with exogenous information. Estimates are based on 2020 tax records from the population of taxpayers. The estimates reported in the table were prepared by DIAN. The OECD had access to a representative sample of 110 695 personal income tax returns and calculated preliminary estimates. The OECD provided DIAN with an initial coding proposal but was not involved in the final calculations. Total revenue forgone from exempt income, non-taxable income, and non-standard deductions cannot be provided because only a small share of all TEs can be measured based on the data currently available and no variable corresponding to the total is available.

* Includes the simulated exempt income for labour income and for income from professional services if the taxpayer choses to deduct this 25% rather than deduct effective costs. Taxpayers that provide professional services with a maximum of two employees can choose to either deduct 25% of income or effective costs.

** Voluntary contributions to mandatory pension funds and the inflationary component are determined by simulating mandatory contributions to pension funds or by subtracting mandatory contributions based on information provided by third parties. In the case of capital and non-labour income the methodology may overestimate the mandatory contributions effectively made and thereby lead to an underestimation of revenue forgone from voluntary contributions to mandatory pension schemes and the inflationary component.

*** Includes donations to those affected by the volcanic activity of the Nevado del Ruiz; betting prizes and equestrian or canine contests and prizes to owners of horses or racing dogs (up to 410 UVT); inheritance (up to 7 700 UVT, 20% of assets up to 2 290 UVT, heirs' and spouse's inheritance allowance up to 3 490 UVT); real estate capital gains (up to 7 500 UVT); raffle of capitalization titles; life insurance compensation (up to 12 500 UVT); income from the sale of shares of participations in a CFC. Note that the estimate also includes assets from divorce which are not considered a TE but should represent a low share of the total amounts reported in the box.

Source: DIAN.

Reporting recommendations

This Section also provides recommendations on how to report revenue forgone from Personal Income Tax expenditures in the TE report:

- Whenever possible, DIAN should report revenue forgone rather than the size of the tax exemptions, non-taxable income, deductions or tax credits that are claimed. Under the PIT with its progressive rate schedule and zero-rate bracket, revenue forgone cannot be easily inferred from the value of the TE.
- The main revenue forgone table (Table 4.3) would present revenue forgone from all PIT TEs that can be measured; the table follows a similar structure as the CIT table.
- For each type of TE, the table also contains a row that records the revenue forgone that cannot be measured on an item-by-item basis ("Other"). Currently, no estimate can be provided in these rows because the aggregate boxes in the tax return (for example, total exempt income) include both TE and non-TE components. As a large fraction of TEs cannot be measured on an item-by-item basis, the revenue forgone linked to the "other" category is likely large. If Colombia were to follow the recommendations made in 4.5, the design of future tax returns would ensure that the aggregated information does not mix TEs and tax provisions that are part of the TE benchmark.
- In the TE report, values would be expressed both in thousand million pesos and as a percentage of GDP.
- Over time, DIAN could add more information in the table by adding the revenue forgone in previous years. This will indicate how the revenue foregone has changed over time. If the calculations for two or more consecutive years are based on the same underlying data source (as is currently the case in the MFMP), this information should be highlighted and the change in revenue forgone between years that are based upon the same underlying data should not be discussed in the text.
- The table could include the sum of all PIT TEs. This total should, however, be interpreted with caution given the limitations of summing different TEs. If the total is provided, the report should explicitly mention that some TEs are not included in the total because of a lack of data (see chapter 5 for further discussion).
- The most recent edition of the MFMP includes revenue foregone from total exempt income across economic sectors and income schedules. Including tables with breakdowns by sector or types of taxpayers constitutes good practice insofar as it is possible to distinguish between tax provisions that are TEs and those that are included in the benchmark. A similar analysis could be included with respect to non-taxable income and special deductions in order to further increase transparency with respect to the types of taxpayers that benefit the most from PIT TEs.

Item-by-item discussion

In addition to the tables that provide an overview of revenue forgone from individual PIT TEs, and in line with the reporting recommendations for the CIT (see Chapter 3), the TE report could include item-specific tables for each TE measured on an item-by-item basis. These tables would include information about the reliability of the revenue forgone estimate. For example, the table would indicate if the estimate is based upon a simulated full take-up of the tax benefit, as it is done for the 25% labour income deduction. Table 4.4 provides an illustrative example.

More specifically, the item-by-item table could include the following elements:[5]

- (i) TE identifier; (ii) Name of the TE; (iii) Revenue forgone in the current year and in the five preceding years; (iv) Tax type; (v) TE type; (vi) Year of implementation; (vii) Year of expiration; (viii) Legal reference; (ix) Reliability of the estimate; (x) Data source used to estimate revenue forgone; (xi) Estimation method; (xii) Paragraph that states why the provision deviates from the benchmark and provides more detail about the TE.

Table 4.4. Suggested presentation of item-by-item PIT revenue forgone

E43 Labour income exemption (25%)

Year	2015	2016	2017	2018	2019	2020
Revenue forgone (COP thousand million)	.	.	.	.	.	7 187*

Tax:	*Personal income tax*	*Legal reference:*	*Art 96, Law 223 of 1995; Art 106, Law 1607 of 2012*
Tax expenditure type:	*Exempt income*	*Estimate reliability:*	*Medium-High*
Implementation:	*1995*	*Data source:*	*Tax returns*
Expiration:	*n/a*	*Estimation method:*	*Microsimulation applying the respective marginal personal tax rate to simulated exemption amount*

Note: **Reason why this measure is not part of benchmark tax system**: Under the benchmark, all sources of income for the individual, including income from employment is subject to taxation. However, twenty-five percent (25%) of the total value of the labour payments (after subtracting from the total value of the labour payments received by the worker, the income not constituting income, the deductions and the other exempt income), limited monthly to 240 UVT, is exempt from taxation.

* Includes the simulated exempt income for labour income and for income from professional services if the taxpayer choses to deduct this 25% rather than deduct effective costs.

Appendix tables

Finally, a comprehensive list of TEs could be included in the annex of the TE report. This list could provide information about the legal reference of the tax provision and explain why the provision is considered a TE. This list would include all TEs, and not just those that are measured on an item-by-item basis. The list could be compiled by building upon the detailed list of PIT TEs included in Annex D of this report, and which is the result of several rounds of input and discussions with DIAN and the Ministry of Finance.

4.4. Distributional analysis

The tax return data allows DIAN to move beyond total revenue forgone estimates for each category and present a distributional analysis of PIT TEs. Figure 4.1 and Figure 4.2 provide an example for four TEs that can currently be measured on an item-by-item basis estimated by DIAN based on OECD recommendations. Figure 4.1 shows the breakdown of taxpayers who claim the TE across gross income deciles and Figure 4.2 plots the share of revenue forgone by gross income decile. Figure 4.3 replicates the analysis for voluntary contributions to the mandatory individual savings scheme (capital income) and the inflationary component (both items are non-taxable income TEs). Deciles are calculated among taxpayers who submit a tax return and the fraction of the population who does not submit any return is excluded.

Figure 4.1. Breakdown of taxpayers claiming the TE by decile of gross income (2020)

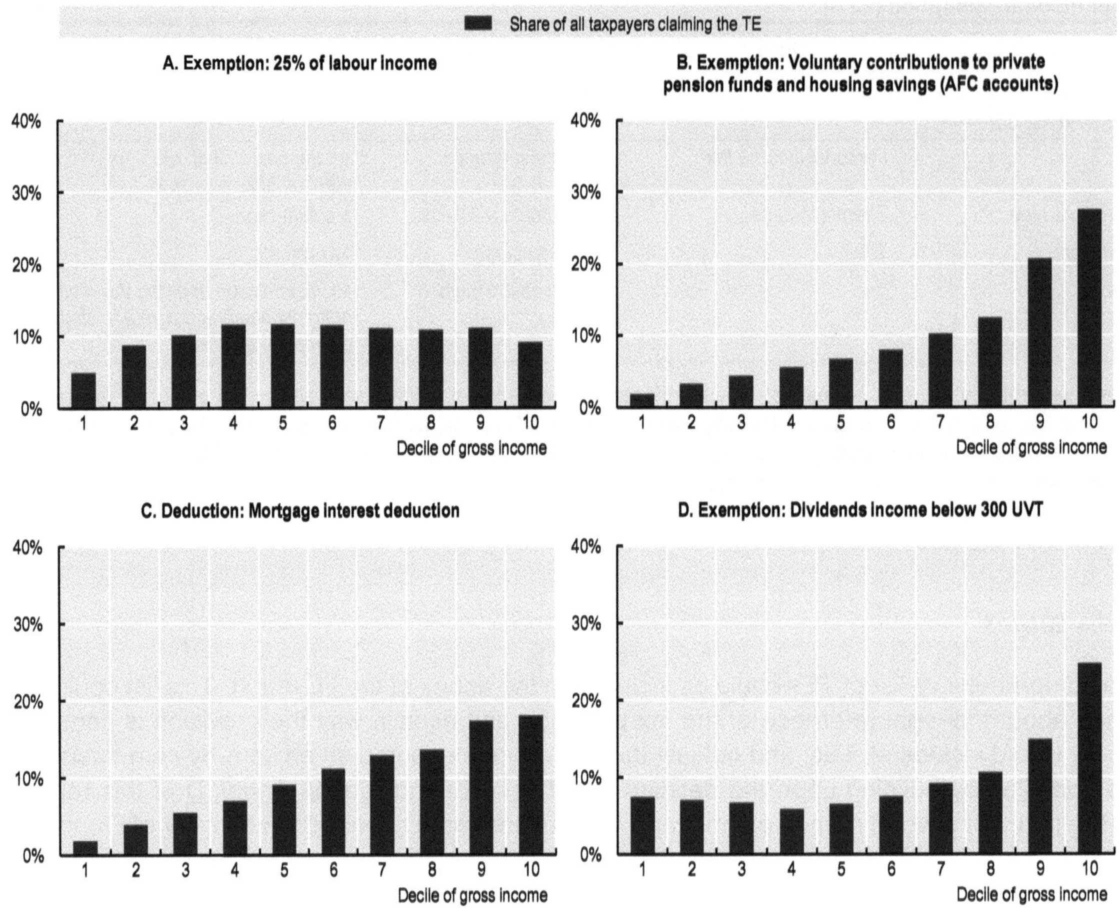

Note: Based on personal income tax returns of the full taxpayer population in 2020. The OECD had access to a representative sample of 110 695 personal income tax returns and calculated preliminary estimates. The OECD provided DIAN with an initial coding proposal but was not involved in the final calculations. Gross income is defined as the sum of gross income from: labour income, income from professional services, capital income, non-labour income, pension income, dividend income and occasional gains.
Source: DIAN.

Figure 4.2. Share of total revenue forgone by gross income decile (2020)

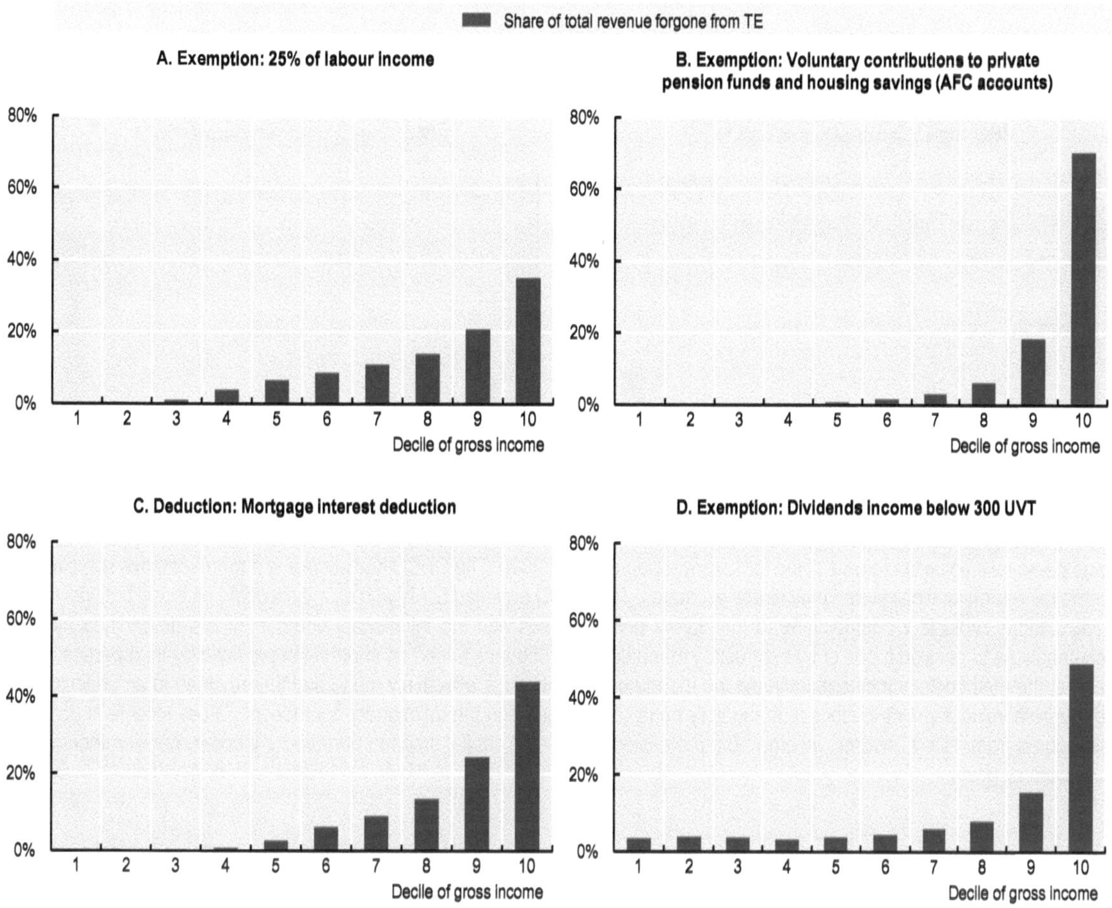

Note: Based on personal income tax returns of the full taxpayer population in 2020. The OECD had access to a representative sample of 110 695 personal income tax returns and calculated preliminary estimates. The OECD provided DIAN with an initial coding proposal but was not involved in the final calculations. Gross income is defined as the sum of gross income from: labour income, income from professional services, capital income, non-labour income, pension income, dividend income and occasional gains.
Source: DIAN.

A distributional analysis of TEs would allow DIAN to examine to which extent tax provisions are progressive, proportional or regressive across the income distribution. For example, the Tax Incentives Commission noted that the 25% labour income exemption is expected to be highly regressive as the amount of the exempt income is increasing with earnings, and the value of the TE is increasing in the taxpayer's marginal PIT rate (OECD, DIAN and Minhacienda, 2021[1]). This observation is confirmed in Figure 4.2.The fact that there are fewer taxpayers in the first three deciles of the gross income distribution who report labour income is consistent with a finding of the Tax Incentives Commission (OECD, DIAN and Minhacienda, 2021[1]). The distributional analysis calls for a more in-depth analysis that would allow making concrete tax policy recommendations. This could include an analysis of the overall statutory and effective tax burden across the income distribution and an evaluation of the possible behavioural responses to particular tax policy reforms.

Figure 4.3. Distributional analysis for non-taxable income: voluntary contributions to the mandatory individual savings scheme (capital income) & inflationary component (2020)

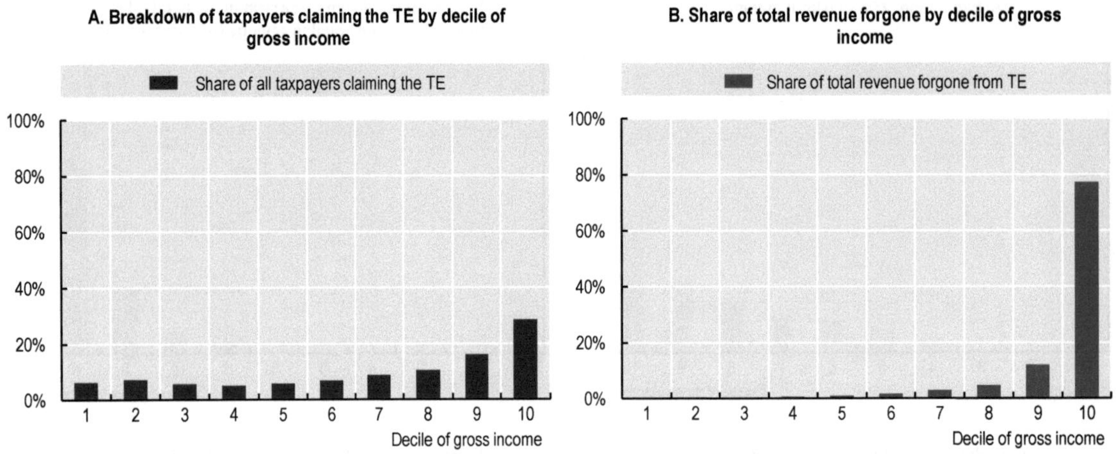

Note: Based on personal income tax returns of the full taxpayer population in 2020. The OECD had access to a representative sample of 110 695 personal income tax returns and calculated preliminary estimates. The OECD provided DIAN with an initial coding proposal but was not involved in the final calculations. Voluntary contributions to mandatory pension funds and the inflationary component are determined by simulating mandatory contributions to pension funds or by subtracting mandatory contributions based on information provided by third parties. In the case of capital income, the methodology may overestimate the mandatory contributions effectively made and thereby lead to an underestimation of revenue forgone from voluntary contributions to mandatory pension schemes and the inflationary component. Gross income is defined as the sum of gross income from: labour income, income from professional services, capital income, non-labour income, pension income, dividend income and occasional gains.
Source: DIAN.

4.5. Strengthening the TE measurement through more and better data

In order to improve the measurement of PIT TEs, DIAN needs to collect more granular data. As Table 4.6 shows, less than 10% of the PIT TEs can be quantified based on the information that taxpayers are required to provide within the income tax return in 2020. This is a result of both the design of the cells within the PIT return and the low share (less than 2%) of taxpayers that are required to submit exogenous information. In order to increase the number of TEs that can be measured on an item-by-item basis, DIAN could undertake the following steps (in decreasing order of priority):

1. **Redesign the PIT return**. A first priority would be to redesign the income tax return that individuals need to file, possibly including the following:

   - *Cells in the income tax return should not combine tax provisions that are TEs and provisions that are considered part of the PIT benchmark. Table 4.6 shows all the boxes that according to the proposed benchmark, include both income from TEs and non- TEs in the 2020 tax return. Once the PIT benchmark is defined, the tax return should distinguish between cells where TEs are filed and cells that ask for information that are part of the benchmark. This would allow DIAN to calculate total revenue forgone from aggregate PIT TE categories (e.g. exempt income, non-taxable income, special deductions and tax credits that are viewed as TEs).*

   - *The tax return should include one single cell for exempt voluntary contributions and one cell for the deduction of mortgage interest. Recently, cells for these items were included in the tax return but they were added for each type of income from the general schedule (labour, professional services, capital and non-labour), which might lead taxpayers to declare these deductions multiple times within the same tax return. More generally, the number of cells in the tax return could be increased, ideally by including a separate Section where taxpayers earning income subject to the general schedule would declare their deductions with respect to the four categories. This would minimize the number of additional boxes and would avoid confusion and multiple reporting of the same item. More detailed tax returns would also enhance DIAN's monitoring and tax auditing possibilities.*

2. **Increase the number of taxpayers that are required to submit exogenous information**. If adding cells to the PIT return would not be feasible in the short run, DIAN could increase the number of taxpayers that provide exogenous information by reducing the gross income thresholds that define who needs to file the exogenous information forms.
3. **Use additional data that allows for breaking down information in cells in the tax return that record both TEs and non TEs, or multiple TEs**. For some TEs, DIAN can already split the information reported within a particular cell in the tax return in its TE and non-TE component. This is for instance the case for mandatory pension contributions that can be distinguished from the voluntary contributions to the mandatory individual savings scheme (Law 1819 of 2016) and the inflationary component. Until it redesigns the tax return, DIAN should evaluate whether it can proxy for more items the share of TEs in the total amount that is declared within a particular cell in the tax return (Table 4.5), as this would allow DIAN to quantify additional TEs on an item-by-item basis. The same strategy could be applied if several TEs remain grouped together in one cell after redesigning the tax return.
4. **Explore additional sources of information**. DIAN should make use of additional information reported by third parties. This can include aggregated information (e.g. returns from voluntary contributions to private insurance), which would allow DIAN to refine the average marginal tax rate approach that it applies to estimate revenue forgone. DIAN can also make use of microdata that can be merged with the tax return data (e.g. the information that employers report on the compulsory contributions they make to pension funds on behalf of their employees or the data collected by the Ministry of Labour on the usage of the 120% first-job for employees who are under twenty-eight years of age).

Table 4.5. Boxes in the PIT return that contain both TEs and non-TE components based on the proposed income benchmark

Box in 2020 PIT return (Form 220)	Content	TE provisions included (Non-exhaustive list)	Non-TE provisions included (Non-exhaustive list)
33, 44, 59, 76	Non-taxable income	• Voluntary contributions to the mandatory individual savings scheme • Inflationary component • Income from the sale of shares of a company listed in the Colombian Stock Exchange when such sale does not represent more than 10% of the total number of shares of the listed company	• Mandatory social security contributions
36, 48, 64, 81	Other exempt income	• Income of officials of international organisations • 25% labour income exemption	• Compensation for work-related accidents or illness • Provision of personal services rendered in another country CAN member • Exempt income from the application of an agreement to avoid double taxation
45, 60, 77	Deductions	• Salaries paid to first-job employees who are under twenty-eight years of age (120%).	• Expenses incurred to earn taxable income (professional services, capital income or non-labour income)
39, 51, 67, 84	Other deductions	• 50% of the financial transaction tax (GMF) • Interest paid on educational loans from the Colombian institute for educational credit and technical studies abroad, aimed at the taxpayer's higher education • Private health insurance contributions	• Deduction for dependents • Severance pay contributions
114	Deductions (occasional gains)	• Average cost of shares • Adjustment of real estate, shares and contributions that are fixed assets of individuals • The fiscal cost of intangible assets formed by taxpayers not required to keep accounts, concerning industrial, literary, artistic and scientific property	• Cost of fixed assets that have not been adjusted
115	Non-taxable income (occasional gains	• Donations to those affected by the volcanic activity of the Nevado del Ruiz • Betting prizes and equestrian or canine contests and prizes to owners of horses or racing dogs (up to 410 UVT) • Inheritance (up to 7 700 UVT, 20% of assets up to 2 290 UVT, heirs' and spouse's inheritance allowance up to 3 490 UVT) • Real estate capital gains (up to 7 500 UVT) • Raffle of capitalization titles • Life insurance compensation (up to 12 500 UVT) • Income from the sale of shares of participations in a CFC • Income from the sale of shares of a company listed in the Colombian Stock Exchange when such sale does not represent more than 10% of the total number of shares of the listed company	• Assets from divorce

Source: OECD based on information provided by DIAN.

Table 4.6. Data availability to measure PIT revenue forgone on an item-by-item basis

Category	PIT TEs currently measurable on an item-by-item basis / All identified PIT TEs
Exempt income	4/40
*Non-taxable income**	4/28
Non-standard deductions	2/34
Deferrals	0/9
Tax credits	2/11
Special regime	0/2
Total	**12/124**

Note: Based on comparing Table 4.3 with the list of identified TEs in Annex D.
* In the case of non-taxable income, revenue forgone from voluntary contributions to pension savings and the inflationary component are measured jointly but counted as two separate items that can currently be measured.

4.6. Additional tax return analysis

Data from individual tax returns can be used by DIAN beyond estimating revenue forgone, by examining taxpayers' behaviour. This type of analysis does not necessarily have to be included in the TE report but it could provide useful additional insights that would enrich the tax policy debate. It could also shed a light on the extent to which taxpayers use TEs strategically in order to reach certain income thresholds in the tax schedule.

The graphs that are included below provide an example of the type of analysis that could be conducted by zooming in on the PIT exempt bracket threshold (Figure 4.4). The aim of the analysis is to assess the extent of bunching behaviour and potential tax planning around the threshold. Figure 4.4 shows that while the distribution of gross income is not particularly concentrated around the exempt bracket threshold, taxable income is significantly concentrated around this threshold both below the threshold but also slightly above it. Bunching analysis could also be carried out for the 40% deduction ceiling or 5 040 UVT, for instance.[6]

Figure 4.4. Distribution of gross and taxable income around exemption threshold (1 090 UVT)

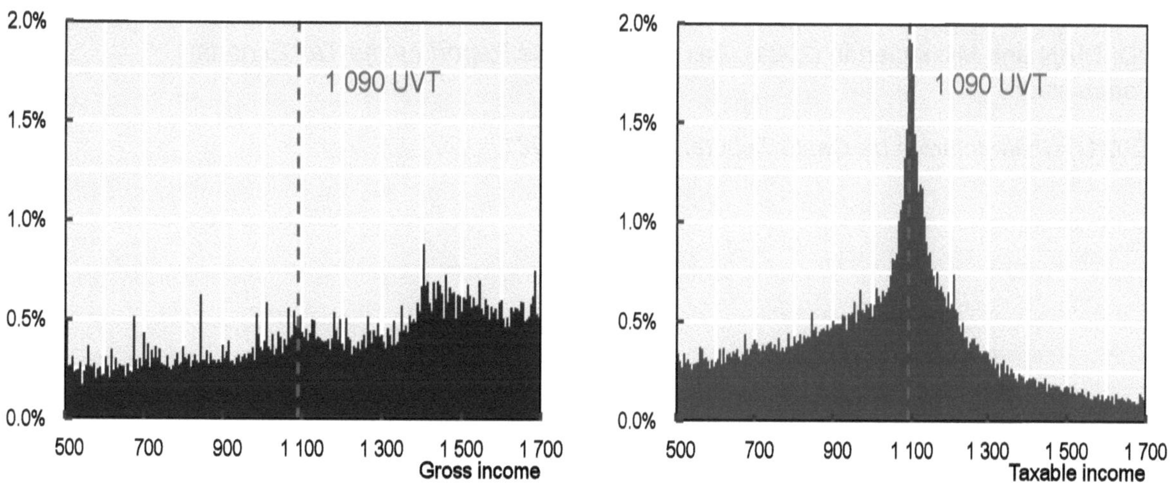

Note: Illustrative example based on a sample of 110 695 income tax records (2020) provided by DIAN. 1 UVT = COP 35 607 (2020). Gross income and taxable income in this case refers to all income taxed under the general PIT general schedule (i.e. labour income, income from professional services, capital income, non-labour income and pension income).
Source: DIAN and own calculations.

4.7. Recommended treatment of the SIMPLE regime

The SIMPLE is a presumptive tax regime that is targeted at unincorporated businesses with gross income below 80 000 UVT per year (about USD 729 000). The SIMPLE is levied on business turnover at rates ranging between 1.8% and 14.5%, varying with turnover and the sector the business operates in. The SIMPLE replaces the income tax and the Municipal Business Turnover tax (ICA), in accordance with the rates determined by the municipal and district councils. Furthermore, taxpayers declare VAT and consumption tax (levied on sales of restaurants and bars) within the tax return of SIMPLE. Employer pension contributions can be credited against the tax liability under SIMPLE. While business costs are not deductible from the turnover-based tax base, income items that are considered "non-taxable" are deductible from the presumptive tax base.

The proposed benchmark considers the SIMPLE regime as a TE even though it is a presumptive regime that aims at strengthening tax compliance by means of tax simplification. However, as the regime is not only targeted at small businesses but reaches also medium-sized businesses, and preferential tax regimes targeted at SMEs are typically viewed as a TE, the same approach is followed regarding SIMPLE.

The estimation of revenue foregone for businesses that pay SIMPLE rather than the income tax is currently not possible as businesses only declare turnover and not their costs, which implies that DIAN cannot determine taxable income. Nevertheless, DIAN could report components of SIMPLE that are viewed as a TE such as the tax credit on mandatory employer pension contributions (art 903 of the Tax Code). The deduction of non-taxable income is also a TE insofar it corresponds to provisions that are not part of the benchmark, such as voluntary contributions to pension funds; once more disaggregated data is available, this provision could also be reported separately as a TE. However, it would be important to signal in the TE report that these individual TEs do not cover the overall TE that corresponds to SIMPLE regime as a whole. Finally, SIMPLE should ideally be included in a separate Section and not be included in either the CIT or PIT sections of the TE report.

References

Australian Government the Treasury (2021), *Tax Benchmarks and Variations Statement 2020.* [4]

Minhacienda (2022), *Marco Fiscal de Mediano Plazo 2022.* [2]

OECD, DIAN and Minhacienda (2021), *Tax Expenditures Report by the Tax Experts Commission.* [1]

SII (2021), *Chile: Informe de Gasto Tributario 2019 a 2021.* [3]

Notes

[1] In line with the proposed benchmark, DIAN has already excluded the tax credit granted for tax payments in foreign jurisdiction from the total tax credit estimate that it provides in the latest MFMP (Minhacienda, 2022[2]).

[2] However, the fact that exempt income is now reported separately from deductions in the 2020 tax return is viewed as an improvement.

[3] The same formula applies to non-standard deductions or special deductions and non-taxable income.

[4] Note that the current report estimated the revenue forgone from this TE both for labour income and for income from professional services if the taxpayer choses to deduct 25%. Taxpayers that provide professional services with a maximum of two employees can choose to either deduct 25% of income or effective costs.

[5] The structure and content of these tables are modelled upon the reporting practices in the Australian TE report (Australian Government the Treasury, 2021[4]).

[6] Whether the 40% of net income ceiling on exempt income and deductions (up to a maximum of 5 040 UVT) is binding or not for a particular taxpayer can currently only be determined for taxpayers who file their tax return online and create a username. Under this modality, the system includes additional questions that allow DIAN to calculate the amount of income that is not subject to the ceiling and, as a result, automatically calculate the amount of deductions that are subject to the ceiling. However, taxpayers who do not create a username are requested to complete the boxes for "limited exempt income and deductions" (*Rentas Exentas y deducciones limitadas*) by themselves and the information is not derived indirectly based on a formula. These boxes combine both the limited exempt income and deductions as well as the exempt income that is not subject to the ceiling. In future tax returns, DIAN may want to ensure that these two items are split and filed separately. Ideally, taxpayers should always have to provide detailed information on income that is not subject to the ceiling.

5 Drafting the First Tax Expenditure Report – Structure and Important Clarifications

This chapter makes a proposal for the structure of the standalone TE report that Colombia is planning to publish on an annual basis, following best practices in other OECD countries. It also includes a set of clarifications that could be added in the report to facilitate the interpretation of the results.

5.1 Suggested report structure

This chapter presents recommendations for the outline of the TE report that Colombia is planning to publish on a regular basis, following best practices in other OECD countries.[1] The TE report should be a standalone report and not an annex of the MFMP. The chapters of this report could be used as a template for the outline of the TE report and for the specific topics it covers. In particular, Colombia's TE report could include the following chapters:

- The first chapter would describe the tax benchmark for all taxes that are covered in the TE report, and in particular the CIT, PIT and VAT, and include a discussion of the standard benchmark principles. The chapter would define key concepts such as *TEs*, *tax benchmark* and *revenue forgone* and describe the main assumptions underlying the revenue forgone method and provide guidance on how to interpret the revenue foregone estimates. It would also briefly discuss the type of data that has been used when estimating tax revenue foregone.
- The second chapter summarizes changes regarding tax policy, the benchmark and the methodology applied to measure revenue forgone compared to the previous TE report. The chapter would first list relevant tax policy reforms introduced in the last year that lead to the creation of new TEs or to the abolishment of existing TEs. It would then zoom in on the changes made to the benchmark compared to the previous editions of the report. This is relevant as it will have an impact on the tax provisions that are identified as TEs. In addition, the chapter could discuss major changes to the methodology applied to measure revenue foregone. Any changes to the data sources that have been used compared to previous editions of the report could also be presented.
- The third chapter would present a summary of the main findings; it would include the main revenue forgone estimates. This chapter could include a summary table that lists the revenue forgone by type of tax and main types of TEs (Table 5.1). This chapter could also include a table that lists the largest TEs and their revenue forgone.
- The following chapters would zoom in on the TEs within the main taxes covered in the report. The report would include a separate chapter for CIT TEs, PIT TEs, VAT TEs and, possibly, TEs within other taxes (including excise duties, property taxes, etc.).
- The report would then include annexes with the details that would be useful background information.

5.2 Other TE reporting recommendations

Relevant clarifications

Some clarifications that would be useful to add in the first chapter of the report include:

- The fact that a tax provision is identified as a TE does not mean the provision needs to be removed or reformed. The TE report aims at providing a comprehensive overview of deviations from the benchmark tax system, and the associated revenue forgone. From a tax policy perspective, certain TEs may be well justified.
- The fact that a tax provision is a TE does not mean the associated revenue forgone can be quantified. For some provisions, measuring revenue forgone is difficult or impossible because the data that would be required to measure the TE is not available. However, concerns regarding costing are not supposed to impact whether a provision is considered a TE or not. Whether or not a tax provision is a TE is solely guided by comparing the current tax system to the benchmark tax

system. If the revenue forgone of a provision cannot be estimated, the provision is nonetheless included in the comprehensive list of TEs in the annex to increase transparency.

- Low revenue forgone does not necessarily mean that the distortions caused by the TE are small. TEs can result in significant distortions that do not show up as revenue forgone.

To reduce the risk of misinterpretation, the report should remind the reader of the limitations of the revenue foregone method that is typically applied to quantify TEs.[2] As a static concept, revenue forgone does not take into account the potential behavioural responses by businesses and consumers to the removal of a TE.[3] In particular, taxpayers may change their behaviour when a specific TE is abolished to, possibly, benefit from another TE. Revenue foregone is therefore not the same as revenue gain.

Revenue forgone tables

This subsection list key recommendations regarding the reporting of revenue forgone:

- The main focus of TE reporting should lie on revenue foregone of the TEs. Less attention should be given (if at all) to the total amount of exempt income and deductions, as the revenue foregone of specific TEs will depend on the tax rate that applies to that specific item.
- Revenue forgone could be summarised as in Table 5.1 and then discussed by type of tax, in line with the reporting suggestions included in the VAT, CIT and PIT chapters. The tables should include both item-by-item estimates and totals by type of TE.
- Values would be expressed both in thousand million pesos and as a percentage of GDP. Previous year estimates could be included if estimates for more than one year are available. If estimates for the latest year are projected this should be clearly stated in the notes to the tables.
- For special regimes, the table *should* include the total number of firms that are subject to each regime as is currently done in the MFMP (Minhacienda, 2022[1]).
- The tables could possibly include revenue foregone for several years. This would allow for an analysis and discussion of the changes over time. However, the reader of the TE report should be made aware of the fact that changes in the benchmark would induce changes in the TEs over time. In addition, if revenue forgone estimates for two consecutive years are based (with adjustments) on the same underlying data source, the change in the estimates will only capture the change in the design of the TE and the tax value that corresponds to this tax provision. It will not capture the extent to which taxpayers have taken up the tax provision.
- An overall total of all measured TEs could be provided as part of Table 5.1 (8 out of 16 OECD countries reviewed in this report provide such a statistic) even though the resulting figure should be interpreted with caution.[4] If the total is provided, the report would explicitly mention that the revenue forgone concept does not take into account the interaction between individual TEs, and that some TEs could not be included in the total because the necessary data was not available.
- A breakdown of CIT and PIT revenue forgone by agents and/ or economic sectors would ideally only be reported once all types of TEs are measured and aggregate revenue forgone from each type of TE can be measured accurately. Otherwise, the tables would present biased results across types of agents and economic sectors.

Table 5.1. Presentation of total revenue forgone in the TE report

	Revenue forgone	
	COP thousand million	% of GDP
CIT		
Exempt income		
Non-taxable income		
Non-standard deductions		
Tax credits		
*Reduced rate***		
*Increased rate***		
PIT		
Exempt income		
Non-taxable income		
Non-standard deductions		
Tax credits		
VAT		
Exclusions		
Exemptions*		
Reduced rates		
Excise taxes		
Total		

* Includes Free Trade Zones.
** Includes the interaction between reduced/increased rates and other TEs.

Revenue forgone item-by-item discussions

Following the format recommended in Table 3.3 and Table 4.4, the individual chapters for each specific tax would include separate tables for each TE that has been measured, including the legal reference, the reason why the provision deviates from the benchmark, the revenue forgone estimate as well as the other information such as the methodology and data used to estimate it.

Distributional analysis

Leveraging the potential of the tax return microdata, the individual chapters for each specific tax could include a distributional analysis of specific TEs. More guidance has been included in the CIT and PIT chapters.

Annex: List of TEs

The annex to the report could include a comprehensive list of all TEs, regardless of whether they have been quantified or not. In addition to their legal reference, these tables could point out why these TEs are not part of the benchmark. Annex C, Annex D and Annex E provide the list of TEs that have been identified in Colombia in the income and VAT. Reduced rates from withholding taxes should be reported in a separate table rather than being included under the income tax.

Annex: Revenue forgone from additional provisions which are part of the benchmark

The annex of the report could include estimates of the tax provisions that are part of the tax benchmark but that are nevertheless interesting to quantify in terms of their foregone tax revenue. For example, even though the zero-rate bracket or the deduction for dependents under the PIT do not constitute a TE, their foregone revenue would be useful input in the tax policy debate. The foregone revenue of these tax provisions could therefore be presented in the annex of the TE report. The same could apply to exempt income from Andean Community treaties.

References

Minhacienda (2022), *Marco Fiscal de Mediano Plazo 2022.* [1]

Notes

[1] Annex A summarizes practices in other OECD countries.

[2] It is standard practise to quantify TEs by means of the static revenue forgone method. The alternative method (tax revenue gain) strives to take into account behavioural responses but its results depend on reliable estimates or assumptions about how precisely taxpayers would react to removing a TE. Regarding VAT, this would for example imply having access to estimates on price elasticities (ideally on the product and industry level), which are not available.

[3] Two other limitations of the revenue forgone method are that it does not account for interdependencies between TEs and the potential non-take up of a tax relief.

[4] Table A A.5 reports practices in sixteen OECD countries on this matter.

Annex A. Benchmark approaches across OECD countries

Three benchmark approaches and their use in OECD countries

Tax expenditures (TEs) are deviations from a benchmark tax system. The benchmark acts as a reference point and should not be interpreted as optimal from a tax policy perspective. A benchmark tax system is typically defined using one, or some combination, of the following three approaches (OECD, DIAN and Minhacienda, 2021[1]):

- **Reference tax law approach**. Under this approach, a country's existing tax system becomes the starting point for defining the benchmark. A TE is an explicit concession that departs from what is considered a generally applicable tax provision under the existing tax law.
- **Conceptual approach**. This approach defines a normative benchmark tax system based on a theoretical concept of comprehensive income or consumption that provides guidance on how tax policy should be defined, irrespective of whether this benchmark accurately reflects existing tax law.
- **Expenditure subsidy approach**. This approach seeks to cost only those concessions that are clearly analogous to an expenditure subsidy. This method is rarely used in practice (see (Australian Government the Treasury, 2021[2]) for an example) and it would likely result in a narrower list of TEs than under the other two approaches.

While most countries follow a reference tax law approach (see Table A A.1), some countries apply a hybrid approach defining the benchmark more broadly than under a legal reference approach by including some of the most fundamental aspects of the tax systems into the benchmark. For example, Canada defines its tax benchmark as the "tax structure that is characterized only by the most fundamental aspects of a tax system" (Department of Finance Canada, 2021[3]). In a similar spirit the Australian TE reports states "The choice of tax benchmark unavoidably involves judgment and therefore, may be contentious in some cases. These judgments are informed by long-standing features of the tax system, practice in TE publications in other jurisdictions and consultation with stakeholders." (Australian Government the Treasury, 2021[2]) Finally, all TE reports that follow a mixed approach indicate that the tax benchmark should not be interpreted as an indication of the way activities or taxpayers ought to be taxed.

Table A A.1. Benchmarking practises in selected countries

Not listed as a TE nor revenue forgone measured	Legal reference	Conceptual	Expenditure subsidy approach	Fundamental aspects of the tax system[1]
Australia				Yes
Austria	Yes		Yes	
Belgium	Yes			
Canada				Yes
Chile				Yes
Costa Rica	Yes			
Czech Republic	Yes			
France	Yes			
Germany			Yes	
Italy	Yes			
Mexico				Yes
Norway				Yes
Spain	Yes			
UK				No
United States	Yes	Yes		

Note: 1. It is not conceptual but it is very broad.
Source: Own research.

Only the United States uses a purely conceptual approach for defining the benchmark but also presents estimates based on a legal reference benchmark. Mixed approaches are found in Australia, Canada, Chile, Mexico and Norway. The rest of countries that were reviewed use the tax law as the benchmark. It is worth noting that among the countries reviewed, the Australian and Canadian TE reports stand out as those that define the benchmark in a more detailed and clear way.

All countries measure TEs using the revenue forgone approach. Unlike most countries, Canada estimates revenue forgone assuming as counterfactual benchmark scenario that the taxpayer choses the optimal alternative solution once the TE is abolished. Australia includes a chapter that includes revenue gain estimates for selected TEs.

The taxes covered vary across TE reports, which is related to the defined benchmark (Table A A.2).

Table A A.2. Taxes covered in tax expenditure reports in selected countries

Benchmark	Personal income tax	Corporate income tax	VAT/GST	Excise taxes	Capital gains tax	Inheritance tax	Net wealth tax	Fringe benefits tax
Australia	√	√	√	√	√			√
Belgium	√	√	√	√				
Canada	√	√	√					
Chile	√	√	√	√				
France	√	√	√	√	√		√	
Germany	√	√	√	√		√		
Mexico	√	√	√	√				
Spain	√	√	√	√	√		√	
United Kingdom	√	√	√	√	√	√		
United States	√	√						

Source: OECD based on country Tax Expenditure Reports.

The United Kingdom and Canada distinguish between structural and non-structural TEs. According to the United Kingdom TE report, while non-structural reliefs help or encourage particular types of individuals, activities or products in order to achieve economic or social objectives, structural reliefs exist to define the scope of the tax, calculate income or profits correctly, make the tax progressive or simplify the tax code.

Unlike all other OECD countries, Germany and France do not consider VAT rate reductions for food as a TE because these countries view these provisions as fundamental features of their tax system based on a general and redistributive logic. France applies the same argument for medicine.

A few countries (e.g. Belgium, Czech Republic, the United Kingdom) list the fact that small traders do not have to register for VAT as a TE, though it is not quantified.

Australia includes most excise taxes as part of the benchmark (e.g. fuel and health taxes). However, it views certain excise rates that are higher than standard treatment as a negative TE. For example, the luxury car tax in Australia is a negative TE as the benchmark tax treatment stipulates that purchases of new motor vehicles are only subject to the GST. The same applies to the 5% customs levy on car imports because "the benchmark tax treatment is that imported goods are subject to the same taxes on consumption as domestically produced goods". In addition concessions to certain goods (e.g. alternative fuels) are classified as a positive TE.

Implications for the treatment of pension systems

In the same way as with other provisions, the treatment of pension systems depends on the benchmark tax system.

Table A A.3. Benchmark choice and tax expenditures linked to the pension system

Benchmark	Contributions are deductible	Returns to pension savings are exempt	Taxation of retirement savings withdrawn at retirement age	Taxation of retirement savings withdrawn in advance
Exempt-Exempt-Taxed (EET)	Not a TE	Not a TE	Not a TE	Not a TE
Taxed-Taxed-Exempt (TTE)	TE	TE	Negative TE	Negative TE

Source: OECD.

The vast majority of countries does not identify a TE regarding the deduction of mandatory social security contributions, the only exemptions being Australia and Spain (and Chile until 2018). While Australia measures both the deduction and the exemption on the returns generated by the contributions, Spain only measures the revenue forgone linked to the deduction of the contribution. In most countries, tax concessions on private health insurance contributions are generally considered a TE.

Table A A.4. Benchmark choices linked to the pension system in selected countries

	Mandatory pension system	Voluntary pension system
Australia	TTE	TTE
Chile (2018)	TTE	TTE
Chile (2020)	EET	TTE
Canada	EET	TTE
France	EET	TTE_NM
Germany	EET	TTE_NM
Italy	EET	TTE
Spain	TTE	TTE
United Kingdom	EET	TTE
United States	EET	TTE

Note: EET stands for Exempt-Exempt-Taxed, TTE stands for Taxed-Taxed-Exempt.
Source: OECD.

Additional practises observed in OECD countries

- The PIT exempt bracket is not considered a TE except in the Czech Republic. Canada does not consider it a TE but still measures it.
- The non-taxation of the unemployment benefit, maternity leave and non-contributory family allowances is considered a TE in Spain.
- If simplified regimes exist, they are generally listed as a TE but often not quantified. This includes simplified accounting methods, special regimes for small farmers, locally different tax regimes, or the differential treatment of international shipping for corporate income taxation.
- What is required by international agreements to avoid double taxation is usually considered part of the benchmark.
- Accelerated-write off schemes for businesses are part of TEs in Australia, France, Germany, Spain and Norway. In the United States, they are TEs under in the conceptual benchmark, but not in the reference law benchmark scenario. This is because a deviation from the economic depreciation rate is only a clear tax expenditure in a conceptual framework.
- Australia lists loss carry-backward as a TE but not loss carry-forward.

Table A A.5. Practices regarding reporting of total revenue forgone

	Total provided
Australia	No
Austria	Yes
Belgium	Yes
Canada	No
Chile	Yes
Costa Rica	Yes
Czech Republic	Yes
France	Yes
Germany	Yes
Italy	No
Mexico	No
New Zealand	No
Norway	No
Spain	Yes
United Kingdom	No
United States	No

Source: OECD.

Benchmark treatment and TEs linked to natural resources in selected OECD countries

The following section summarizes the benchmark treatment of natural resource-related income in three resource rich countries, namely in Canada, the United States, and Australia. Examples of TEs that the countries identify based on their benchmark are listed in italics.[1]

Canada

- Under the income tax benchmark, businesses are allowed to depreciate natural resource assets based on the useful life of the asset. This also applies to successful exploration expenses, which need to be capitalized and amortized over time. Unsuccessful exploration can be expensed immediately.
  - *Businesses in the natural gas, mining and oil sands sector can depreciate certain investments at higher rates than implied by their useful life. This provision is considered a TE.*
  - *Until 2018, businesses engaged in successful exploration projects were able to fully deduct the respective expenses (intangible pre-production development expenses) when they are incurred. As a benchmark deviation, the provision is listed as a TE. In practice, Canada notes that it is often not possible to determine whether or not exploration activities have been successful in the year when the expenses are incurred, since it is often several years afterwards before decisions on production are made.*
  - *The deductible depletion allowance (phased out) that was calculated as a percent of gross profits ("percentage depletion") is listed as a TE as the deduction is unrelated to the actual cost incurred.*
- The benchmark tax system does not allow credits for particular activities, investments, or industries.
  - *Provisions like the Corporate Mineral Exploration and Development Tax Credit or provincial tax credits are listed as TEs.*

- The unit of taxation is the business that carries out the business activity.
  - *The provision that allowed natural resource businesses to transfer certain unused tax deductions to their equity investors is listed as a TE. These "flow-through shares" were typically issued by corporations, which are not yet profitable and therefore not able to immediately use the deductions themselves.*

United States

- Under the benchmark, expenses incurred to explore and develop natural resource properties need to be capitalized and amortized over time in accordance with their economic life. The benchmark tax treatment stipulates "cost depletion" which allows businesses to reduce the value of capitalized expenses following the percentage of resources extracted from the property.
  - *Independent fuel producers and royalty owners can calculate annual deductions as a percentage of gross income ("percentage depletion"). These deductions are not related to the actual cost incurred and, over the life of the asset, can exceed the total cost of the investment. As the benchmark would ask businesses to amortize the capitalized expenses gradually following their decline in economic value, the excess of percentage over cost depletion is considered a TE.*
  - *Current law allows immediate expensing of intangible drilling costs for successful investments in domestic oil and gas wells (even though some limits to immediate expensing apply to integrated oil companies). The same applies to eligible exploration and development costs for domestic coal mines and other natural fuel deposits. As expensing allows the taxpayer to recover costs sooner than under the benchmark treatment, these provisions are listed as TEs.*
  - *Some oil companies can amortize geological and geophysical expenditures incurred in connection with oil and gas exploration over two years. As this span is generally shorter than the economic life of the assets, the rule is considered a TE.*
- The benchmark system limits the deductibility of losses from passive activities against non-passive income (e.g., wages, interest, and dividends).
  - *The exception from the passive loss limitation provided for a working interest in an oil or gas property that the taxpayer holds directly or through an entity that does not limit the liability of the taxpayer with respect to the interest is a TE.*
- The benchmark tax system does not allow credits for particular activities, investments, or industries.
  - *The Enhanced oil recovery credit, the Energy production credit, the Marginal wells credit, the Energy investment credit as well as the Credit for investment in clean coal facilities are listed as TEs.*
- The benchmark system taxes all income under the regular tax rate schedule.
  - *Certain sales of coal under royalty contracts are taxed as capital gains rather than ordinary income, and so benefit from the preferentially low 20 percent maximum tax rate on capital gains. This provision is listed as a TE.*

Australia

- Under the benchmark, expenditure on a depreciating asset is deductible over the effective life of the asset. Business capital expenditures not elsewhere recognised within the taxation laws are deductible over five years.

  - *The immediate deductibility of expenditure on exploration or prospecting for the purpose of mining (including for petroleum) and quarrying as well as of the assets used for the same purposes is considered a TE.*
- The benchmark system taxes all income under the regular tax rate schedule.
  - *Under the benchmark, government payments to taxpayers are generally subject to tax. Eligible companies are able to create exploration credits by giving up a portion of their tax losses relating to their exploration expenditure, which can then be distributed to investors. A TE arises because payments made under a refundable tax offset are exempt from tax.*
- The natural resources benchmark (separate from the corporate income tax) is a 40 per cent tax rate on the economic rents earned on the extraction of petroleum resources including natural gas. The natural resources benchmark includes immediate expensing of project expenditures and losses can be carried forward.
  - *If losses are carried forward because they cannot be utilised immediately, the benchmark treatment would uplift them at the long-term government bond rate (a proxy for the risk-free rate). Under the petroleum resource rent tax, a significant amount of expenditure is uplifted at rates that exceed the long-term government bond rate. These rules are listed as TEs.*
  - *Provisions in the calculation of the gas transfer price (if there is no arm's length transaction to determine the price of that gas) that reduce the estimated upstream gas price by half the difference between the estimated 'upstream' price and the estimated 'downstream' price where the upstream price is the higher are considered TEs.*
- Under the natural resource benchmark, crude oil excise is treated as a prepayment of the petroleum resource rent tax (PRRT) liabilities.
  - *To the extent that the crude oil excise exceeds the PRRT payable in a year, a negative tax benchmark variation will arise for that period. Where crude oil excise credits are carried forward and used to reduce PRRT in later periods, a TE will arise in the year the carried forward credit is utilised.*

Asset-specific tax depreciation rates and economic depreciation rates in Colombia and in the literature

As per chapter 1, the tax depreciation of an asset that is aligned with the asset's loss in economic value over time is considered part of the benchmark tax system. Such a treatment is common in TE analysis in OECD countries as it allows identifying TEs linked to enhanced, accelerated or decelerated tax depreciation. DIAN has shared with the OECD the set of standard tax depreciation rates applicable in Colombia. The table below (Table A A.6) compares the tax depreciation rates in Colombia to estimates of economic depreciation published by the Bureau of Economic Analysis (BEA) in the United States (Giandrea et al., 2018[4]). Where a comparison was possible, the tax depreciation rates in Colombia do not deviate significantly from the economic depreciation of the assets. In particular, the standard tax depreciation rates do not appear excessively high. Therefore, no TEs have been identified in the report linked to the standard tax depreciation rules currently in place in Colombia. Instead, several specific accelerated and enhanced depreciation provisions have been identified as TEs by means of a detailed analysis of tax provisions in the Colombian tax system.

Table A A.6. Standard tax depreciation rates in Colombia compared to economic depreciation rates

Asset	Annual tax depreciation rate in Colombia	Equivalent useful life in Colombia	Economic depreciation rate (Giandrea et al., 2018[4])
Constructions and Buildings	2.22%	45 years	1.76-3.14% (non-residential), 1.14 – 4.55% (residential)
Aqueduct, plant and networks	2.50%	40 years	1.76-3.14%
Transport routes	2.50%	40 years	2.02-2.25%
Fleet and air equipment	3.33%	30 years	6.6-13.75%
Fleet and railroad equipment	5%	20 years	5.89%
Fleet and river equipment	6.67%	15 years	6.11%
Armament and surveillance equipment	10%	10 years	
Electrical equipment	10%	10 years	12.25%
Fleet and land transport equipment	10%	10 years	10.09-12.25%
Machinery, equipment	10%	10 years	6.86-12.25%
Furniture and appliances	10%	10 years	12.25%
Scientific medical equipment	12.50%	8 years	13.5%-14%
Containers, packaging and tools	20%	5 years	9.17-20.09%
Computer equipment	20%	5 years	12.25-35.2%
Data processing networks	20%	5 years	
Communication equipment	20%	5 years	11%-15%

Note: Asset categories have been matched to the best extent possible. Note that the Bureau of Economic Analysis (Giandrea et al., 2018[4]) provides a more granular asset breakdown and records economic depreciation in the United States, which can deviate from economic depreciation in Colombia.
Source: DIAN and (Giandrea et al., 2018[4]).

References

Australian Government the Treasury (2021), *Tax Benchmarks and Variations Statement 2020.* [2]

Department of Finance Canada (2021), *Report on Federal Tax Expenditures - Concepts, Estimates, Evaluations.* [3]

Giandrea, M. et al. (2018), "Incorporating Canadian Capital Asset Depreciation Rates into US Capital and Multifactor Productivity Measures: A Collaborative Investigation", *Fifth World KLEMS Conference.* [4]

OECD, DIAN and Minhacienda (2021), *Tax Expenditures Report by the Tax Experts Commission.* [1]

Notes

[1] The information is based on country TE reports (but the information has not been validated by the respective OECD member countries) and information available in the IBFD Tax Research Platform.

Annex B. VAT revenue forgone linked to the Free Trade Zone exemption

The illustrations on the following pages visualize how the interaction of VAT exclusions and the FTZ exemption give raise to VAT revenue forgone in scenarios 3 and 4. Arrows represent financial flows. For simplicity, the illustrations only focus on FTZ users purchasing inputs from the national territory but the same reasoning holds for inputs purchased from outside Colombia.

Scenario 1

Infographic A B.1. Domestic consumption of non-excluded goods produced in Free Trade Zones

A. With Free Trade Zones

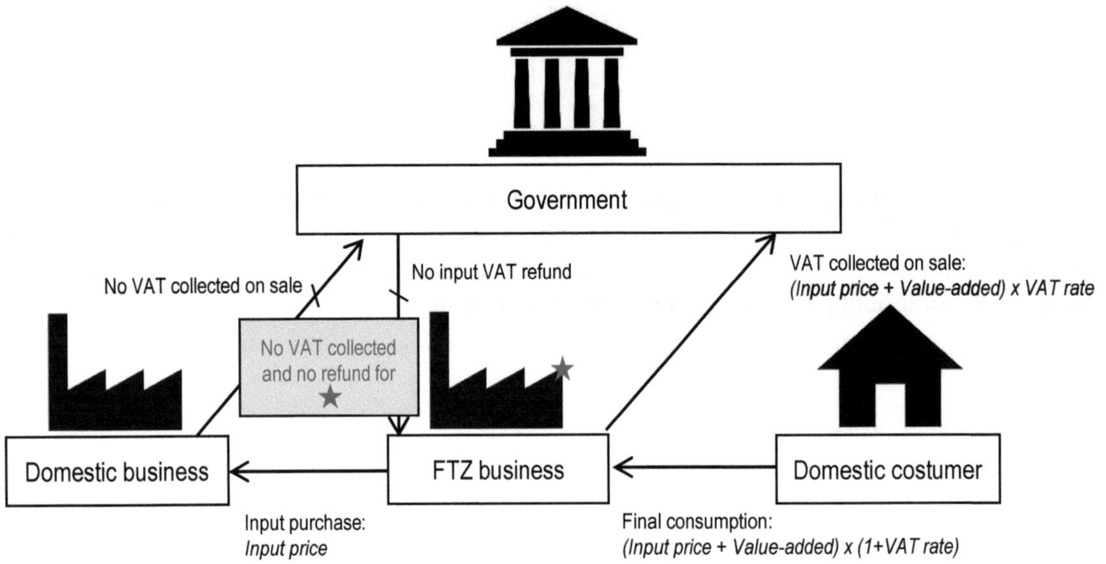

B. Without Free Trade Zones

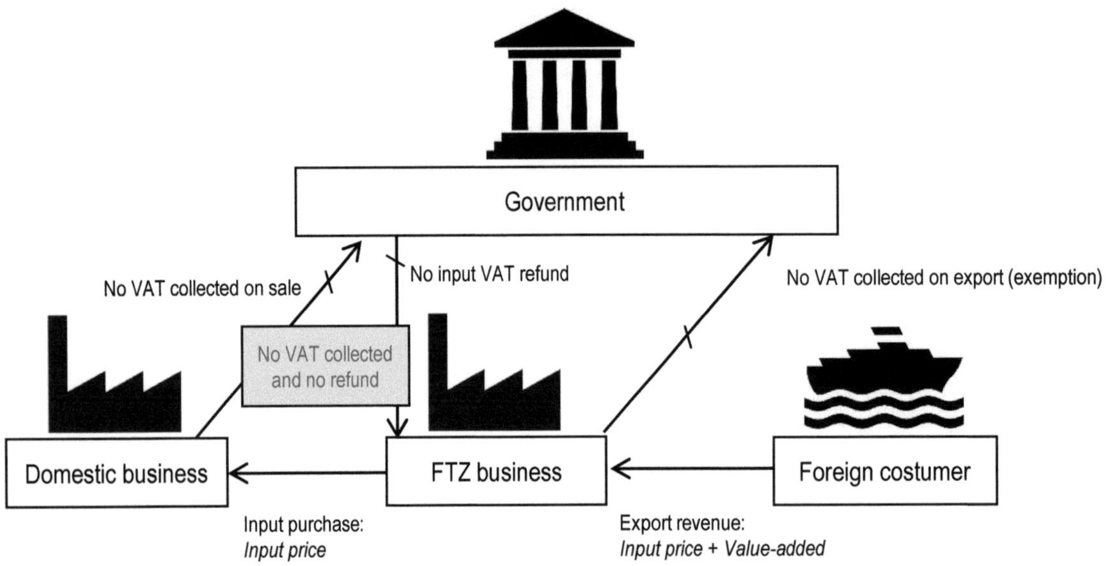

Source: OECD.

Result: As revenue forgone is a static concept that does not take into account behavioural responses such as price changes or the relocation of businesses, revenue forgone from FTZs is zero in the absence of VAT exclusions. Businesses can recover the input VAT paid in the absence of FTZs. The same applies to output goods taxed at reduced or zero rates. The FTZ does not increase the revenue forgone caused by these provisions.

Scenario 2

Infographic A B.2. Export of goods produced in Free Trade Zones

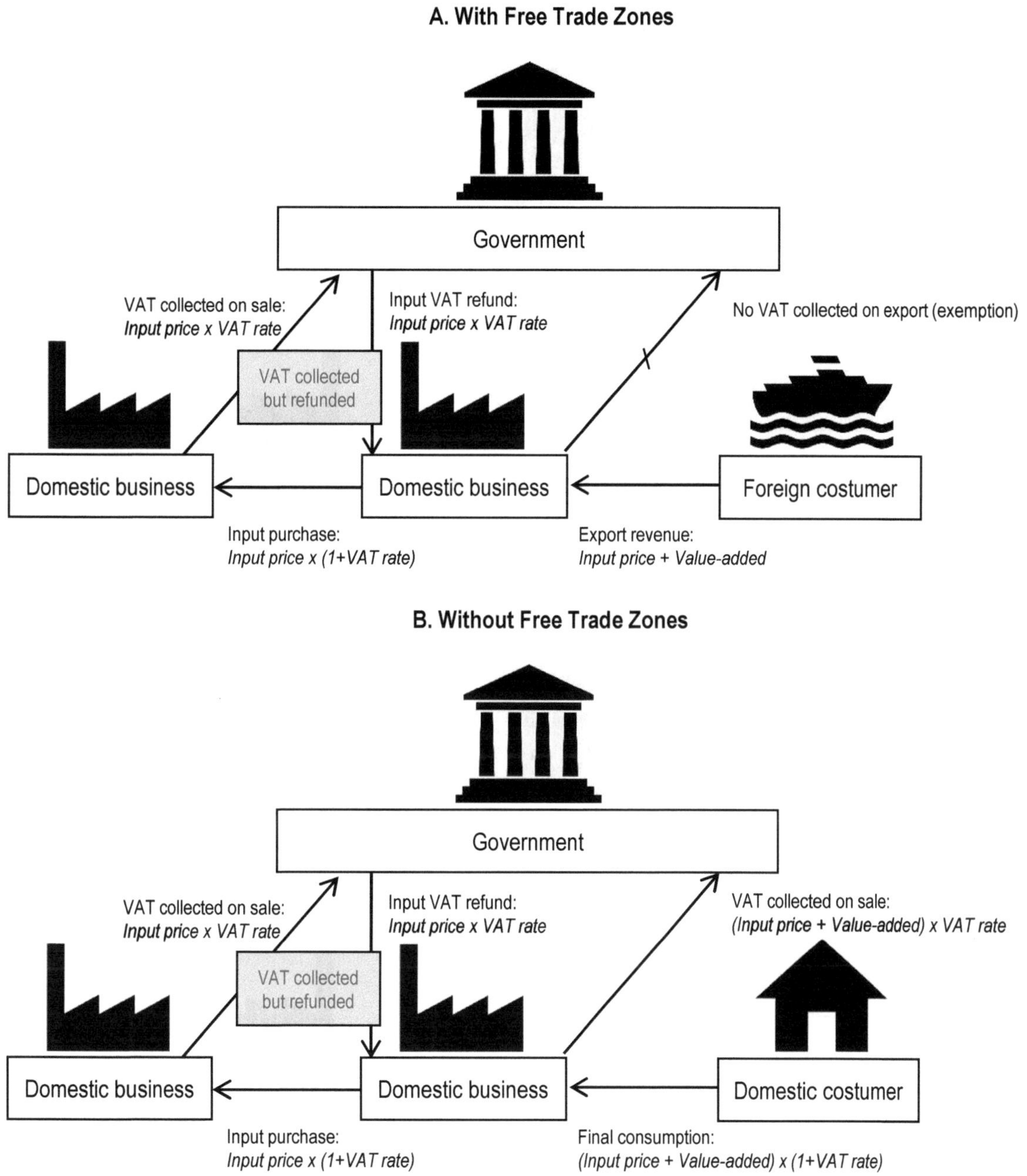

Source: OECD.

Result: Revenue forgone from FTZs is zero in the case of goods produced for export purposes as the VAT exemption on exports is part of the benchmark. Businesses can recover the input VAT paid in the absence of FTZs.

Scenario 3

Infographic A B.3. Sale of excluded goods from domestic to Free Trade Zone businesses

A. With Free Trade Zones

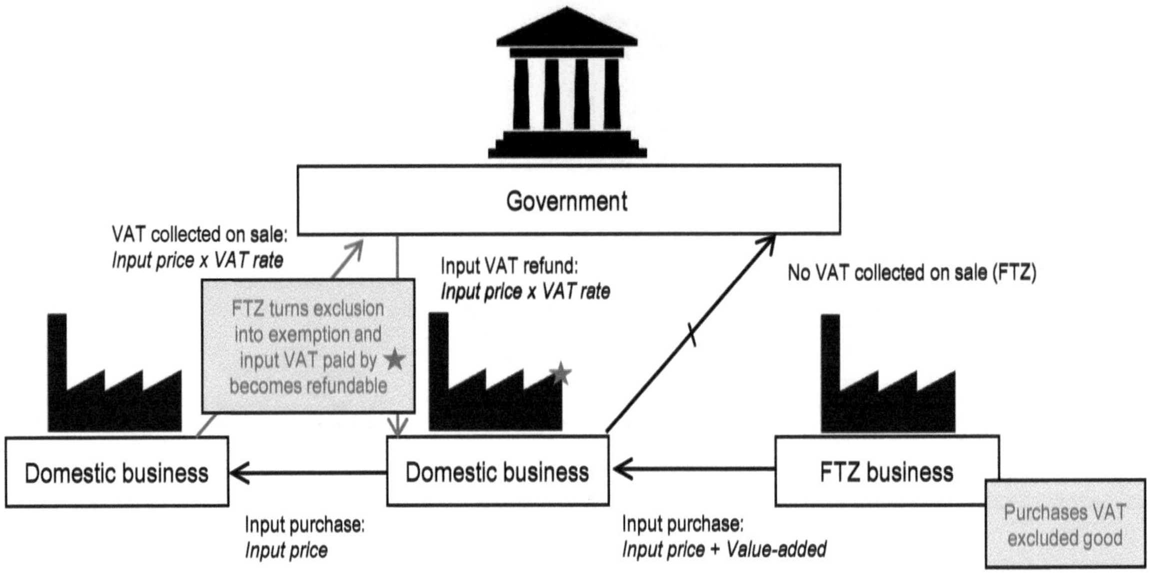

B. Without Free Trade Zones

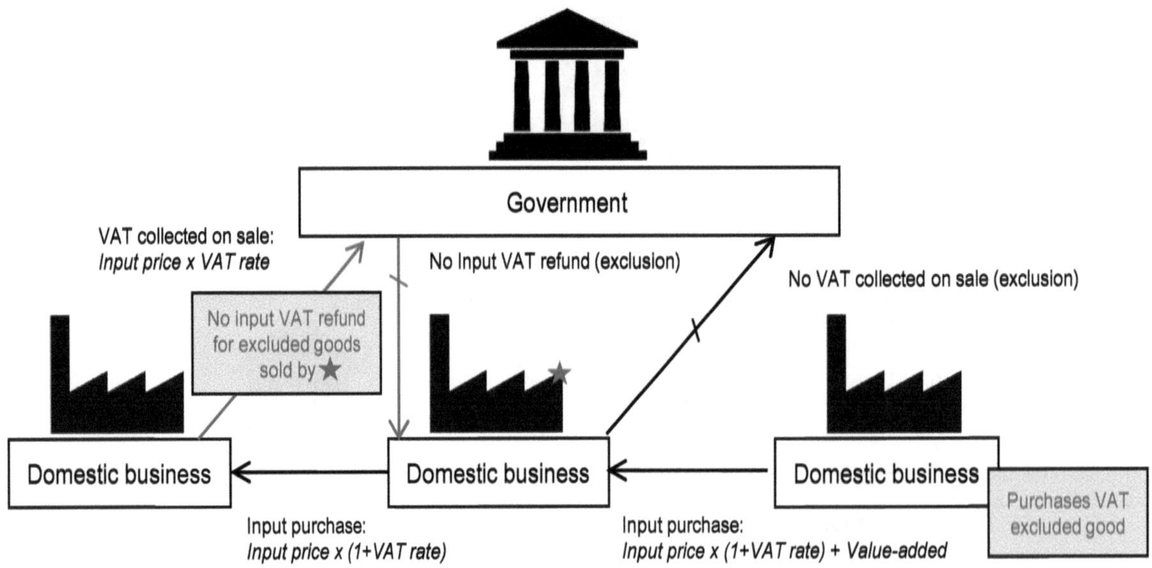

Source: OECD

Result: Revenue forgone increases if FTZ businesses purchase excluded goods from domestic businesses. Domestic businesses are allowed to reclaim input VAT if excluded goods are sold to FTZs (the exclusion turns into an exemption). Without the FTZ, input VAT paid on the production of excluded goods cannot be recovered. The fact that the non-recoverability of input VAT might lead to higher pre-tax price when the good is sold to the final consumer (and VAT is levied again on the transaction) is disregarded by the static concept of revenue forgone.

Scenario 4

Infographic A B.4. Domestic consumption of excluded goods produced in Free Trade Zones

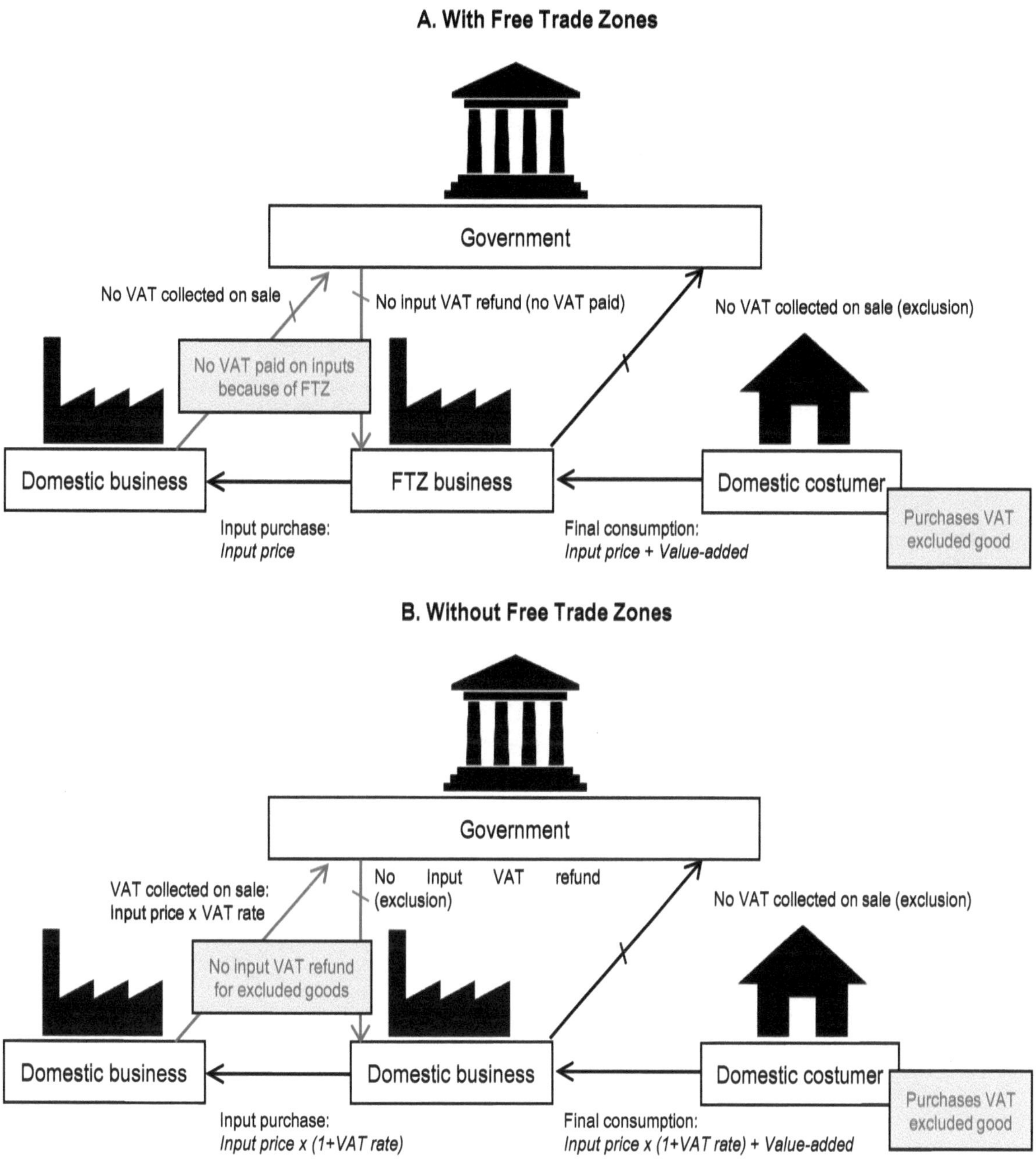

Source: OECD.

Result: Revenue forgone increases if FTZ businesses produce excluded goods, which are then sold to the domestic market. This is because the input VAT paid on the production of an excluded good would not have been recoverable by a domestic business. FTZ businesses, on the other hand, do not pay input VAT) in the first place. We show the scenario in which FTZs purchase inputs from domestic businesses but the same logic would apply if these inputs were imports from abroad.

Annex C. List of Corporate Income Tax Expenditures

This Annex includes the complete list of Corporate Income Tax Expenditures that were identified in Colombia as part of the project.

Table A C.1. Identified Corporate Income Tax Expenditures (legal persons)

ID	Type	Tax Expenditure	Legal Reference (Law/Article)		Revenue forgone estimate available
E1	Exempt income	**Agrotourism services (20 years).** A 20-year exemption for income derived from the provision of agroturism services.	Law 788 of 2002	18	
E2	Exempt income	**Creative industries (orange economy, 7 years).** A 7-year exemption for income obtained by the creative industries (so called orange economy). This exemption applies to companies exclusively engaged in the development of 1 of the 27 business activities defined as creative industry which include but are not limited to: jewelry manufacturing; book publishing; film, music, radio and television production; software development; architecture and engineering and other activities related to technical consultancy; theatre and other cultural activities; cultural tourism activities.	Law 2010 of 2019	91	X
E3	Exempt income	**Dividends distributed by non-resident to a CHC.** Dividends or shares distributed by entities not resident in Colombia to a Colombian Holding Company (CHC) will be exempt from income tax.	Law 2010 of 2019	77	
E4	Exempt income	**Hotels constructed between 2002-2017 (30 years).** A 30-year exemption for income generated by new hotels that were built within the following 15 years as of the entry into force of Law 788 of 2002.	Law 788 of 2002	18	X

ID	Type	Tax Expenditure	Legal Reference (Law/Article)		Revenue forgone estimate available
E5	Exempt income	**Hotels renovated between 2002-2017 (30 years).** A 30-year exemption for income generated by refurbished hotels that were built within the following 15 years as of the entry into force of Law 788 of 2002.	Law 788 de 2002	18	X
E6	Exempt income	**Income received by authors, translators and copyright holders of certain books.** Income that authors and translators, both Colombian and foreign resident in Colombia, receive from copyrights for books of a scientific or cultural nature edited and printed in Colombia. Copyright and translation rights of national or foreign authors of books, published and printed in Colombia.	Law 98 of 1993	28	X
E7	Exempt income	**Investment in higher agricultural productivity (10 years).** A 10-year exemption for income derived from investments made that increase productivity in the farming sector.	Law 2010 of 2019	91	X
E8	Exempt income	**Investment in sawmills and related investment in the lumber industry.** Investments in new sawmills and processing plants directly related to the use of new forest plantations, including guadua, rubber and cashew, and for those who have plantations of timber trees and fruit trees, that must be duly registered with the competent authority.	Law 2010 of 2019	91	X
E9	Exempt income	**Low-income housing.** With respect to low-income housing, the following should be included: the profit on the first sale of the VIS, and the financial returns generated in the first 5 years by loans for the acquisition of VIS.	235-2 TC		X
E10	Exempt income	**Non-profit entities (special regime).** Exemption on the net profit or surplus.	Law 1819 of 2019	146	X

ID	Type	Tax Expenditure	Legal Reference (Law/Article)		Revenue forgone estimate available
E11	Exempt income	**Property received by way of donations (up to 2 290 UVT).** 20% of the property and rights received by way of donations and other inter vivos legal acts celebrated free of charge, without such amount exceeding the equivalent of two thousand two hundred ninety (2 290) UVT.	Law 1607 of 2012	104	
E12	Exempt income	**Sale of property for public interest projects**. Any gains from the sale of property earmarked for public interest projects or social interest projects (social interest housing projects).	Law 2010 of 2019	91	X
E13	Exempt income	**Sale of renewable electricity (15 years).** A 15-years exemption, as of 2017, for income derived from the sale of electrical energy, carried out by generating companies, derived from wind energy, biomass or agricultural, solar, geothermal or marine waste, according to the definitions of Law 1715 of 2014 and Decree 2755 of 2003.	Law 2010 of 2019	91	X
E14	Exempt income	**Sale of shares in a CHC.** The income derived from the sale or transfer of the shares or participations in a Colombian Holding Company (CHC) will be exempt except for the value corresponding to the profits obtained from activities carried out in Colombia	Law 2010 of 2019	77	
E15	Exempt income	**Sale of shares in non-resident entity by a CHC.** Income derived from the sale or transfer of a Colombian Holding Company (CHC)'s stake in entities not resident in Colombia will be exempt from income tax.	Law 2010 of 2019	77	
E16	Exempt income	**Waterway transport services (15 years).** A 15-years exemption, as of 2019, for income obtained from the provision of fluvial transport services with boats and low draft slabs.	Law 2010 of 2019	91	X

ID	Type	Tax Expenditure	Legal Reference (Law/Article)		Revenue forgone estimate available
NT1	Non-taxable income	**Bonds for Peace.** Yields from bonds for peace.	Law 487 of 1987	5	
NT2	Non-taxable income	**Bonds for Security.** Yields originating from Bonos para la Seguridad bonds will be considered non-taxable income.	Law 345 of 1996	4	
NT3	Non-taxable income	**Compensation received as a result of eradication or renewal of crops**. Indemnification or compensation received as a result of eradication or renewal of crops, or for the control of pests, when this is part of programs aimed at protecting national agricultural production and such payments are made with public resources.	Law 223 of 1995	70	X
NT4	Non-taxable income	**Contribution of capital surplus of shares or quotas.** Contribution of capital surplus of shares or quotas will not result in taxable income or give rise to the tax basis of the shares or quotas issued.	Law 1607 of 2012	91	
NT5	Non-taxable income	**Contributions by National Television Commission to regional stations.** Income received by regional television organizations from contributions made by the National Television Commission to stimulate and promote public television.	Law 488 of 1998	40	X
NT6	Non-taxable income	**Derivatives with CSE-listed companies as underlying.** The income that comes from the negotiation of derivatives that are securities and whose underlying is represented exclusively in shares listed in a Colombian stock exchange (CSE), indices or participations in funds or collective portfolios that reflect the behavior of said shares, are not taxable income.	Law 1430 of 2000	37	X

ID	Type	Tax Expenditure	Legal Reference (Law/Article)		Revenue forgone estimate available
NT7	Non-taxable income	**Distribution of gains from shares from companies listed in the Colombian Stock Exchange.** Distribution of profits in shares, provided from the capitalization of the revaluation's account, is made by companies listed in the Colombian Stock Exchange.seed ca	Law 1819 of 2016	37	X
NT8	Non-taxable income	**Donations to projects approved by the Multilateral Fund of the Montreal Protocol.** Donations in cash received by individuals or entities that participate in the execution and development of projects approved by the Multilateral Fund of the Montreal Protocol (protecting the ozone layer), through any executing agency, bilateral or multilateral, are non-taxable income.	Law 488 of 1998	32	X
NT9	Non-taxable income	**Forest Incentive Certificates.** As it constitutes an acknowledgment by the state of the environmental benefits originated by reforestation, the income from Forest Incentive Certificates are not taxable income.	Law 139 of 1994	8	X
NT10	Non-taxable income	**Incentives for rural capitalization.**	Law 788 of 2002	20	X
NT11	Non-taxable income	**Income distributed to employee shareholders.** Companies may define a system of incentives through which workers can participate in the capital of companies. For these purposes, the profits that are distributed through shares, will not be taxed with the income tax to the employer, up to the equivalent of 10% of the profit generated.	Law 789 of 2002	44	X
NT12	Non-taxable income	**Income from horizontal properties, boards of co-owners, administrators of buildings organized in horizontal property or of residential complexes.**	Law 1819 of 2016, Law 2010 of 2019	143 and 83	

ID	Type	Tax Expenditure	Legal Reference (Law/Article)		Revenue forgone estimate available
NT13	Non-taxable income	**Inflationary component if capitalized.**	Decree 2686 of 1999	10	X
NT14	Non-taxable income	**Investments in the exploration of mining and hydrocarbon.** Certificates of investment given by the ministry of finance to new investments in the exploration of mining and hydrocarbon.	Law 1819 of 2016	365	
NT15	Non-taxable income	**Liquidation of a limited liability company.** Income provided from the liquidation of a limited liability company up to the amount of capital contribution made by the shareholder.	Decree 2053 of 1974	43	X
NT16	Non-taxable income	**Public funding for urban mass transport network.**	Law 488 of 1998	29	X
NT17	Non-taxable income	**Resources managed by Fogafín and Fogacoop.** Income provided from the resources managed by Fogafín and Fogacoop in trust accounts will not be considered for calculating their income tax. The same applies to the resources transferred by the state to Fogafín from the General Nation's Budget that is destined to stabilize the public banks.	Law 788 of 2002	11	X
NT18	Non-taxable income	**Sale of CSE-listed company shares.** Income provided from the sale of shares of a company listed in the Colombian Stock Exchange (CSE) when such sale does not represent more than 10% of the total number of shares of the listed company.	Law 633 of 2000	9	X

ID	Type	Tax Expenditure	Legal Reference (Law/Article)		Revenue forgone estimate available
NT19	Non-taxable income	**Sale of expropriated real estate.** The income obtained in the voluntary sale of real estate expropriated is a non-taxable income.	Law 388 of 1997	67	X
NT20	Non-taxable income	**Sale of properties in Nevado del Ruiz area.** The income obtained from the sale of properties located in the areas affected by the Nevado del Ruiz volcanic activity is non-taxable income.	Decree 2512 of 1987	5	
NT21	Non-taxable income	**Seed capital provided by the state.** Non-taxable income is the non-reimbursable economic support provided by the State, as seed capital for the venture and as capital for the strengthening of the company.	Ley 1429 de 2014	16	X
NT22	Non-taxable income	**State contributions to cover obligations of public entities in liquidation.** When the Nation assumes obligations in charge of public entities in liquidation, including those derived from the assignment of assets, liabilities and contracts made by the entity in liquidation / State contributions when they are made to take responsibility for the obligations of public entities in liquidation.	Law 633 of 2000	77	X
NT23	Non-taxable income	**Subsidies from Agro Ingreso Seguro program.** The subsidies and aid granted by the government in the program Agro Ingreso Seguro, AIS, and those from the incentive to storage and the incentive to rural capitalization provided for in Law 101 of 1993 are non-taxable income.	Law 1111 of 2006	58	X
NT24	Non-taxable income	**Support for scientific, technological or innovative projects.** The resources that the taxpayer receives to be used for the development of projects classified as scientific, technological or innovative, according to the conditions defined by the National Council of Tax Benefits in Science, Technology and Innovation, are non-taxable income.	Law 1450 of 2011	37	X

ID	Type	Tax Expenditure	Legal Reference (Law/Article)		Revenue forgone estimate available
DD1	Deduction	**Attentions to customers, suppliers and employees**. Attentions to customers, suppliers and employees, such as gifts, courtesies, parties, meetings and celebrations. The maximum amount to be deducted for all of these concepts is 1% of net and effectively realized tax income.	Law 1819 of 2016	63	X
DD2	Deduction	**Carbon tax.** For the taxpayer, the carbon tax is deductible from the income tax as the greater value of the cost of the good.	Law 1819 of 2016	Paragraph 2, 222	X
DD3	Deduction	**Contributions.** Exemption from health, SENA and ICBF contributions when hiring workers earning up to 10 minimum monthly salaries.	Law 1819 of 2016	65	
DD4	Deduction	**Donations to libraries.** Donations to the National Network of Public Libraries and the National Public Library.	Law 1819 of 2016	75	X
DD5	Deduction	**Donations to the entrepreneurship and innovation agency of the government.** Taxpayers can deduct the value of donations made to the entrepreneurship and innovation agency of the government iNNpulsa, after verification and approval by the Ministry of Commerce, Industry and Tourism.	Law 2069 of 2020	40	
DD6	Deduction	**Education for children of employees.** Deduction for investment payments made to programs or centers for attention, stimulation and integral development and/or initial education for minors under seven years of age, established by companies exclusively for the children of their employees.	Law 2010 of 2019	87	

ID	Type	Tax Expenditure	Legal Reference (Law/Article)		Revenue forgone estimate available
DD7	Deduction	**Education for employees.** Deductions for payments destined to scholarship programs for total or partial studies and forgivable credits for education, established by legal entities for the benefit of their employees or members of the employee's family nucleus.	Law 2010 of 2019	87	X
DD8	Deduction	**Education in area of activity.** Deduction for contributions made by companies to primary, secondary and high school education institutions recognized by the Ministry of Education, and technical, technological and higher education institutions that meet the requirements established by the Ministry of Education, and that are justified by benefiting the communities and areas of influence where the productive or commercial activity of the legal entity is carried out.	Law 2010 of 2019	87	X
DD9	Deduction	**Financial transaction tax (50%).** 50% of the financial transaction tax (GMF).	Law 2010 of 2019	86	X
DD10	Deduction	**Investments in air transportation in remote areas.** Deduction for investments made for air transportation in remote areas of the country	Law 633 of 2000	97	
DD11	Deduction	**Investments in detention centers.** Companies or individuals can deduct from their gross income the value of the new investments made in the year, in detention centers, as long as they are effectively used for work and education programs for inmates, and individuals are linked to the company. post-prison sentences who have observed good behavior certified by the detention center. The deduction may not exceed (15%) per year of the net income.	Law 633 of 2000	98	X
DD12	Deduction	**Investments in real productive fixed assets (30%).** Deduction for investments in real productive fixed assets (legal stability contracts Law 963/05).	Law 863 of 2003	68	X

ID	Type	Tax Expenditure	Legal Reference (Law/Article)		Revenue forgone estimate available
DD13	Deduction (and Deferral if Investment)	**Investments or donations to Colombian film projects (165%).** Taxpayers who make investments or donations to Colombian production or co-production film projects approved by the Ministry of Culture can deduct from their tax (165%) of the real value invested or donated.	Law 814 of 2003 Law 1607 of 2012	16 195	
DD14	Deduction	**Maintenance and conservation of assets declared as in cultural interest.** The owners of movable and immovable property declared as of cultural interest, can deduct the totality of the expenses for the elaboration of the Special Protection Plans and for the maintenance and conservation of these assets, even if this is not causally related to the activity that produces the income.	Law 1185 of 2008	14	X
DD15	Deduction	**Mutual investment fund contributions.** Deduction of the amount of the contribution to the mutual investment fund.	Law 75 of 1986	7	X
DD16	Deduction	**Real-estate valuation.**	Law 74 of 1994	4	
DD17	Deduction	**Receivables of public utilities companies to the new companies created to preserve the continuity in public services.** Contribution of outstanding receivables of the intervened public utilities companies to the new companies that are created in order to preserve the continuity in the rendering of the public service, as well as any other outstanding receivables of the intervened company. In these cases, the new companies may apply Articles 145 and 146 of the Tax Statute with respect to the tax balances of the credits contributed.	Law 2010 of 2019	145	
DD18	Deduction	**Royalties paid for the exploitation of non-renewable natural resources.** Deduction for royalties paid for the exploitation of non-renewable natural resources.	TC	107	

ID	Type	Tax Expenditure	Legal Reference (Law/Article)		Revenue forgone estimate available
DD19	Deduction	**Salaries paid to first-job employees who are under twenty-eight years of age (120%).** Deduction of 120% of the payments that the employer makes for salary, in relationship with employees who are under twenty-eight (28) years of age, as long as in the case of the person's first job.	Law 2010 of 2019	88	
DD20	Deduction	**Salaries paid to senior citizens without pension (120%).** Deduction of 120% of salaries for hiring a senior citizen without pension.	Law 2040 of 2020	2	
DD21	Deduction	**Salaries, social benefits and other labor payments, paid to female workers who are victims of proven violence (200%).** Employers who employ female workers who are victims of proven violence, can deduct from their income 200% of the value of wages and social benefits paid during the year, since the employment relationship exists, and up to a period of three years.	Law 1257 of 2008	23	X
DD22	Deduction	**Salaries, social benefits and other labor payments, paid to widows and orphans of members of the Armed Forces killed in combat, kidnapped or missing (200%).** Deduction equivalent to 200% for salaries, social benefits and other labor payments, paid to widows and orphans of members of the Armed Forces killed in combat, kidnapped or missing.	Law 6 of 1992	127	X
DD23	Deduction	**Salaries, social benefits and other labor payments, paid to workers hired as apprentices or in training (130%).** Employers may deduct annually from their taxable income, up to 130% of the expenses for salaries and social benefits of workers hired as apprentices, in addition to those legally provided for, in professional training programs previously approved by the National Apprenticeship Service SENA.	Law 115 of 1994	189	X
DD24	Deduction	**Salaries, social benefits and other labor payments, paid to workers with a proven disability of no less than 25% (200%).** Employers who employ workers with a proven disability of no less than 25% can deduct from their income 200% of the value of wages and social benefits paid during the year to workers with a disability, as long as it subsists.	Law 361 of 1997	31	X

ID	Type	Tax Expenditure	Legal Reference (Law/Article)		Revenue forgone estimate available
DD25	Deduction	**Taxes, fees and contributions.** Taxes, fees and contributions paid that have a causal relationship with the economic activity, other than ICA and GMF.	Law 2010 of 2019	86	X
DD26	Deduction	**Projects for taxes (Option 3).**	Law 2010 of 2019	79	X
DF1	Deferral	**Accelerated depreciation of machinery, equipment and civil works of projects of unconventional energy sources.** Deduction for accelerated depreciation of machinery, equipment and civil works of projects of unconventional energy sources. The annual depreciation rate will be no higher than (33.33%) as a global annual rate.	Law 1715 of 2014 Law 2099 of 2021	14 11	
DF2	Deferral	**Accelerated tax depreciation allowances.**	Law 1819 of 2016	83	
DF3	Deferrals	**Investment in hydrogen.** Special 50% deduction for green and blue hydrogen investments	Law 2099 of 2021	21	
DF4	Deferrals	**Investment in non-conventional energy sources.** Taxpayers obliged to submit a tax return who directly make investments in non-conventional energy sources can deduct from their income, in a period not exceeding 15 years, from the following year in which the investment has come into operation, the 50% of the total investment made.	Law 1715 of 2014 Law 2099 of 2021	11 8	

ID	Type	Tax Expenditure	Legal Reference (Law/Article)		Revenue forgone estimate available
DF5	Deferrals	**Investments in expansion or opening of bookstores.** The totally new own investment, made by individuals or companies in expansion or opening of new bookstores or branches of those already established, is deductible from the investor's gross income up to a value equivalent to 10 000 UVT (USD$ 90 770).	Law 98 of 1993	30	
DF6	Deferral	**Investments in exploration, development and construction of mines and oil and gas fields.** Amortization of investments in exploration, development and construction of mines and oil and gas fields. E.T., art. 143-1.	Law 1819 of 2016	86	
DF7	Deferral	**Investments in hydrogen.** Accelerated depreciation for green and blue hydrogen investments	Law 2099 of 2021	21	
DF8	Deferral	**Investments under mega-investment regime.** The taxpayers of the mega-investment regime, who make the new investments, can depreciate their fixed assets in a maximum period of two (2) years, regardless of the useful life of the asset.	Law 2010 of 2019	75	
DF9	Deferral	**Investment in research, technological development and innovation.** Taxpayers can deduct the value of investments made in research, technological development and innovation, according to the conditions of the National Council of Tax Benefits in Science, Technology and Innovation (CNBT). This is deductible in the taxable period in which is carried out.	Law 6 of 1992 Law 1955 of 2019	4 170	
C1	Tax credit	**Donation to sports and recreational or cultural organizations or non-profit legal entities.** For donation to sports and recreational or cultural organizations or non-profit legal entities, E.T., art. 126-2, paragraph 3.	Law 488 of 1998	37	X

ID	Type	Tax Expenditure	Legal Reference (Law/Article)		Revenue forgone estimate available
C2	Tax credit	**Donation to support the immunization of the population against Covid-19 (50%).** Tax credit equivalent to 50% of the donation made to achieve the immunization of the population Colombia against Covid-19 and any other pandemic.	Law 2064 of 2020	40	
C3	Tax credit	**Donation to the General Gustavo Matamoros D' Costa Foundation and other foundations dedicated to the defense and protection of human rights**. Donation to the General Gustavo Matamoros D' Costa Corporation and other foundations dedicated to the defense and protection of human rights. E.T., art 126-2, paragraph 1.	Law 488 of 1998	37	X
C4	Tax credit	**Donations to certain non-profits (25%).** 25% of donations granted to non-profit entities qualified under the CIT special tax regime and to CIT non-taxpayers stated in articles 22 and 23 of the Colombian Tax Code.	Law 1819 of 2016	105	X
C5	Tax credit	**Donations to higher education and science (25%).** 25% of donations made through institutions of higher education or the Colombian Institute of Educational Credit and Technical Studies Abroad (ICETEX), addressed to programs of scholarships or forgivable credits, that are approved by the Ministry of Education, and that benefit students from 1, 2 and 3 economic levels. 25% of donations received by the National Fund for the Financing of Science, Technology and Innovation, Francisco José de Caldas Fund, that are destined to the financing of science, technology and innovation projects.	Law 1955 of 2019	174	X
C6	Tax credit	**Donations to the entrepreneurship and innovation agency (25%).** Tax Credit equivalent to 25% of the value of donations made to the entrepreneurship and innovation agency of the government *iNNpulsa*, after verification and approval by the Ministry of Commerce, Industry and Tourism.	Law 2069 of 2020	40	
C7	Tax credit	**Foreign audio-visual productions in Colombia.** Foreign audio-visual works fully or partially produced or post-produced in Colombia are entitled to an income tax credit equal to 35% of the amount invested in Colombia.	Law 1556 of 2012 Law 1955 of 2019	9 178	

ID	Type	Tax Expenditure	Legal Reference (Law/Article)		Revenue forgone estimate available
C8	Tax credit	**Input VAT paid on fixed capital assets**. Capital goods input VAT paid on the import, formation, construction or acquisition of real productive fixed assets can be credited in the tax year in which they pay the VAT or in any subsequent tax years.	Law 2010 of 2019	95	X
C9	Tax credit	**Investment by public service companies (40%).** 40% of investments made in the respective tax year by the domiciliary public service companies that provide the aqueduct and sewerage services to aqueduct and sewerage companies of the regional order.	Law 788 of 2002	104	X
C10	Tax credit	**Investment by SMEs in research & development (50%).** A 2-year tax credit of the 50% of investments made in research, technological development or innovation certified by the National Council for Tax Benefits in Science, Technology and Innovation made by micro, small and medium businesses.	Law 1955 of 2019	168	
C11	Tax credit	**Investment in environmental conservation and tourism (25%).** 25% tax discount on investments made in environmental control, conservation and improvement in tourism activities.	Law 2068 of 2020	42	
C12	Tax credit	**Investment in environmental protection (25%).** 25% of the investments made in control, conservation and improvement of the environment, provided that the investment is certified by the environmental authority.	Law 1819 of 2016	103	X
C13	Tax credit	**Investment in research, technological development or innovation (25%)**. 25% of investments made in research, technological development or innovation certified by the National Council for Tax Benefits in Science, Technology and Innovation. On the other hand, 25% of the remuneration payments made to personnel hired with a doctorate degree.	Law 1955 of 2019	171	X

ID	Type	Tax Expenditure	Legal Reference (Law/Article)		Revenue forgone estimate available
C14	Tax credit	**Local turnover tax (ICA, 50%).** 50% of local turnover tax (municipal tax) paid in the corresponding tax year	Law 2010 of 2019 Law 2155 of 2021	86	X
C15	Tax credit	**Salaries paid by SMEs to personnel with doctorate degree (50%).** A 2-year tax credit of the 50% of the remuneration payments made by micro, small and medium businesses to personnel hired with a doctorate degree.	Law 1955 of 2019	168	
C16	Tax credit	**Scholarships and support for talented athletes (100%).**100% tax credit for scholarships and maintenance for talented athletes or sports reserves.	Law 1955 of 2019	190	
SR1	Special regime / Reduced rate	**Free Trade Zones (20%).** 20% income tax rate for legal entities that are free trade zone users.	Law 1819 of 2016	101	X
SR2	Special regime / Reduced rate	**Free Trade Zone in Cúcuta (15%).** Income tax rate of 15% for legal entities that are users of free trade zones created in the Municipality of Cúcuta between January 2017 and December 2021.	Law 1819 of 2016	101	
SR3	Special regime / Reduced rate	**Hotels (9%).** Income tax rate of 9% for national and assimilated companies, permanent establishments and foreign legal entities, for the rendering of new or remodeled hotel services.	Law 2068 of 2020	41	X

ID	Type	Tax Expenditure	Legal Reference (Law/Article)		Revenue forgone estimate available
SR4	Special regime / Reduced rate	**Medical care, food, nursing, lodging, physiotherapy, recovery and other assistance services provided by old age tourism centers (9%).** Income tax rate of 9% for national and assimilated companies, permanent establishments and foreign legal entities, for services such as medical care, food, nursing, lodging, physiotherapy, recovery and other assistance services.	Law 2068 of 2020	41	X
SR5	Special regime / Reduced rate	**Mega-investments (9% or 27%).** Income tax rate on mega-investment projects (27% and 9% for hotels).	Law 2010 of 2019	75	
SR6	Special regime / Reduced rate	**Publication industry (9%).** The income tax rate applicable to publishing companies incorporated in Colombia as legal entities, whose economic activity and corporate purpose is exclusively the publishing of books, magazines, pamphlets or serialized collectibles of a scientific or cultural nature, under the terms of Law 98 of 1993, will be 9%.	Law 1819 of 2016	100	X
SR7	Special regime / Reduced rate	**Perennial crops (9%).** A preferential income tax rate of 9% for new perennial crops cultivated before fiscal year 2014. The tax incentive applies for ten years after the start of the crops' production and applies to rubber, palm oil, cocoa, citrus trees and other fruit trees.	Law 1819 of 2016	100	X
SR8	Special regime	**Stability contracts.**	Law 963 of 2005		X
SR9	Special regime / Reduced rate	**State-owned alcohol production and gambling (9%).** Income tax rate of 9% in industrial and commercial companies of the State and Mixed Economy Companies of the Departmental, Municipal and District order, in which the participation of the State is higher than 90%, which exercise monopolies of luck and chance and liquor and alcohol.	Law 1819 of 2016	100	X

ID	Type	Tax Expenditure	Legal Reference (Law/Article)		Revenue forgone estimate available
SR10	Special regime / Reduced rate	**Theme parks, ecotourism parks, agro-tourism and nautical docks (9%).** Income tax rate of 9% for national and assimilated companies, permanent establishments and foreign legal entities, for new theme park projects or remodeled, new ecotourism and agrotourism parks and new nautical docks.	Law 2068 of 2020	41	X
SR11	Special regime / Reduced rate	**Non-profit organisations / Special regime (20%).** Income tax rate on the net profit or surplus of the entities under the special tax regime. Surpluses not invested or allocated in the development of the non-profit organization's "worthy purpose" are subject to a 20% CIT rate.	Law 1819 of 2019	146	X
SR12	Special regime / Reduced rate	**Cooperatives, their associations, unions, central leagues, higher financial organizations, mutual associations, cooperative auxiliary institutions, cooperative confederations (20%)**. Special single tax rate for cooperatives, their associations, unions, central leagues, higher financial organizations, mutual associations, cooperative auxiliary institutions, cooperative confederations, as provided for in the cooperative legislation, supervised by a superintendence or control agency (20%).	Law 1819 of 2016	142	X
SR13	Special regime	**Dividends distributed from profits that would have been taxed in a mega-investment project**. Income tax rate for dividends distributed to partners or shareholders from profits that would have been taxed in a mega-investment project.	Law 2010 of 2019	75	
SR14	Special regime / Reduced rate	**First sale of land, real estate or real estate units that are new constructions (9%).** Income tax rate of 9% for national and similar companies, permanent establishments and foreign legal entities, for profits on the first sale of land, real estate or real estate units that are new constructions for a term of 10 years.	Law 2068 of 2020	41	
SR15	Special regime	**Foreign portfolio equity investments in public or private fixed-income securities**. Income from foreign portfolio equity investments in public or private fixed-income securities.	Law 1607 of 2012	125	

ID	Type	Tax Expenditure	Legal Reference (Law/Article)		Revenue forgone estimate available
SR16	Special regime	**Infrastructure projects in Special Economic Export Zones.** Infrastructure projects that qualify as eligible in the Special Economic Export Zones are treated as industrial users of goods and services.	Law 677 of 2001	16	
SR17	Special regime / Reduced rate	**International maritime transportation services provided by vessels or naval artifacts registered in the Colombian registry (2%).** Income tax rate of 2% for national and similar companies, permanent establishments and foreign legal entities, for international maritime transportation services provided by vessels or naval artifacts registered in the Colombian registry.	Law 2133 of 2021	30	
SR18	Special regime / Reduced rate	**Micro and small ZOMAC (0%).** The 0% rate was applied between 2017 and 2021. The following rates apply for the subsequent time periods: 25% of the standard CIT rate (2022-2024), 50% of the standard CIT rate (2025-2027), standard CIT rate (starting 2028). **Medium and large ZOMAC (50% of the standard rate).** The rate (50% of the standard rate) was applied between 2017 and 2021. The following rates apply for the subsequent time periods: 75% of the standard CIT rate (2022-2027), standard CIT rate (starting 2028).	Law 1819 of 2016	237	X
SR19	Special regime / Reduced rate	**Reorganization agreements.** The reductions, discounts or capital reductions, fines, penalties or interest obtained by debtors will be taxed in all cases as occasional income, when such yields, profits, reductions, discounts or reductions are presented or are the result and part of the reorganization agreements entered into or modified within the framework of the regime of Law 1116 of 2006, Decree 560 of 2020 and Legislative Decree 772 of 2020.	Decree 772 of 2020	15	
SR20	Special regime / Reduced rate	**ZESE (0%, first 5 years).** **ZESE (50% of the standard rate, 6-10 years)**	Law 1955 of 2019	268	X
SR21	Special regime / Increased rate (Negative TE)	**Financial sector surtax (32%+4%).**	Law 2155 of 2021		X

ID	Type	Tax Expenditure	Legal Reference (Law/Article)		Revenue forgone estimate available
O1	Other	**Associations.** Income from the National Society of the Colombian Red Cross and its federated system, public improvement societies, parents' associations, community action organizations, civil defense boards, alumni associations, associations of community homes and children's homes of the Colombian Family Welfare Institute or authorized by the latter, and associations of senior citizens authorized by the Colombian Family Welfare Institute.	Law 2010 of 2019	83	
O2	Other	**Contributions to family compensation funds.** Income from contributions to family compensation funds.	Law 21 of 1982		
O3	Other	**Cost of labor in coffee growing sector.** For the determination of the cost in coffee plantations, it is presumed by law that forty percent (40%) of the value of the income taxed by the producer, in each taxable year, corresponds to the costs and deductions inherent to the workforce.	Law 1819 of 2016	46	
O4	Other	**Income obtained from the sale of foreign goods introduced from abroad to International Logistics Distribution Centers.** Income obtained from the sale of foreign goods owned by foreign companies or persons without residence in the country, which have been introduced from abroad to International Logistics Distribution Centers, located in international airports, seaports and river ports located only in the departments of Guanía, Vaupés, Putumayo and Amazonas.	Law 2010 of 2019	84	
O5	Other	**International air or maritime transportation.** For Colombian tax resident companies, income from international air or maritime transportation.	Law 2010 of 2019	84	
O6	Other	**Labor unions, trade associations, employee funds, mutual investment funds, churches and religious denominations.** Income from: labor unions, trade associations, employee funds, mutual investment funds, churches and religious denominations recognized by the Ministry of the Interior or by law, political parties or movements approved by the National Electoral Council, associations and federations of Departments and Municipalities, societies or entities of alcoholics anonymous, public establishments and in general any decentralized official establishment.	Law 1819 of 2016	145	

ID	Type	Tax Expenditure	Legal Reference (Law/Article)		Revenue forgone estimate available
O7	Other	**Loans made through Bancoldex, Finagro and Findeter.** Loans for foreign trade operations and import of services, made through Bancoldex, Finagro and Findeter.	Law 2010 of 2019	84	
O8	Other	**Loans obtained from non-residents.** Loans obtained from non-residents, denominated and/or disbursed in legal or foreign currency, by financial corporations, financial cooperatives, financial cooperatives, commercial financing companies, banks, Bancoldex, Finagro, Findeter and commercial companies subject to the surveillance of the Superintendence of Companies under a prudential regulation regime, whose exclusive purpose is the origination of loans and whose indebtedness is destined to the development of their corporate purpose.	Law 2010 of 2019	84	
O9	Other	**Repair and maintenance of equipment abroad.** Income derived from technical services for repair and maintenance of equipment rendered abroad.	Law 2010 of 2019	84	
O10	Special regime	**Simple Regime (RST).** The SIMPLE regime is a preferential tax regime for small and medium enterprises.	Ley 2010 de 2019	74	

Annex D. List of Personal Income Tax Expenditures

This Annex includes the complete list of Personal Income Tax Expenditures that were identified in Colombia as part of the project.

Table A D.1. Identified Personal Income Tax Expenditures (natural persons)

ID	Type	Tax Expenditure	Legal Reference (Law/Article)		Revenue forgone estimate available
E1	Exempt income	**Benefits from Retirement and Disability Pension Fund.** The benefits received by a taxpayer from a Retirement and Disability Pension Fund, due to a pension plan and due to old age, disability, widowhood, or orphan hood, are assimilated to retirement pensions for the purposes of the provisions of the numeral 5 of article 206.	Legislative Decree 2512 of 1987	4	
E2	Exempt income	**Betting prizes and equestrian or canine contests and prizes to owners of horses or racing dogs (up to 410 UVT).** Prizes for equestrian or canine bets and competitions, obtained from horse or dog races, in legally established racetracks or dog tracks, whose value does not exceed 410 UVT (approximately USD$ 4 100), are not subject to capital gains tax or tax withholding.	Law 6 of 1992	8	
E3	Exempt income	**Capitalized income in cinematographic industry (50%).** The income that the cinematographic industrialists (producers, distributors and exhibitors) obtain, and that is capitalized or reserved to develop new productions or investments in the cinematographic sector, will be exempt up to fifty percent (50%) of the value of income tax.	Law 397 of 1997	46	
E4	Exempt income	**Difference between market value and historical cost in property sales.** The value of transferred property is based upon the historical cost and not the current market value of the property.	Legislative Decree 2053 of 1974 Law 1111 of 2006	26 116 20	

ID	Type	Tax Expenditure	Legal Reference (Law/Article)		Revenue forgone estimate available
E5	Exempt income	**Dividends (up to 300 UVT).** Dividends paid to an individual shareholder that do not exceed 300 UVT (about US 2 900) are not taxed under the 10% dividend withholding tax.	Law 1819 of 2016 Law 2010 of 2019	6 35	X
E6	Exempt income	**Donations to those affected by the volcanic activity of the Nevado del Ruiz.** Donations in favor of people affected by the volcanic activity of the Nevado del Ruiz made by the Reconstruction Fund, "RESURGIR", or the entities that work in the rehabilitation of the areas affected by it, are exempt from capital gains tax.	Law 44 of 1987	4	
E7	Exempt income	**Income received by authors, translators and copyright holders of certain books.** The income that authors and translators, both Colombian and foreign resident in Colombia, receive from authors and translators, for books of a scientific or cultural nature edited and printed in Colombia, for each title and for each year.	Law 1819 of 2016 Law 2010 of 2019	99 91	
E8	Exempt income	**Inheritance (20% of assets up to 2 290 UVT).** 20 percent of the value of the assets and rights received by individuals other than the heirs and / or the surviving spouse for inheritances and bequests, and 20% of the assets and rights received for donations and other acts, limited to 2 290 UVT (USD 22 000)	Law 75 of 1986. Law 1607 of 2012.	72 104.	
E9	Exempt income	**Inheritance (heirs' and spouse's inheritance allowance up to 3 490 UVT).** The equivalent of the first 3 490 UVT (USD 34 000) of the value of the allowances that each of the heirs and the surviving spouse received.	Law 75 of 1986. Law 1607 of 2012.	72 104.	
E10	Exempt income	**Inheritance (up to 7 700 UVT).** The equivalent of the first 7 700 UVT (USD 74 000) of a rural property and the equivalent of the first 7 700 UVT in the inheritance are exempt from taxation.	Law 75 of 1986. Law 1607 of 2012.	72 104.	

ID	Type	Tax Expenditure	Legal Reference (Law/Article)		Revenue forgone estimate available
E11	Exempt income	**Investment in sawmills and related investment in the lumber industry.** Exempt income for investment in new sawmills, processing plants and plantations of timber trees and trees in fruit production.	Law 1819 of 2016 Law 2010 of 2019	99 91	
E12	Exempt income	**Labor income deduction.** 25% of labor income is deductible; this deduction cannot be higher than 2 880 UVT per year.	Law 223 of 1995. Law 1607 of 2012	96 6	X
E13	Exempt income	**Life insurance compensation (up to 12 500 UVT).** Life insurance compensations are exempt up to 12 500 UVT (about USD 120 000). Compensations in excess of this amount are treated as occasional income.	Law 2010 of 2019	36	
E14	Exempt income	**Maternity leave payments.**	Law 75 of 1986.	35	
E15	Exempt income	**Other exempt income recognized in international agreements ratified by Colombia.**	CAN Decision 578 of 2004 Law 2061 of 2020 Law 1939 of 2018 Law 1690 of 2013 Law 1667 of 2013 Law 1668 of 2013 Law 1568 of 2012 Law 1459 of 2011 Law 1344 of 2009 Law 1082 of 2006 Law 2004 of 2019 Law 1692 of 2013 Law 1261 of 2008.		
E16	Exempt income	**Pensions (up to 12 000 UVT).** Pension income below 1 000 UVT per month or 12 000 UVT per year (about USD 116 000 per year) is tax exempt (i.e. there is a tax allowance of 12 000 UVT per year). The tax expenditure is equal to the difference between the 1 000 UVT zero-rate bracket and the standard zero-rate bracket under the PIT.	Law 75 of 198 Law 223 of 1995.	35 96	X

ID	Type	Tax Expenditure	Legal Reference (Law/Article)		Revenue forgone estimate available
E17	Exempt income	**Private use of a company car.** Transport reimbursements are exempt from individual income tax provided that the employee provides the employer with invoices to support the reimbursement. This includes the private use of a company car made available by the employer, tickets for fuel costs and maintenance, and the payment of the insurance premium in respect of a vehicle used by the employee for work purposes.	Decree 2663 of 1950 Law 50 of 1990	129 15	
E18	Exempt income	**Real estate capital gains (up to 7 500 UVT).** Realized capital gains from the sale of homes up to 7 500 UVT (about USD 72 000).	Law 1607 of 2012	105	
E19	Exempt income	**Return from contributions to voluntary pension schemes.** The return from contributions to voluntary pension schemes.	Law 49 of 1990 Law 1819 of 2016	9 15	
E20	Exempt income	**Salaries and emoluments paid by the Development Bank of Latin America.** The salaries and emoluments paid by the Development Bank of Latin America to the Directors, their alternates and the officials and employees thereof, who are not citizens or nationals of the country where the Bank has its headquarters or offices, are exempt from taxes.	Law 103 of 1968	52	
E21	Exempt income	**Salaries and emoluments paid by the International Bank for Reconstruction and Development.** Salaries and emoluments paid by the International Bank for Reconstruction and Development to the Executive Directors, alternates, officers or employees of the Bank itself who are not citizens, subjects or other nationals of the respective country are not taxed, nor is any tax established in relation to such salaries and emoluments.	Law 76 of 1946	7	
E22	Exempt income	**Salaries and emoluments paid by the United Nations Organization**. Are exempt from taxes on salaries and emoluments paid by the United Nations Organization to its officials. This is not subject to the limit of 40% or 5040 UVT.	Law 62 of 1973	5	

ID	Type	Tax Expenditure	Legal Reference (Law/Article)		Revenue forgone estimate available
E23	Exempt income	**Salaries by the Council of the Organization of American States.** The Representatives of the Governments in the Council of the Organization of American States, the Representatives in the organs of the Council, the personnel that make up the Representations, as well as the Secretary General and the Assistant Secretary General of the Organization, shall enjoy the privileges and immunities necessary to carry out their functions independently. This Includes the labor income receive by the officials of OEA.	Law 1 of 1951	104	
E24	Exempt income	**Salary of headmasters and professors at public universities (50%).** In the case of headmasters and professors at public universities, a percentage equivalent to 50% of their salary will be considered exempt representation expenses (not subject to 40% ceiling).	Law 2010 of 2019	32	
E25	Exempt income	**Salary of judges, prosecutors and judicial attorneys (50%).** In the case of judges of the High Courts, their prosecutors and judicial attorneys, a percentage equivalent to 50% of their salary will be considered exempt representation expenses (not subject to 40% ceiling).	Law 2010 of 2019	32	
E26	Exempt income	**Salary of officials in other international organizations.** The exemption of the remuneration of officials in international organizations. Residual classification of the exempt income that applies to officials of international organizations not included in other rows.			
E27	Exempt income	**Salary received above basic salary in the military.** Excess of basic salary received by officers, non-commissioned officers, and professional soldiers of the Military (not subject to 40% ceiling).	Law 75 of 1986 Law 2010 of 2019	35 32	
E28	Exempt income	**Salary received above basic salary in the national police.** Excess of basic salary received by officers, non-commissioned officers, executive level personnel, patrolmen and agents of the national police (not subject to 40% ceiling).	Law 75 of 1986. Law 2010 of 2019.	35 32	

ID	Type	Tax Expenditure	Legal Reference (Law/Article)		Revenue forgone estimate available
E29	Exempt income	**Sale of property for public interest projects.** The profit in the sale of properties destined to the development of social interest housing projects and / or priority interest housing; it is exempt income.	Law 1819 of 2016 Law 2010 of 2019	99 91	
E30	Exempt income	**Sale of property for urban renewal projects.** The profit in the sale of properties for the development of urban renewal projects is exempt income.	Law 1819 of 2016 Law 2010 of 2019	99 91	
E31	Exempt income	**Sale of shares in CHC (excluding profits from activity in Colombia).** The income derived from the sale of shares or participations owned in a Colombian Holding Company are exempt income, except for the value corresponding to the profits obtained from the profits obtained in Colombia.	Law 2010 of 2019	77	
E32	Exempt income	**Services rendered in new hotels.** Exempt income for services rendered in new hotels.	Law 788 of 2002	18	
E33	Exempt income	**Services rendered in remodeled and / or expanded hotels.** Exempt income for services rendered in remodeled and / or expanded hotels. It corresponds to the proportion that represents the value of the remodeling and / or expansion in the fiscal cost of the property.	Law 788 of 2002	18	
E34	Exempt income	**Severance payments and interest earned on severance payments.** Severance payments and interest earned on severance payments provided they are received by employees whose average monthly salary in the previous 6 months does not exceed 350 UVT.	Law 75 of 1986.	35	

ID	Type	Tax Expenditure	Legal Reference (Law/Article)		Revenue forgone estimate available
E35	Exempt income	**Social benefits received by the members of the Military or the national Police.** Social benefits received by the members of the military or the national police while being in active duty or retirement (not subject to 40% ceiling).	Law 75 of 1986 Law 2010 of 2019.	35 32	
E36	Exempt income	**Top government officials.** Exemptions on certain income from top government positions.	Law 1607 of 2012. Law 2010 of 2019.	7 33	
E37	Exempt income	**Urban dwelling owned by the deceased (up to 7 700 UVT).** 7 700 UVTs of the value of the deceased's urban dwelling is not taxed under the capital gains tax.	Law 75 of 1986. Law 1607 of 2012	72 104.	
E38	Exempt income	**Use of new forest plantations.** The use of new forest plantations, including guadua, rubber and cashew, is a exempt income, according to the qualification issued by the regional autonomous corporation or the competent entity.	Law 1819 of 2016 Law 2010 of 2019	99 91	
E39	Exempt income	**Voluntary contributions to private pension funds and AFC housing savings.** Voluntary contributions to private pension funds made by the employee and contributions to housing savings (AFC accounts) are considered exempt income. The deductions are subject to permanence requirements and cannot exceed 30% of general gross income and cannot exceed 3 800 UVT (approximately USD 37 000).	Law 49 of 1990 and Law 488 of 1998 Law 1819 of 2016	9 and 23 15 and16	X
E40	Exempt income	**Waterway transport services.** The income from the provision of the river transport service with boats and slabs of low draft is exempt income, for a term of fifteen (15) years as of 2019.	Law 1819 of 2016 Law 2010 of 2019	99 91	

ID	Type	Tax Expenditure	Legal Reference (Law/Article)		Revenue forgone estimate available
NT1	Non-taxable income	**Capitalization processes.** The income that is distributed through shares will not be taxed with income tax to the employer, up to the equivalent of 10% of the profit generated. The profits derived from these actions will not be subject to tax within the 5 years in which they are transferred to the worker and he retains his ownership, nor will they be part of the base to settle any other tax.	Law 789 of 2002	44	
NT2	Non-taxable income	**Compensation for working with intelligence services.** Compensation for supply of data to the intelligence sections of the State / Government bodies.	Law 223 of 1995	252	
NT3	Non-taxable income	**Derivatives with CSE-listed companies as underlying.** The income that comes from the negotiation of derivatives that are securities and whose underlying is represented exclusively in shares listed in a Colombian stock exchange, indices or participations in funds or collective portfolios that reflect the behavior of said shares, are not taxable income.	Law 1430 of 2010	37	
NT5	Non-taxable income	**Dividends derived from mega-Investments.** Dividends from mega-investments are not taxed under the dividend withholding tax (i.e. the 7.5% when dividends are distributed to another corporation or 10% when distributed to an individual shareholder).	Law 2010 of 2019	75	
NT6	Non-taxable income	**Dividends distributed by a CHC to a non-resident.** The premium of the placement of shares or dividends distributed by a Colombian Holding Company to a non-resident individual are foreign source income, which is not taxed in Colombia.	Law 2010 of 2019	77	
NT7	Non-taxable income	**Donations to political parties.** Donations for Political Parties, Movements and Campaigns. The sums that individuals receive from third parties, exclusively destined to finance the operation of parties, political movements and social groups that nominate candidates and those that the candidates receive for the same purpose for the financing of political campaigns for the planned popular elections. In the National Constitution, this is non-taxable income for the beneficiary if it is shown that it has been used for these activities.	Law 223 of 1995	248	

ID	Type	Tax Expenditure	Legal Reference (Law/Article)		Revenue forgone estimate available
NT8	Non-taxable income	**Donations to projects approved by the Multilateral Fund of the Montreal Protocol.** Donations in cash received by individuals or entities that participate in the execution and development of projects approved by the Multilateral Fund of the Montreal Protocol (protecting the ozone layer), through any executing agency, bilateral or multilateral, are non-taxable income.	Law 488 of 1998	32	
NT9	Non-taxable income	**Forest Incentive Certificates.** As it constitutes an acknowledgment by the state of the environmental benefits originated by reforestation, the income from Forest Incentive Certificates are not taxable income.	Law 139 of 1994	8 Literal C	
NT10	Non-taxable income	**Inflation on capitalized income and interest.** Inflationary component if capitalized and on interests paid by financial entities and investment funds.	Law 75 of 1986 Decree 2512 of 1987	27 6	X
NT11	Non-taxable income	**Payments by employer for food.** Payments made by the employer to employees or their families for food up to a monthly amount of 41 UVTs are exempt income of the employee. This tax treatment only applies to employees with employment income below 310 UVTs per month.	Law 488 of 1998 Law 788 of 2002	6 84	X
NT12	Non-taxable income	**Property sales (1978-1986).** Income obtained from the sale of immovable property acquired since 1978 to 1986, where the percentage of non-taxable income decreases from 1978 (100% non-taxable) to 1986 (10% non-taxable).	Law 75 of 1986	64, Paragraph 2	
NT13	Non-taxable income	**Raffle of capitalization titles in closed groups.** In raffles for closed groups of capitalization titles and in any other raffle in which there is total certainty of being favored, what is received by way of raffle is non-taxable income.	Decree 187 of 1975 Decree 400 of 1975	113 11	

ID	Type	Tax Expenditure	Legal Reference (Law/Article)		Revenue forgone estimate available
NT14	Non-taxable income	**Raffle of capitalization titles.** For taxpayers who are favored in a raffle of capitalization titles, only the difference between the prize received and what is paid in installments corresponding to the favored title is an occasional gain.	Legislative Decree 2348 of 1974	1	
NT15	Non-taxable income	**Raffles or contests carried out by the Tax Administration.** The Tax Administration may carry out raffles or contests; the income from prizes obtained in the raffles, sweepstakes or contests carried out under the Fiscal Prize, are not taxable income.	Law 49 of 1990	36	
NT16	Non-taxable income	**Rural Capitalization Incentive.** The Rural Capitalization Incentive (ICR), provided for in Law 101 of 1993, is non-taxable income.	Law 788 of 2002	20	
NT17	Non-taxable income	**Sale of CSE-listed company shares.** Income provided from the sale of shares of a company listed in the Colombian Stock Exchange (CSE) when such sale does not represent more than 10% of the total number of shares of the listed company.	Law 633 of 2000.	9	
NT18	Non-taxable income	**Sale of expropriated real estate.** The income obtained in the voluntary sale of real estate expropriated is a non-taxable income.	Law 388 of 1997	67, Paragraph 2.	
NT19	Non-taxable income	**Sale of properties in Nevado del Ruiz area.** The income obtained from the sale of properties located in the areas affected by the Nevado del Ruiz volcanic activity is non-taxable income.	Extraordinary Decree of 1987	5	

ID	Type	Tax Expenditure	Legal Reference (Law/Article)		Revenue forgone estimate available
NT20	Non-taxable income	**Sale of real estate destined for public interest.** The income from the sale of real estate destined for public utility or social interest purposes is non-taxable income, if the negotiation occurs through voluntary sale.	Law 9 of 1989 Law 3 of 1991	15 35	
NT21	Non-taxable income	**Sale of shares in CFC**. Income from the sale of shares or participations in the CFC is non-taxable income.	Law 1819 of 2016	139	
NT22	Non-taxable income	**Sale of shares in CHC by non-residents.** For non-resident partners or shareholders, income derived from the sale of shares or participations owned in a Colombian Holding Company is foreign source income, which is not taxed in Colombia.	Law 2010 of 2019	77	
NT23	Non-taxable income	**Voluntary contributions to the mandatory individual savings scheme.** Voluntary contributions to the mandatory individual savings scheme are non-taxable income (so they are not limited to the 40% overall deduction ceiling), but the deduction itself cannot exceed 25% of general gross income, nor 2 500 UVT.	Law 1819 of 2016	13	X
NT24	Non-taxable income	**Scientific, technological or innovation work.** Non-taxable income is remuneration of the individuals for work of a scientific, technological or innovation.	Law 1450 of 2011	37	
NT25	Non-taxable income	**Seed capital provided by the state.** Non-taxable income is the non-reimbursable economic support provided by the State, as seed capital for the venture and as capital for the strengthening of the company.	Law 1429 of 2010	16	

ID	Type	Tax Expenditure	Legal Reference (Law/Article)		Revenue forgone estimate available
NT26	Non-taxable income	**Student support.** Economic support for students provided by the state.	Law 1819 of 2016.	11	
NT27	Non-taxable income	**Subsidies from Agro Ingreso Seguro program.** The subsidies and aid granted by the government in the program Agro Ingreso Seguro, AIS, and those from the incentive to storage and the incentive to rural capitalization provided for in Law 101 of 1993 are non-taxable income.	Law 1111 of 2006	58	
NT28	Non-taxable income	**Support for scientific, technological or innovative projects.** The resources that the taxpayer receives to be used for the development of projects classified as scientific, technological or innovative, according to the conditions defined by the National Council of Tax Benefits in Science, Technology and Innovation, are non-taxable income.	Law 1450 of 2011	37	
DD1	Deduction / Non-standard deduction	**Adjustment of real estate, shares and contributions that are fixed assets of individuals.** For purposes of determining the income or capital gain, as the case may be, from the sale of real estate and shares or contributions, which have the character of fixed assets, taxpayers who are individuals may adjust the acquisition cost of such assets, in the percentage increase in the value of the real estate, or in the percentage increase in the consumer price index for employees, respectively, that has been registered in the period between January 1 of the year in which the property was acquired good and January 1 of the year in which it is sold. The cost thus adjusted, may be increased with the value of the improvements and valuation contributions that have been paid, in the case of real estate. When the taxpayer chooses to determine the fiscal cost of real estate, contributions or shares in companies, based on the provisions of this article, the sum thus determined must appear as equity value in their income statements, notwithstanding that in years may make use of the alternative provided for in article 72 of this Statute, fulfilling the requirements demanded therein. The percentage increases applicable to the cost of acquisition of real estate, shares or contributions, provided for in this article, will be published by the government based on the certification issued in this regard, the Agustín Codazzi Geographical Institute and the Department National Statistics Administration DANE, respectively. The adjustments made in accordance with the first paragraph of article 70, will not be applicable to determine the income or occasional profit provided for in this article. At the time of the sale of the property, the depreciation that has been deducted for tax purposes will be subtracted from the fiscal cost determined in accordance with this article.	Law 75 of 1986 Legislative Decree 2687 of 1988	64 65	

ID	Type	Tax Expenditure	Legal Reference (Law/Article)		Revenue forgone estimate available
DD2	Deduction / Non-standard deduction	**Agricultural parafiscal contributions to stabilization funds.** Deduction for agricultural parafiscal contributions made by producers to stabilization funds.	Law 101 of 1993	29	
DD3	Deduction / Non-standard deduction	**Amortization in abandoned or withdrawn natural resource projects.** When such explorations are abandoned or withdrawn, the unamortized balance of the investments made in exploration will continue to be amortized at the annual rate of ten percent (10%).	Legislative Decree 2310 of 1974	10	
DD4	Deduction / Non-standard deduction	**Assessment as fiscal cost.** The assessment declared for purposes of the Unified Predial Tax, and the values formed or updated by the cadastral authorities, may be taken as fiscal cost for the determination of the income or capital gain that occurs in the alienation of properties that constitute real estate assets for the taxpayer. For these purposes, the self-assessment or assessment acceptable as a tax expense will be the one that appears in the declaration of the Unified Tax on Real Estate and/or income declaration, as the case may be, corresponding to the year prior to the alienation. For these purposes, corrections or additions to the affidavits or unformed assessment will not be taken into account. If the assessment or self-assessment is taken as the fiscal cost, at the time of the sale of the property, the depreciation that has been deducted for fiscal purposes will be subtracted from the fiscal cost.	Law 14 of 1983	13, 14, and 23	
DD5	Deduction / Non-standard deduction	**Attentions to customers, suppliers and employees.** Attentions to customers, suppliers and employees, such as gifts, courtesies, parties, meetings and celebrations. The maximum amount to be deducted for all of these concepts is 1% of net and effectively realized tax income.	Law 1819 of 2016	63	
DD6	Deduction / Non-standard deduction	**Average cost of shares.** When the taxpayer has within his equity shares of the same company whose costs are different, he must take the average of such costs as the cost of disposal.	Legislative Decree 2247 of 1974	55	
DD7	Deduction / Non-standard deduction	**Carbon tax.** For the taxpayer, the carbon tax is deductible from the income tax as the greater value of the cost of the good.	Law 1819 of 2016	Paragraph 2, 222	

ID	Type	Tax Expenditure	Legal Reference (Law/Article)		Revenue forgone estimate available
DD8	Deduction / Non-standard deduction	**Cost of labor in coffee growing sector.** For the determination of the cost in coffee plantations, it is presumed by law that forty percent (40%) of the value of the income taxed by the producer, in each taxable year, corresponds to the costs and deductions inherent to the workforce.	Law 1819 of 2016	46	
DD9	Deduction / Non-standard deduction	**Depletion in mining, gases other than hydrocarbons and natural deposits.** Deduction for depletion in mining, gases other than hydrocarbons and natural deposits.	Legislative Decree 2310 of 1974	11	
DD10	Deduction / Non-standard deduction	**Determination of the fiscal cost of the elements of property, plant and equipment and investment properties.** The tax cost of items of property, plant and equipment, and investment property, for taxpayers who are required to keep accounts, is the acquisition price plus directly attributable costs until the asset is available for use, except for the initial estimate of the costs of dismantling and removal of the element, as well as the rehabilitation of the place on which it sits, if applicable. Additionally, improvements, major repairs and inspections, which must be capitalized in accordance with the accounting technique and that comply with the provisions of the tax code, will be part of the cost of the asset. In subsequent measurements of these assets, the cost thus determined will be maintained. When these assets are sold, the value of the adjustments related to the UVT, which is dealt with in article 70 of the tax code, is added to the previous result; and, when applicable, depreciation or amortization is subtracted, as long as it has been deducted for tax purposes. Investment properties that are measured for accounting purposes under the fair value model, for tax purposes will be measured at cost. For taxpayers not required to keep accounts, the cost of the goods disposed of fixed or immobilized assets, is constituted by the acquisition price or the cost declared in the immediately previous year, as the case may be, plus the following values: a) The cost of additions and improvements, in the case of personal property; b) The cost of construction, improvements, non-deducted locative repairs and that of contributions for valuation, in the case of real estate.	Law 1819 of 2016	48	
DD11	Deduction / Non-standard deduction	**Donations directed to scholarship programs.** Deduction for donations directed to scholarship programs or condonable educational loans.	Law 6 of 1992	4	

ID	Type	Tax Expenditure	Legal Reference (Law/Article)		Revenue forgone estimate available
DD12	Deduction / Non-standard deduction	**Donations made for the sponsorship of Natural Parks and Conservation of Natural Forests**. Taxpayers who make donations to the Special Administrative Unit of the System of National Natural Parks, in order to finance Colombia's natural parks and conserve natural forests, can deduct 30% from the income tax of the value of the donations made during the taxable period.	Law 1536 of 2012	6	
DD13	Deduction / Non-standard deduction	**Donations made to the entrepreneurship and innovation agency of the government.** Taxpayers can deduct the value of donations made to the entrepreneurship and innovation agency of the government *iNNpulsa*, after verification and approval by the Ministry of Commerce, Industry and Tourism.	Law 2069 of 2020	40	
DD14	Deduction / Non-standard deduction	**Donations received through Icetex.** Taxpayers can deduct the value of donations received through Icetex, directed to programs of scholarships that finance the training and education of those who enter the Public Force.	Law 2130 of 2021	2	
DD15	Deduction / Enhanced deduction	**Donations to organizations dedicated to the defense, protection and promotion of human rights and access to justice, amateur sports organizations, sports clubs, sports federations or associations (125%).** Donations to the General Gustavo Matamoros D'Costa Corporation and to foundations and organizations dedicated to the defense, protection and promotion of human rights and access to justice, amateur sports organizations, sports clubs, sports federations or associations, and the Colombian Olympic Committee, and the recreational or cultural organizations can deduct 125% of the value of the donation.	Law 6 of 1992 Law 488 of 1998 Law 223 of 1995 Law 181 of 1995	137 37 278 76	
DD16	Deduction / Non-standard deduction	**Donations to support science, technology and innovation.** Taxpayers can deduct the donations received by the National Financing Fund for the Science, Technology and Innovation, Francisco José de Caldas Fund, aimed at financing of Science, Technology and Innovation Programs and / or Projects, according to the conditions of the National Council of Tax Benefits in Science, Technology and Innovation (CNBT). This is deductible in the taxable period in which it is carried out.	Law 6 of 1992 Law 1955 of 2019	4 170	
DD17	Deduction / Non-standard deduction	**Financial transaction tax (50%).** 50% of the financial transaction tax (GMF).	Decree 2053 of 1974 Decree 2348 of 1974 Law 75 of 1986 Law 2010 of 2019	48 56 5 39 86	

ID	Type	Tax Expenditure	Legal Reference (Law/Article)		Revenue forgone estimate available
DD18	Deduction / Non-standard deduction	**Fiscal cost of formed intangible assets.** The fiscal cost of intangible assets formed by taxpayers not required to keep accounts, concerning industrial, literary, artistic and scientific property, such as invention patents, trademarks, copyrights and other intangibles, is presumed to be constituted by thirty percent (30%) of the sale value.	Legislative Decree 2053 of 1974 Law 1819 of 2016	25 55	
DD19	Deduction / Non-standard deduction	**Interest paid on educational loans.** Interest paid on educational loans from the Colombian institute for educational credit and technical studies abroad, aimed at the taxpayer's higher education. The deduction cannot exceed 100 UVT per year.	Legislative Decree 2053 of 1974 Law 2010 of 2019	47 89	
DD20	Deduction / Non-standard deduction	**Investments in detention centers.** Companies or individuals can deduct from their gross income the value of the new investments made in the year, in detention centers, as long as they are effectively used for work and education programs for inmates, and individuals are linked to the company. The deduction may not exceed (15%) per year of the net income.	Law 633 of 2000	98	
DD21	Deduction / Enhanced deduction	**Investments or donations in creative economy projects (165%).** Deduction equivalent to 165% for investments or donations in creative economy projects as defined by the Ministry of Culture.	Law 1955 of 2019	180	
DD22	Deduction / Enhanced deduction	**Investments or donations to Colombian film projects (165%).** Taxpayers who make investments or donations to Colombian production or co-production film projects approved by the Ministry of Culture can deduct from their tax (165%) of the real value invested or donated.	Law 814 of 1993 Law 1607 of 2012	16 195	
DD23	Deduction / Non-standard deduction	**Maintenance and conservation of assets declared as in cultural interest.** The owners of movable and immovable property declared as of cultural interest, can deduct the totality of the expenses for the elaboration of the Special Protection Plans and for the maintenance and conservation of these assets, even if this is not causally related to the activity that produces the income.	Law 1185 of 2008	14	

ID	Type	Tax Expenditure	Legal Reference (Law/Article)		Revenue forgone estimate available
DD24	Deduction / Non-standard deduction	**Mortgage interest relief (up to 1 200 UVT).** Mortgage interest relief, the deduction is limited to 1 200 UVT per year.	Decree 2053 of 1974 Law 75 of 1986 Law 2010 of 2019	47 40 89	X
DD25	Deduction / Non-standard deduction	**Natural resource exhaustion in contracts in force as of October 28, 1974.** Normal deductions for exhaustion in contracts in force as of October 28, 1974. The taxpayer can deduct a fixed percentage of 10% of the natural product extracted from the oil field or another deduction rate based on a technical estimate of the cost of operating units. This cannot exceed 35% of net income.	Legislative Decree 2310 of 1974	6	
DD26	Deduction / Non-standard deduction	**Private health insurance contribution (up to 192 UVT).** Voluntary payments for additional health insurance paid to private health insurers that provide supplementary services to mandatory health insurance, to protect the worker, his partner, his children and dependents. The tax deduction cannot exceed 192 UVT per year.	Law 6 of 1992 Law 1607 of 2012	120 15	
DD27	Deduction / Enhanced deduction	**Salaries paid to first-job employees who are under twenty-eight years of age (120%).** Deduction of 120% of the payments that the employer makes for salary, in relationship with employees who are under twenty-eight (28) years of age, as long as in the case of the person's first job.	Law 2010 of 2019	88	
DD28	Deduction / Enhanced deduction	**Salaries, social benefits and other labor payments, paid to female workers who are victims of proven violence (200%).** Employers who employ female workers who are victims of proven violence, can deduct from their income 200% of the value of wages and social benefits paid during the year, since the employment relationship exists, and up to a period of three years.	Law 1257 of 2008	23	
DD29	Deduction / Enhanced deduction	**Salaries, social benefits and other labor payments, paid to widows and orphans of members of the Armed Forces killed in combat, kidnapped or missing (200%).** Deduction equivalent to 200% for salaries, social benefits and other labor payments, paid to widows and orphans of members of the Armed Forces killed in combat, kidnapped or missing.	Law 6 of 1992	127	

ID	Type	Tax Expenditure	Legal Reference (Law/Article)		Revenue forgone estimate available
DD30	Deduction / Enhanced deduction	**Salaries, social benefits and other labor payments, paid to workers with a proven disability of no less than 25% (200%).** Employers who employ workers with a proven disability of no less than 25% can deduct from their income 200% of the value of wages and social benefits paid during the year to workers with a disability, as long as it subsists.	Law 361 of 1997	31	
DD31	Deduction / Non-standard deduction	**Special depletion deductions.** Once the exploitation period has started, this deduction will be suspended; but the unamortized balance of the corresponding investments will be taken as an integral cost of the amount of the taxpayer's investments, amortizable by the normal and special depletion deductions.	Legislative Decree 2310 of 1974	10	
DD32	Deduction / Non-standard deduction	**Special Exhaustion Factor in Hydrocarbon Exploitation.** In addition to the annual deduction for normal depletion, the taxpayer can deduct a special depletion factor applicable year by year at a rate equivalent to 15% or 18% of the gross value of the natural product extracted; the normal deduction and the special deduction cannot exceed 50% of net income.	Law 75 of 1986	45	
DD33	Deduction / Non-standard deduction	**Studies of employees in Higher Education institutions.** The individuals or companies that finance the studies of their employees in Higher Education institutions, for tax purposes, may deduct this amount from their operating costs.	Law 30 of 1992	124	
DD34	Deduction / Non-standard deduction	**Value of the income in kind:** The value of payments or credits in kind that constitute income is determined by the commercial value of the species at the time of delivery. If species are given in payment of obligations agreed in money, their value is determined, unless proven otherwise, by the price set in the contract.	Legislative Decree 2053 of 1974	27	
DF1	Deferrals	**Accelerated depreciation of machinery, equipment and civil works of projects of unconventional energy sources.** Deduction for accelerated depreciation of machinery, equipment and civil works of projects of unconventional energy sources. The annual depreciation rate will be no higher than (33.33%) as a global annual rate.	Law 1715 of 2014 Law 2099 of 2021	14 11	

ID	Type	Tax Expenditure	Legal Reference (Law/Article)		Revenue forgone estimate available
DF2	Deferrals	**Depletion in exploitation of mines or gases other than hydrocarbons and natural deposits in contracts in force as of October 28, 1974.** Deduction for Depletion in Exploitation of Mines or Gases other than hydrocarbons and natural deposits in contracts in force as of October 28, 1974. This deduction is equal to 10% of the total value of the year's production calculated at the mine head, less royalties or Leases paid, the deduction cannot exceed 35% of net income.	Legislative Decree 2310 of 1974	12	
DF3	Deferrals	**Investment in expansion or opening of bookstores.** The totally new own investment, made by individuals or companies in expansion or opening of new bookstores or branches of those already established, is deductible from the investor's gross income up to a value equivalent to 10 000 UVT (USD$ 90 770).	Law 98 of 1993	30	
DF4	Deferrals	**Investment in non-conventional energy sources.** Taxpayers obliged to submit a tax return who directly make investments in non-conventional energy sources can deduct from their income, in a period not exceeding 15 years, from the following year in which the investment has come into operation, the 50% of the total investment made.	Law 1715 of 2014 Law 2099 of 2021	11 8	
DF5	Deferrals	**Investment in performing arts infrastructure.** Investments made in infrastructure projects for enabled stages or infrastructure for existing enabled stages, specifically intended for public performances of the performing arts, will be deductible from income tax by 100%.	Law 493 of 2011	4	
DF6	Deferrals	**Investment in research, technological development and innovation.** Taxpayers can deduct the value of investments made in research, technological development and innovation, according to the conditions of the National Council of Tax Benefits in Science, Technology and Innovation (CNBT). This is deductible in the taxable period in which is carried out.	Law 6 of 1992 Law 1955 of 2019	4 170	
DF7	Deferrals	**Investment such as prepaid expenses, establishment expenses, research, development and innovation.** Deduction for investments such as prepaid expenses, establishment expenses, research, development and innovation, applies to taxpayers who keep accounting. For all cases, the aliquot to be deducted per year cannot exceed 20% of the fiscal cost.	Law 1819 of 2016	84	

ID	Type	Tax Expenditure	Legal Reference (Law/Article)		Revenue forgone estimate available
DF8	Deferrals	**Investments under mega-investment regime.** The taxpayers of the mega-investment regime, who make the new investments, can depreciate their fixed assets in a maximum period of two (2) years, regardless of the useful life of the asset.	Law 2010 of 2019	75	
DF9	Deferrals	**Petroleum exploration in contracts in force as of October 28, 1974.** Deduction for Petroleum Exploration in Contracts in Force as of October 28, 1974. In the case of explorations in search of petroleum carried out from the 1st. of January 1955 that correspond to areas whose oil subsoil has been recognized as privately owned or to concessions or associations in force on October 28, 1974, directly by individuals or by companies with farms in production, a deduction is granted for amortization of investments of all kinds, made in explorations charged to the income of farms in the country, a rate of ten percent (10%) of the respective investment.	Legislative Decree 2310 of 1974	10	
C1	Tax credit	**Donation to support the immunization of the population against Covid-19 (50%).** Tax credit equivalent to 50% of the donation made to achieve the immunization of the population Colombia against Covid-19 and any other pandemic.	Law 2064 of 2020	40	
C2	Tax credit	**Donations received through Icetex (25%).** Tax credit equivalent to 25% of the value of donations received through Icetex, directed to programs of scholarships that finance the training and education of those who enter the Public Force.	Law 2130 of 2021	2	
C3	Tax credit	**Donations to certain non-profits (25%).** 25% of donations granted to non-profit entities qualified under the CIT special tax regime and to CIT non-taxpayers stated in articles 22 and 23 of the Colombian Tax Code.	Law 1819 of 2016	105	
C4	Tax credit	**Donations to higher education and science (25%).** 25% of donations made through institutions of higher education or the Colombian Institute of Educational Credit and Technical Studies Abroad (ICETEX), addressed to programs of scholarships or forgivable credits, that are approved by the Ministry of Education, and that benefit students from 1, 2 and 3 economic levels. 25% of donations received by the National Fund for the Financing of Science, Technology and Innovation, Francisco José de Caldas Fund, that are destined to the financing of science, technology and innovation projects.	Law 1955 of 2019	171	

ID	Type	Tax Expenditure	Legal Reference (Law/Article)		Revenue forgone estimate available
C5	Tax credit	**Donations to support science, technology and innovation (25%).** Tax Credit equivalent to 25% of the value of donations received by the National Financing Fund for the Science, Technology and Innovation, Francisco José de Caldas Fund, aimed at financing of Science, Technology and Innovation Programs and / or Projects, according to the conditions of the National Council of Tax Benefits in Science, Technology and Innovation (CNBT).	Law 1819 of 2016 Law 1955 of 2019	104 171	
C6	Tax credit	**Donations to the entrepreneurship and innovation agency (25%).**Tax credit of 25% of the donations made to the entrepreneurship and innovation agency of the government *iNNpulsa.*	Law 2069 of 2020	41	
C7	Tax credit	**Input VAT paid on fixed capital assets.** Capital goods input VAT paid on the import, formation, construction or acquisition of real productive fixed assets can be credited in the tax year in which they pay the VAT or in any subsequent tax years.	Law 2010 of 2019	95	
C8	Tax credit	**Investment in research, technological development and innovation (25%).** Tax credit equivalent to 25% of the value of investments made in research, technological development and innovation, according to the conditions of the National Council of Tax Benefits in Science, Technology and Innovation (CNBT). The excess originated in the tax credit can be taken in the 4 taxable periods to the one in which the investment was made.	Law 1819 of 2016 Law 1955 of 2019	104 171	X
C9	Tax credit	**Remuneration to the employment with a doctorate degree.** 25% of the remuneration corresponding to the employment of personnel with a doctorate degree in income-contributing companies, as long as the criteria and conditions defined by the CNBT for this purpose are met and their employment is associated with the development of activities of R+D+i. (Research + Development + Innovation)	Law 1955 of 2019	171	
C10	Tax credit	**Local turnover tax (50%-100%).** 50% of local turnover tax (municipal tax) paid in the corresponding tax year (2020 and 2021). 100% of local turnover tax (municipal tax) paid from 2022.	Law 2010 of 2019	86	

ID	Type	Tax Expenditure	Legal Reference (Law/Article)		Revenue forgone estimate available
C11	Tax credit	**Scholarships and support for talented athletes.** Tax credit for agreements with Coldeportes to assign study scholarships and support for talented athletes or sports reserves.	Law 1955 of 2019	190	
SR1	Special regime / Increased rate (Negative TE)	**Withholding tax (CIT recapture tax)** Dividends, are taxed first at the CIT rate of 32% in 2020, (31% in 2021 and 30% as from 2022 onwards) and then again at a withholding tax rate of 10% for dividends exceeding 300 UVTs while dividends below that amount are not taxed.	Law 1819 of 2016 Law 2010 of 2019	6 35	
SR2	Special regime	**Simple Regime (RST).** The SIMPLE regime is a preferential tax regime for small and medium enterprises.	Law 2010 of 2019	74	

Annex E. List of Tax Expenditures in the Value-Added Tax

This Annex includes the complete list of Value-Added Tax Expenditures that were identified in Colombia as part of the project.

Table A E.1. Identified Tax Expenditures in the Value-Added Tax

ID	Type	Tax Expenditure	Legal Reference (Law/Identifier/Date)	
1	Exclusion (goods)	Live swine	Art. 424 CTC	01.03
2	Exclusion (goods)	Live sheep and goats	Art. 424 CTC	01.04
3	Exclusion (goods)	Live poultry, that is to say, fowls of the species Gallus domesticus, ducks, geese, turkeys and guinea fowls.	Art. 424 CTC	01.05
4	Exclusion (goods)	Other live animals	Art. 424 CTC	01.06

ID	Type	Tax Expenditure	Legal Reference (Law/Identifier/Date)	
5	Exclusion (goods)	Live fish except ornamental fish of subheadings 03.01.11.00.00 and 03.01.19.00.00.	Art. 424 CTC	03.01
6	Exclusion (goods)	Albacore or long finned tunas	Art. 424 CTC	03.03.41.00.00
7	Exclusion (goods)	Yellowfin tunas	Art. 424 CTC	03.03.42.00.00
8	Exclusion (goods)	Atlantic and Pacific bluefin tunas	Art. 424 CTC	03.03.45.00.00
9	Exclusion (goods)	Fish, dried, salted or in brine; smoked fish, whether or not cooked before or during the smoking process	Art. 424 CTC	03.05
10	Exclusion (goods)	Products consisting of natural milk constituents,	Art. 424 CTC	04.04.90.00.00

ID	Type	Tax Expenditure	Legal Reference (Law/Identifier/Date)	
11	Exclusion (goods)	Natural honey	Art. 424 CTC	04.09
12	Exclusion (goods)	Bovine semen	Art. 424 CTC	05.11.10.00.00
13	Exclusion (goods)	Bulbs, tubers, tuberous roots, corms, crowns and rhizomes, dormant, in growth or in flower; chicory plants and roots other than roots of heading 12.12	Art. 424 CTC	06.01
14	Exclusion (goods)	Other live plants (including their roots), cuttings and slips; mushroom spawn	Art. 424 CTC	06.02.90.90.00
15	Exclusion (goods)	Trees, shrubs and bushes, grafted or not, of kinds which bear edible fruit or nuts	Art. 424 CTC	06.02.20.00.00
16	Exclusion (goods)	Potatoes, fresh or chilled.	Art. 424 CTC	07.01

ID	Type	Tax Expenditure	Legal Reference (Law/Identifier/Date)	
17	Exclusion (goods)	Tomatoes, fresh or chilled.	Art. 424 CTC	07.02
18	Exclusion (goods)	Onions, shallots, garlic, leeks and other alliaceous vegetables, fresh or chilled.	Art. 424 CTC	07.03
19	Exclusion (goods)	Cabbages, cauliflowers, kohlrabi, kale and similar edible brassicas, fresh or chilled.	Art. 424 CTC	07.04
20	Exclusion (goods)	Lettuce (Lactuca sativa) and chicory (Cichorium spp.), fresh or chilled.	Art. 424 CTC	07.05
21	Exclusion (goods)	Carrots, turnips, salad beetroot, salsify, celeriac, radishes and similar edible roots, fresh or chilled.	Art. 424 CTC	07.06
22	Exclusion (goods)	Cucumbers and gherkins, fresh or chilled	Art. 424 CTC	07.07

ID	Type	Tax Expenditure	Legal Reference (Law/Identifier/Date)	
23	Exclusion (goods)	Leguminous vegetables, shelled or unshelled, fresh or chilled.	Art. 424 CTC	07.08
24	Exclusion (goods)	Other vegetables, fresh or chilled.	Art. 424 CTC	07.09
25	Exclusion (goods)	Dried vegetables, whole, cut, sliced, broken or in powder, but not further prepared.	Art. 424 CTC	07.12
26	Exclusion (goods)	Dried leguminous vegetables, shelled, whether or not skinned or split.	Art. 424 CTC	07.13
27	Exclusion (goods)	Manioc, arrowroot, salep, Jerusalem artichokes, sweet potatoes and similar roots and tubers with high starch or inulin content, fresh, chilled, frozen or dried, whether or not sliced or in the form of pellets; sago pith.	Art. 424 CTC	07.14
28	Exclusion (goods)	Coconuts, Brazil nuts and cashew nuts, fresh or dried, whether or not shelled or peeled in the inner shell	Art. 424 CTC	08.01.12.00.00

ID	Type	Tax Expenditure	Legal Reference (Law/Identifier/Date)	
29	Exclusion (goods)	Other coconuts	Art. 424 CTC	08.01.19.00.00
30	Exclusion (goods)	Bananas, including plantains, fresh or dried.	Art. 424 CTC	08.03
31	Exclusion (goods)	Dates, figs, pineapples, avocados, guavas, mangoes and mangosteens, fresh or dried.	Art. 424 CTC	08.04
32	Exclusion (goods)	Citrus fruit, fresh or dried.	Art. 424 CTC	08.05
33	Exclusion (goods)	Grapes, fresh or dried.	Art. 424 CTC	08.06
34	Exclusion (goods)	Melons (including watermelons) and papaws (papayas), fresh.	Art. 424 CTC	08.07

ID	Type	Tax Expenditure	Legal Reference (Law/Identifier/Date)	
35	Exclusion (goods)	Apples, pears and quinces, fresh.	Art. 424 CTC	08.08
36	Exclusion (goods)	Apricots, cherries, peaches (including nectarines), plums and sloes, fresh.	Art. 424 CTC	08.09
37	Exclusion (goods)	Other fruit, fresh.	Art. 424 CTC	08.10
38	Exclusion (goods)	Coffee not roasted, not decaffeinated	Art. 424 CTC	09.01.11
39	Exclusion (goods)	Seeds of coriander : Neither crushed nor ground	Art. 424 CTC	09.09.21.10.00
40	Exclusion (goods)	Durum wheat	Art. 424 CTC	10.01.11.00.00

ID	Type	Tax Expenditure	Legal Reference (Law/Identifier/Date)	
41	Exclusion (goods)	Other durum wheat seeds	Art. 424 CTC	10.01.91.00.00
42	Exclusion (goods)	Rye seed	Art. 424 CTC	10.02.10.00.00
43	Exclusion (goods)	Barley	Art. 424 CTC	10.03
44	Exclusion (goods)	Oats seed	Art. 424 CTC	10.04.10.00.00
45	Exclusion (goods)	Corn seed	Art. 424 CTC	10.05.10.00.00
46	Exclusion (goods)	Corn for human consumption	Art. 424 CTC	10.05.90

ID	Type	Tax Expenditure	Legal Reference (Law/Identifier/Date)	
47	Exclusion (goods)	Rice	Art. 424 CTC	10.06
48	Exclusion (goods)	Rice seed	Art. 424 CTC	10.06.10.10.00
49	Exclusion (goods)	Rice in the husk (paddy or rough)	Art. 424 CTC	10.06.10.90.00
50	Exclusion (goods)	Grain sorghum seed	Art. 424 CTC	10.07.10.00.00
51	Exclusion (goods)	Maize (corn) hulled, pearled, sliced or kibbled for human consumption	Art. 424 CTC	11.04.23.00.00
52	Exclusion (goods)	Soya beans seeds	Art. 424 CTC	12.01.10.00.00

ID	Type	Tax Expenditure	Legal Reference (Law/Identifier/Date)	
53	Exclusion (goods)	Ground-nuts seeds	Art. 424 CTC	12.02.30.00.00
54	Exclusion (goods)	Copra	Art. 424 CTC	12.03
55	Exclusion (goods)	Linseed, whether or not broken	Art. 424 CTC	12.04.00.10.00
56	Exclusion (goods)	Rape or colza seeds, whether or not broken	Art. 424 CTC	12.05
57	Exclusion (goods)	Sunflower seeds, whether or not broken.	Art. 424 CTC	12.06.00.10.00
58	Exclusion (goods)	Palm nuts and kerne seeds	Art. 424 CTC	12.07.10.10.00

ID	Type	Tax Expenditure	Legal Reference (Law/Identifier/Date)	
59	Exclusion (goods)	Cotton seeds	Art. 424 CTC	12.07.21.00.00
60	Exclusion (goods)	Castor oil seeds	Art. 424 CTC	12.07.30.10.00
61	Exclusion (goods)	Sesamum seeds	Art. 424 CTC	12.07.40.10.00
62	Exclusion (goods)	Mustard seed	Art. 424 CTC	12.07.50.10.00
63	Exclusion (goods)	Safflower (Carthamus tinctorius) seed	Art. 424 CTC	12.07.60.10.00
64	Exclusion (goods)	Melon seeds	Art. 424 CTC	12.07.70.10.00

ID	Type	Tax Expenditure	Legal Reference (Law/Identifier/Date)	
65	Exclusion (goods)	Other melon seeds	Art. 424 CTC	12.07.99.10.00
66	Exclusion (goods)	Seeds, fruit and spores, of a kind used for sowing	Art. 424 CTC	12.09
67	Exclusion (goods)	Fescue seeds	Art. 424 CTC	12.12.93.00.00
68	Exclusion (goods)	Cane or beet sugar and chemically pure sucrose, in solid form.	Art. 424 CTC	17.01.13.00.00
69	Exclusion (goods)	Cocoa beans, whole or broken, raw or roasted.	Art. 424 CTC	18.01.00.11.00
70	Exclusion (goods)	Cocoa beans, whole or broken, raw or roasted.	Art. 424 CTC	18.01.00.19.00

ID	Type	Tax Expenditure	Legal Reference (Law/Identifier/Date)	
71	Exclusion (goods)	Bienestarina.	Art. 424 CTC	19.01.10.91.00
72	Exclusion (goods)	Milk based artisanal products	Art. 424 CTC	19.01.90.20.00
73	Exclusion (goods)	Bread, pastry, cakes, biscuits and other bakers' wares, whether or not containing cocoa; communion wafers, empty cachets of a kind suitable for pharmaceutical use, sealing wafers, rice paper and similar products	Art. 424 CTC	19.05
74	Exclusion (goods)	Jams, fruit jellies, marmalades, fruit or nut purée and fruit or nut pastes, obtained by cooking, whether or not containing added sugar or other sweetening matter	Art. 424 CTC	20.07
75	Exclusion (goods)	Waters, including natural or artificial mineral waters and aerated waters, not containing added sugar or other sweetening matter nor flavored; ice and snow	Art. 424 CTC	22.01
76	Exclusion (goods)	Salt (including table salt and denatured salt) and pure sodium chloride, whether or not in aqueous solution or containing added anti-caking or free-flowing agents; sea water.	Art. 424 CTC	25.01

ID	Type	Tax Expenditure	Legal Reference (Law/Identifier/Date)	
77	Exclusion (goods)	Sulphur of all kinds, other than sublimed sulphur, precipitated sulphur and colloidal sulphur.	Art. 424 CTC	25.03
78	Exclusion (goods)	Natural calcium phosphates, natural aluminium calcium phosphates and phosphatic chalk	Art. 424 CTC	25.10
79	Exclusion (goods)	Dolomite, whether or not calcined or sintered, including dolomite roughly trimmed or merely cut, by sawing or otherwise, into blocks or slabs of a rectangular (including square) shape	Art. 424 CTC	25.18.10.00.00
80	Exclusion (goods)	Coal; briquettes, ovoids and similar solid fuels manufactured from coa	Art. 424 CTC	27.01
81	Exclusion (goods)	Coke and semi-coke of coal, of lignite or of peat, whether or not agglomerated; retort carbon	Art. 424 CTC	27.04.00.10.00
82	Exclusion (goods)	Coke and semi-coke of coal, of lignite or of peat, whether or not agglomerated; retort carbon	Art. 424 CTC	27.04.00.20.00

ID	Type	Tax Expenditure	Legal Reference (Law/Identifier/Date)	
83	Exclusion (goods)	Liquefied natural gas	Art. 424 CTC	27.11.11.00.00
84	Exclusion (goods)	Propane gas	Art. 424 CTC	27.11.12.00.00
85	Exclusion (goods)	Liquefied butanes	Art. 424 CTC	27.11.13.00.00
86	Exclusion (goods)	Natural gas in gaseous state	Art. 424 CTC	27.11.21.00.00
87	Exclusion (goods)	Propane gas and butane gas in gaseous state	Art. 424 CTC	27.11.29
88	Exclusion (goods)	Electrical energy	Art. 424 CTC	27.16

ID	Type	Tax Expenditure	Legal Reference (Law/Identifier/Date)	
89	Exclusion (goods)	Radiative material for medical purposes	Art. 424 CTC	28.44.40
90	Exclusion (goods)	Wadding, gauze, bandages and similar articles (for example, dressings, adhesive plasters, poultices), impregnated or coated with pharmaceutical substances or put up in forms or packing for retail sale for medical, surgical, dental or veterinary purposes	Art. 424 CTC	30.05
91	Exclusion (goods)	Animal or vegetable fertilisers, whether or not mixed together or chemically treated; fertilisers produced by the mixing or chemical treatment of animal or vegetable products.	Art. 424 CTC	31.01
92	Exclusion (goods)	Mineral or chemical fertilisers, nitrogenous.	Art. 424 CTC	31.02
93	Exclusion (goods)	Mineral or chemical fertilisers, phosphatic	Art. 424 CTC	31.03
94	Exclusion (goods)	Mineral or chemical fertilisers, potassic	Art. 424 CTC	31.04

ID	Type	Tax Expenditure	Legal Reference (Law/Identifier/Date)	
95	Exclusion (goods)	Mineral or chemical fertilisers containing two or three of the fertilising elements nitrogen, phosphorus and potassium; other fertilisers; goods of this Chapter in tablets or similar forms or in packages of a gross weight not exceeding 10 kg	Art. 424 CTC	31.05
96	Exclusion (goods)	Insecticides, rodenticides, fungicides, herbicides, anti-sprouting products and plant-growth regulators, disinfectants and similar products, put up in forms or packings for retail sale or as preparations or articles (for example, sulphur-treated bands, wicks and candles, and fly-papers)	Art. 424 CTC	38.08
97	Exclusion (goods)	Diagnostic or laboratory reagents on a backing, prepared diagnostic or laboratory reagents whether or not on a backing, whether or not put up in the form of kits, other than those of heading 30.06; certified reference materials	Art. 424 CTC	38.22.00.90.00
98	Exclusion (goods)	Natural rubber, balata, gutta-percha, guayule, chicle and similar natural gums, in primary forms or in plates, sheets or strip.	Art. 424 CTC	40.01
99	Exclusion (goods)	New pneumatic tires, of rubber of a kind used on agricultural or forestry vehicles and machines	Art. 424 CTC	40.11.70.00.00
100	Exclusion (goods)	Sheath contraceptives	Art. 424 CTC	40.14.10.00.00

ID	Type	Tax Expenditure	Legal Reference (Law/Identifier/Date)	
101	Exclusion (goods)	Newsprint, in rolls or sheets.	Art. 424 CTC	48.01.00.00.00
102	Exclusion (goods)	Uncoated paper and paperboard, of a kind used for writing, printing or other graphic purposes, and non-perforated punch cards and punch tape paper, in rolls or rectangular (including square) sheets, of any size, other than paper of heading 48.01 or 48.03; hand-made paper and paperboard in rolls	Art. 424 CTC	48.02.61.90.00
103	Exclusion (goods)	Coconut, abaca (Manila hemp or Musa textiles Nee), ramie and other vegetable textile fibres, not elsewhere specified or included, raw or processed but not spun; tow, noils and waste of these fibres (including yarn waste and garnetted stock).	Art. 424 CTC	53.05.00.90.00
104	Exclusion (goods)	Woven fabrics of other vegetable textile fibres; woven fabrics of paper yarn.	Art. 424 CTC	53.11.00.00.00
105	Exclusion (goods)	Knotted netting of twine, cordage or rope; made up fishing nets and other made up nets, of textile materials - made up fishing nets	Art. 424 CTC	56.08.11.00.00
106	Exclusion (goods)	Packaging made in jute, hemp or fique	Art. 424 CTC	59.11.90.90.00

ID	Type	Tax Expenditure	Legal Reference (Law/Identifier/Date)	
107	Exclusion (goods)	Sacks and bags, of a kind used for the packing of goods of jute	Art. 424 CTC	63.05.10.10.00
108	Exclusion (goods)	Sacks and bags, of a kind used for the packing of goods of hemp	Art. 424 CTC	63.05.90.10.00
109	Exclusion (goods)	Sacks and bags, of a kind used for the packing of goods of fique	Art. 424 CTC	63.05.90.90.00
110	Exclusion (goods)	Ceramic building bricks, flooring blocks, support or filler tiles and the like.	Art. 424 CTC	69.04.10.00.00
111	Exclusion (goods)	Coins of legal tender	Art. 424 CTC	71.18.90.00.00
112	Exclusion (goods)	Outboard motors up to 115HP.	Art. 424 CTC	84.07.21.00.00

ID	Type	Tax Expenditure	Legal Reference (Law/Identifier/Date)	
113	Exclusion (goods)	Diesel marine propulsion engines up to 150H P.	Art. 424 CTC	84.08.10.00.00
114	Exclusion (goods)	Agricultural or horticultural mechanical appliances (whether or not hand-operated) for projecting, dispersing or spraying liquids or powders; fire extinguishers, whether or not charged; spray guns and similar appliances; steam or sand blasting machines and similar jet projecting machines	Art. 424 CTC	84.24.82.21.00
115	Exclusion (goods)	Other dispersing systems	Art. 424 CTC	84.24.82.29.00
116	Exclusion (goods)	Aspersores y goteros, para sistemas de riego.	Art. 424 CTC	84.24.90.10.00
117	Exclusion (goods)	Other mowers, including cutter bars for tractor mounting	Art. 424 CTC	84.33.20.00.00
118	Exclusion (goods)	Other haymaking machinery	Art. 424 CTC	84.33.30.00.00

ID	Type	Tax Expenditure	Legal Reference (Law/Identifier/Date)	
119	Exclusion (goods)	Straw or fodder balers, including pick-up balers	Art. 424 CTC	84.33.40.00.00
120	Exclusion (goods)	Combine harvester-threshers	Art. 424 CTC	84.33.51.00.00
121	Exclusion (goods)	Other threshing machinery	Art. 424 CTC	84.33.52.00.00
122	Exclusion (goods)	Root or tuber harvesting machines	Art. 424 CTC	84.33.53.00.00
123	Exclusion (goods)	Other harvesting machinery; threshing machinery	Art. 424 CTC	84.33.59
124	Exclusion (goods)	Machines for cleaning, sorting or grading eggs, fruit or other agricultural produce	Art. 424 CTC	84.33.60

ID	Type	Tax Expenditure	Legal Reference (Law/Identifier/Date)	
125	Exclusion (goods)	Parts of harvesting or threshing machinery, including straw or fodder balers; grass or hay mowers; machines for cleaning, sorting or grading eggs, fruit or other agricultural produce	Art. 424 CTC	84.33.90
126	Exclusion (goods)	Machinery for preparing animal feeding stuffs	Art. 424 CTC	84.36.10.00.00
127	Exclusion (goods)	Other agricultural, horticultural, forestry, poultry-keeping or bee-keeping machinery, including germination plant fitted with mechanical or thermal equipment; poultry incubators and brooders.	Art. 424 CTC	84.36.80
128	Exclusion (goods)	Other agricultural, horticultural, forestry, poultry-keeping or bee-keeping machinery, including germination plant fitted with mechanical or thermal equipment; poultry incubators and brooders.	Art. 424 CTC	84.36.99.00.00
129	Exclusion (goods)	Machines for cleaning, sorting or grading seed, grain or dried leguminous vegetables	Art. 424 CTC	84.37.10
130	Exclusion (goods)	Tractors for agricultural use of the subheadings 87.01.91.00.00, 87.01.92.00.00, 87.01.93.00.00, 87.01.94.00.00, 87.01.95.00.00.	Art. 424 CTC	87.01

ID	Type	Tax Expenditure	Legal Reference (Law/Identifier/Date)	
131	Exclusion (goods)	Carriages for disabled persons, whether or not motorised or otherwise mechanically propelled.	Art. 424 CTC	87.13
132	Exclusion (goods)	Parts and accessories of vehicles or carriages for disabled persons	Art. 424 CTC	87.14.20.00.00
133	Exclusion (goods)	Self-loading or self-unloading trailers and semi-trailers for agricultural purposes	Art. 424 CTC	87.16.20.00.00
134	Exclusion (goods)	Contact lenses	Art. 424 CTC	90.01.30.00.00
135	Exclusion (goods)	Spectacle lenses of glass	Art. 424 CTC	90.01.40.00.00
136	Exclusion (goods)	Spectacle lenses of other materials	Art. 424 CTC	90.01.50.00.00

ID	Type	Tax Expenditure	Legal Reference (Law/Identifier/Date)	
137	Exclusion (goods)	Syringes, needles, catheters, cannulae for renal dialysis	Art. 424 CTC	90.18.39.00.00
138	Exclusion (goods)	Blood infusion equipment	Art. 424 CTC	90.18.90.90.00
139	Exclusion (goods)	Orthopaedic appliances, including crutches, surgical belts and trusses; splints and other fracture appliances; artificial parts of the body; hearing aids and other appliances which are worn or carried, or implanted in the body, to compensate for a defect or disability	Art. 424 CTC	90.21
140	Exclusion (goods)	Pencils and crayons, with leads encased in a sheath	Art. 424 CTC	96.09.10.00.00
141	Exclusion (goods)	Chemical raw materials for the production of pesticides and insecticides of heading 38.08 and of fertilizers of headings 31.01 to 31.05 and for the production of medicines of headings 29.36, 29.41, 30.01, 30.03, 30.04 and 30.06.	Art. 424 CTC	
142	Exclusion (goods)	The raw materials for the production of vaccines	Art. 424 CTC	

ID	Type	Tax Expenditure	Legal Reference (Law/Identifier/Date)	
143	Exclusion (goods)	All nutritional support products (including dietary supplements and nutritional supplements in liquid, solid, granulated, gaseous, powder presentations) of the special regimen intended to be administered entirely, for patients with specific pathologies or with special conditions; and foods for special medical purposes for patients requiring short- or long-term enteral tube nutrition. Classified by subheadings 21.06.90.79.00, 21.06.90.90.00 and 22.02.90.99.00.	Art. 424 CTC	
144	Exclusion (goods)	Contraceptive devices for female use.	Art. 424 CTC	
145	Exclusion (goods)	Desktop or laptop computers, which value does not exceed 50 UVT (USD 465 approx.)	Art. 424 CTC	
146	Exclusion (goods)	Smart mobile devices (tablets and cell phones) whose value does not exceed 22 UVT (USD 210 approx.)	Art. 424 CTC	
147	Exclusion (goods)	The national or imported equipment and elements that are used for the construction, installation, assembly and operation of control and monitoring systems, necessary for compliance with the provisions, regulations and environmental standards in force, for which such condition must be accredited before the Ministry of Environment and Sustainable Development.	Art. 424 CTC	
148	Exclusion (goods)	Food for human and animal consumption that are imported from the countries near to the departments of Vichada, Guajira, Guainía and Vaupés, as long as they are used exclusively for local consumption in those departments.	Art. 424 CTC	

ID	Type	Tax Expenditure	Legal Reference (Law/Identifier/Date)	
141	Exclusion (goods)	Food for human consumption donated to food banks, in accordance with the regulations issued by the government.	Art. 424 CTC	
142	Exclusion (goods)	Vehicles, motor vehicles, intended for public passenger transport, intended only for replacement. Small transporters who own less than 3 vehicles will be entitled to this benefit and only for the purposes of the replacement of only one, and for a single time. This benefit will be valid until 2019.	Art. 424 CTC	
143	Exclusion (goods)	Objects with artistic, cultural and historical interest purchased by the museums part of the National Museum Network	Art. 424 CTC	
144	Exclusion (goods)	Sale of immovable property	Art. 424 CTC	
145	Exclusion (goods)	Human and animal consumption, clothing, hygiene items and medicines for human or veterinary use, construction materials that are introduced and commercialized to the departments of Guainía, Guaviare, Vaupés and Vichada, as long as they are used exclusively for consumption within the Department.	Art. 424 CTC	
146	Exclusion (goods)	The aviation fuel supplied for passenger and cargo air transport service with origin and destination to the departments of Guainía, Amazonas, Vaupés, San Andrés Islas and Providencia, Arauca and Vichada.	Art. 424 CTC	

ID	Type	Tax Expenditure	Legal Reference (Law/Identifier/Date)	
147	Exclusion (goods)	Products that are purchased or introduced to the department of Amazonas within the framework of the Colombian-Peruvian agreement and the agreement with the Federative Republic of Brazil.	Art. 424 CTC	
148	Exclusion (goods)	The sale of machinery and equipment for the development of projects or activities that are registered in the national registry for the reduction of greenhouse gas emissions defined in article 155 of Law 1753 of 2015, which generate and certify reductions in Greenhouse Gases - GHG, according to regulations issued by the Ministry of the Environment and Sustainable Development.	Art. 424 CTC	
141	Exclusion (goods)	Bicycles, electric bicycles, electric scooters, skates, skateboards, electric skateboards, scooters, and electric scooters, up to 50 UVT (USD 470 approx.)	Art. 424 CTC	
142	Exclusion (goods)	Goods sold by distributors, engaged in the wholesale marketing of books, magazines, brochures or serial collectibles of a scientific or cultural nature.	Art. 424 CTC	
1	Exclusion (services)	Medical, dental, hospital, clinical and laboratory services for human health.	Art. 476 CTC	
2	Exclusion (services)	The administration services of State funds and services related to social security in accordance with the provisions of Law 100 of 1993.	Art. 476 CTC	

ID	Type	Tax Expenditure	Legal Reference (Law/Identifier/Date)	
3	Exclusion (services)	The mandatory health plans of the social security system in health issued by entities authorized by the National Superintendency of Health, the services provided by occupational risk managers and insurance and reinsurance services for disability and survivors,	Art. 476 CTC	
4	Exclusion (services)	Commissions for intermediation for the placement of health plans of the general social security system in health issued by entities legally authorized by the National Superintendency of Health, which are not subject to VAT.	Art. 476 CTC	
5	Exclusion (services)	The education services provided by preschool, primary, middle and intermediate, higher and special or non-formal education establishments, recognized as such by the government, and the education services provided by individuals to those establishments. Also excluded are the services provided by educational establishments related to restaurants, coffee shops and transportation, as well as those provided pursuant to Laws 30 of 1992 and 115 of 1994.	Art. 476 CTC	
6	Exclusion (services)	Virtual education services for the development of digital content.	Art. 476 CTC	
7	Exclusion (services)	Internet connection and access services for residential users in level 3	Art. 476 CTC	
8	Exclusion (services)	In the case of local telephone service, the first 325 monthly minutes of the local telephone service billed to users of levels 1, 2 and 3 and the telephone service provided from public telephones are excluded from the tax.	Art. 476 CTC	

ID	Type	Tax Expenditure	Legal Reference (Law/Identifier/Date)	
9	Exclusion (services)	The public, land, river and maritime transport service of people in the national territory, and the national and international public or private transport of maritime, river, land and air cargo. Likewise, the transport of gas and hydrocarbons is excluded.	Art. 476 CTC	
10	Exclusion (services)	National air transport of passengers to or from national routes where there is no organized land transport.	Art. 476 CTC	
11	Exclusion (services)	Public energy services. Energy and utilities of energy based on gas or other inputs.	Art. 476 CTC	
12	Exclusion (services)	Water for the provision of the public aqueduct and sewerage service, public aqueduct and sewerage services, public cleaning services and public garbage collection services.	Art. 476 CTC	
13	Exclusion (services)	Gas for the provision of the home gas public service and home gas service, either conducted by pipeline or distributed in cylinders.	Art. 476 CTC	
14	Exclusion (services)	Food services, contracted with public resources, destined for the penitentiary system, social assistance, public education schools, the military forces, national police, child development centers, public geriatric centers, public hospitals, and community kitchens.	Art. 476 CTC	

ID	Type	Tax Expenditure	Legal Reference (Law/Identifier/Date)	
15	Exclusion (services)	The property rental service for housing and the rental of spaces for exhibitions and national craft shows, including artistic and cultural events.	Art. 476 CTC	
16	Exclusion (services)	Interest and financial income from credit operations, provided that they are not part of the taxable base indicated in article 447, and financial leasing (leasing).	Art. 476 CTC	
17	Exclusion (services)	Intermediation services for the payment of incentives or conditional cash transfers under government's social programs.	Art. 476 CTC	
18	Exclusion (services)	Tickets to the cinema, sporting and cultural events, including musicals and family recreation, and bull, horse and canine shows.	Art. 476 CTC	
19	Exclusion (services)	Funeral services, cremation, burial and exhumation of corpses, rental and maintenance of tombs and mausoleums.	Art. 476 CTC	
20	Exclusion (services)	Acquisition of software licenses for the commercial development of digital content, in accordance with the regulations issued by the Ministry of Information Technologies and Communications.	Art. 476 CTC	

ID	Type	Tax Expenditure	Legal Reference (Law/Identifier/Date)	
21	Exclusion (services)	Provision of web pages, hosting, cloud computing (cloud computing)	Art. 476 CTC	
22	Exclusion (services)	The commissions paid for the services provided for the development of asset securitization processes through universalities and trusts whose payment is made exclusively from the resources of such universalities or trusts.	Art. 476 CTC	
23	Exclusion (services)	The commissions received by trust companies, investment management companies and stock brokers for the administration of collective investment funds	Art. 476 CTC	
24	Exclusion (services)	Some agricultural services, provided that they are intended for the adaptation of land, agricultural and fishing production and the marketing of the respective products.	Art. 476 CTC	
25	Exclusion (services)	The commercialization of live animals and the slaughter service.	Art. 476 CTC	
26	Exclusion (services)	Hotel and tourism services that are provided in special customs regime zones	Art. 476 CTC	

ID	Type	Tax Expenditure	Legal Reference (Law/Identifier/Date)	
27	Exclusion (services)	Exchange operations of purchase and sale of currencies, as well as exchange operations on financial derivative instruments	Art. 476 CTC	
28	Exclusion (services)	The commissions received for the use of credit and debit cards.	Art. 476 CTC	
29	Exclusion (services)	Sports promotion and development services provided by sports clubs defined in article 2 of Decree Law 1228 of 1995.	Art. 476 CTC	
30	Exclusion (services)	The repair and maintenance services of ships and naval parts, both maritime and fluvial under the Colombian flag,	Art. 476 CTC	
31	Exclusion (services)	Advertising services in newspapers that register advertising sales as of December 31 of the immediately preceding year of less than 180 000 UVT. Advertising on radio stations whose sales are less than 30 000 UVT as of December 31 of the immediately preceding year and regional television channel programmers whose sales are less than 60 000 UVT as of December 31 of the immediately preceding yea	Art. 476 CTC	
32	Exclusion (services)	Reinsurance contract brokerage services.	Art. 476 CTC	

ID	Type	Tax Expenditure	Legal Reference (Law/Identifier/Date)	
33	Exclusion (services)	Services taxed under the "National Consumption Tax	Art. 426 CTC	
1	Exclusion (imports)	Imports of raw materials in exportation plans regulated in Decree 444 of 1967	Art. 428 CTC	
2	Exclusion (imports)	Imports for diplomatic missions use.	Art. 428 CTC	
3	Exclusion (imports)	Imports of weapons and war material for the national defense	Art. 428 CTC	
4	Exclusion (imports)	Temporary import of machinery for basic industries.	Art. 428 CTC	
5	Exclusion (imports)	Imports of machinery and equipment for recycling and waste disposal and treatment, water treatment, atmospheric emissions for the recovery of rivers and improved environment	Art. 428 CTC	

ID	Type	Tax Expenditure	Legal Reference (Law/Identifier/Date)	
6	Exclusion (imports)	Ordinary importation of industrial machinery that is not produced in the country, destined for the transformation of raw materials, by highly exporting users.	Art. 428 CTC	
7	Exclusion (imports)	The importation of goods and equipment under the development of international cooperation agreements, treaties or agreements in force for Colombia, destined for the government or for public law entities	Art. 428 CTC	
8	Exclusion (imports)	The importation of machinery and equipment for the development of projects or activities that are exporters of carbon emission reduction certificates and that contribute to reducing the emission of greenhouse gases and therefore to sustainable development.	Art. 428 CTC	
9	Exclusion (imports)	Imports of urgent postal traffic objects of less than USD 200	Art. 428 CTC	
1	Exemption (goods)	Live bovine animals.	Art. 477 CTC	01.02
2	Exemption (goods)	1 day old chicks	Art. 477 CTC	01.05.11.00.00

ID	Type	Tax Expenditure	Legal Reference (Law/Identifier/Date)	
3	Exemption (goods)	Meat of bovine animals, fresh or chilled.	Art. 477 CTC	02.01
4	Exemption (goods)	Meat of bovine animals, frozen.	Art. 477 CTC	02.02
5	Exemption (goods)	Meat of swine, fresh, chilled or frozen.	Art. 477 CTC	02.03
6	Exemption (goods)	Meat of sheep or goats, fresh, chilled or frozen	Art. 477 CTC	02.04
7	Exemption (goods)	Edible offal of bovine animals, swine, sheep, goats, horses, asses, mules or hinnies, fresh, chilled or frozen.	Art. 477 CTC	02.06
8	Exemption (goods)	Meat and edible offal, of the poultry of heading 01.05, fresh, chilled or frozen	Art. 477 CTC	02.07

ID	Type	Tax Expenditure	Legal Reference (Law/Identifier/Date)	
9	Exemption (goods)	Meat and edible meat offal, fresh, chilled or frozen of rabbits or hares	Art. 477 CTC	02.08.10.00.00
10	Exemption (goods)	Meat and edible meat offal, fresh, chilled or frozen of guinea pigs	Art. 477 CTC	02.08.90.00.00
11	Exemption (goods)	Fish, fresh or chilled, excluding fish fillets and other fish meat of heading 03.04.	Art. 477 CTC	03.02
12	Exemption (goods)	Fish, frozen, excluding fish fillets and other fish meat of heading 03.04. Except tuna of subheadings 03.03.41.00.00, 03.03.42.00.00 and 03.03.45.00.00.	Art. 477 CTC	03.03
13	Exemption (goods)	Fish fillets and other fish meat (whether or not minced), fresh, chilled or frozen	Art. 477 CTC	03.04
14	Exemption (goods)	Farmed shrimp	Art. 477 CTC	03.06

ID	Type	Tax Expenditure	Legal Reference (Law/Identifier/Date)	
15	Exemption (goods)	Milk and cream, not concentrated nor containing added sugar or other sweetening matter	Art. 477 CTC	04.01
16	Exemption (goods)	Milk and cream, concentrated or containing added sugar or other sweetening matter	Art. 477 CTC	04.02
17	Exemption (goods)	Cheese and curd Fresh (unripened or uncured) cheese, including whey cheese, and curd	Art. 477 CTC	04.06.10.00.00
18	Exemption (goods)	Fertilised eggs for incubation of fowls of the species Gallus domesticus	Art. 477 CTC	04.07.11.00.00
19	Exemption (goods)	Fertilised eggs for incubation of other birds	Art. 477 CTC	04.07.19.00.00
20	Exemption (goods)	Fresh eggs of fowls of the species Gallus domesticus	Art. 477 CTC	04.07.21.90.00

ID	Type	Tax Expenditure	Legal Reference (Law/Identifier/Date)	
21	Exemption (goods)	Fresh eggs of fowls of other birds	Art. 477 CTC	04.07.29.90.00
22	Exemption (goods)	Rice for human consumption (except for paddy rice of heading 10.06.10.90.00 and rice for sowing of heading 10.06.10.10.00, which retain the quality of VAT excluded)	Art. 477 CTC	10.06
23	Exemption (goods)	Milk formulas for children up to 12 months of age, only formula or humanized milk.	Art. 477 CTC	19.01.10.10.00
24	Exemption (goods)	Only infant milk based formulas.	Art. 477 CTC	19.01.10.99.00
25	Exemption (goods)	Provitamins and vitamins, natural or reproduced by synthesis (including natural concentrates), derivatives thereof used primarily as vitamins, and intermixtures of the foregoing, whether or not in any solvent.	Art. 477 CTC	29.36
26	Exemption (goods)	Antibiotics.	Art. 477 CTC	29.41

ID	Type	Tax Expenditure	Legal Reference (Law/Identifier/Date)	
27	Exemption (goods)	Glands and other organs for organo-therapeutic uses, dried, whether or not powdered; extracts of glands or other organs or of their secretions for organo-therapeutic uses; heparin and its salts; other human or animal substances prepared for therapeutic or prophylactic uses, not elsewhere specified or included.	Art. 477 CTC	30.01
28	Exemption (goods)	Human blood; animal blood prepared for therapeutic, prophylactic or diagnostic uses; antisera, other blood fractions and immunological products, whether or not modified or obtained by means of biotechnological processes; vaccines, toxins, cultures of micro-organisms (excluding yeasts) and similar products; cell cultures, whether or not modified.	Art. 477 CTC	30.02
29	Exemption (goods)	Medicaments (excluding goods of heading 30.02, 30.05 or 30.06) consisting of two or more constituents which have been mixed together for therapeutic or prophylactic uses, not put up in measured doses or in forms or packing for retail sale	Art. 477 CTC	30.03
30	Exemption (goods)	Medicaments (excluding goods of heading 30.02, 30.05 or 30.06) consisting of mixed or unmixed products for therapeutic or prophylactic uses, put up in measured doses (including those in the form of transdermal administration systems) or in forms or packing for retail sale	Art. 477 CTC	30.04
31	Exemption (goods)	Pharmaceutical goods specified in Note 4 to this Chapter	Art. 477 CTC	30.06
32	Exemption (goods)	Power inverter for solar power system with panels	Art. 477 CTC	85.04.40.90.90

ID	Type	Tax Expenditure	Legal Reference (Law/Identifier/Date)	
33	Exemption (goods)	Solar panels	Art. 477 CTC	85.41.40.10.00
34	Exemption (goods)	Charge controller for solar energy system with panels.	Art. 477 CTC	90.32.89.90.00
35	Exemption (goods)	Weapons of war, except revolvers, pistols and knives, for the exclusive use of the Military forces and the national police	Art. 477 CTC	93.01
36	Exemption (goods)	Sanitary napkins and pads	Art. 477 CTC	96.19
37	Exemption (goods)	Fuel alcohol destined to be mixed with gasoline for motor vehicles; and biofuel of vegetable or animal origin for use in diesel engines of national production destined to be mixed with diesel	Art. 477 CTC	
38	Exemption (goods)	Ammunition and war material or reserved and therefore for private use and the following items belonging to the Military Forces and the national police	Art. 477 CTC	

ID	Type	Tax Expenditure	Legal Reference (Law/Identifier/Date)	
39	Exemption (goods)	Complete passenger public transport motor vehicles and individually purchased motorized chassis and bodywork to form a new complete public passenger transport motor vehicle. This benefit will be applicable to sales made to small carriers that own up to two (2) vehicles and for the purposes of replacing one or two of their own vehicles, only once.	Art. 477 CTC	
40	Exemption (goods)	The motor vehicles of public or private service, of complete cargo transport and the chassis with motor and the bodywork purchased individually to make up a new complete motor vehicle of cargo transport of more than 10.5 tons of gross vehicle weight. This benefit will be applicable to sales made to small carriers that own up to two (2) vehicles and for the purposes of replacing one or two of their own vehicles, only once.	Art. 477 CTC	
41	Exemption (goods)	Bicycles and their parts; motorcycles and their parts and motorcycles and their parts, which are introduced and sold in the departments of Amazonas, Guainía, Guaviare, Vaupés and Vichada, as long as they are intended exclusively for consumption within the same department and motorcycles and motorcycles are registered in the Department. The goods indicated above that are imported into the national customs territory and later exclusively destined to these departments will also be exempt.	Art. 477 CTC	
42	Exemption (goods)	Human and animal consumption, clothing, hygiene items and medicines for human or veterinary use, construction materials that are introduced and marketed to the department of Amazonas, as long as they are destined exclusively for consumption within the same department.	Art. 477 CTC	
43	Exemption (goods)	Books and magazines of a scientific and cultural nature,	Art. 477 CTC	
44	Exemption (goods)	Movable tangible property that is exported; (the retreading service and repair services to maritime vessels and aerodynamics, of foreign flag or registration), and the sale in the country of export goods to international marketing companies provided that they have to be effectively exported.	Art. 477 CTC	

ID	Type	Tax Expenditure	Legal Reference (Law/Identifier/Date)	
45	Exemption (goods)	Imports of goods and equipment for sports, health, scientific and technological research, and education, donated in favor of official or non-profit entities, by national persons or entities or by foreign entities, persons or governments.	Art. 477 CTC	
46	Exemption (goods)	Imports of goods and equipment for national security destined for the Public Force	Art. 477 CTC	
47	Exemption (goods)	Import of goods and equipment that are carried out in development of agreements, treaties, international and inter-institutional agreements or cooperation projects, donated in favor of g government or entities of public law of the national order	Art. 477 CTC	
1	Exemption (services)	Services that are provided in the country and are used exclusively abroad by companies or people without business or activities in Colombia	Art. 481 CTC	
2	Exemption (services)	Tourist services provided to residents abroad that are used in Colombian territory, originated in packages sold by operating agencies or hotels registered in the national tourism registry	Art. 481 CTC	
3	Exemption (services)	Tourist packages sold by hotels registered in the national tourism registry to operating agencies, provided that the tourist services have to be used in the national territory by residents abroad;	Art. 481 CTC	

ID	Type	Tax Expenditure	Legal Reference (Law/Identifier/Date)	
4	Exemption (services)	Internet connection and access services from fixed networks of residential subscribers in socioeconomic levels 1 and 2.	Art. 481 CTC	
1	Reduced rate (goods)	Coffee, whether or not roasted or decaffeinated; coffee husks and skins; coffee substitutes containing coffee in any proportion.	Art. 468-1 CTC	09.01
2	Reduced rate (goods)	Wheat and meslin.	Art. 468-1 CTC	10.01
3	Reduced rate (goods)	Rye	Art. 468-1 CTC	10.02.90.00.00
4	Reduced rate (goods)	Oats	Art. 468-1 CTC	10.04.90.00.00
5	Reduced rate (goods)	Maize (corn) for industrial purposes	Art. 468-1 CTC	10.05.90

ID	Type	Tax Expenditure	Legal Reference (Law/Identifier/Date)	
6	Reduced rate (goods)	Maize (corn) for industrial use	Art. 468-1 CTC	10.06
7	Reduced rate (goods)	Grain sorghum.	Art. 468-1 CTC	10.07.90.00.00
8	Reduced rate (goods)	Buckwheat, millet and canary seeds; other cereals	Art. 468-1 CTC	10.08
9	Reduced rate (goods)	Wheat or meslin flour	Art. 468-1 CTC	11.01.00.00.00
10	Reduced rate (goods)	Cereal flours other than of wheat or meslin	Art. 468-1 CTC	11.02
11	Reduced rate (goods)	Rolled or flaked grains of oats	Art. 468-1 CTC	11.04.12.00.00

ID	Type	Tax Expenditure	Legal Reference (Law/Identifier/Date)	
12	Reduced rate (goods)	Soya beans, whether or not broken.	Art. 468-1 CTC	12.01.90.00.00
13	Reduced rate (goods)	Palm nuts and kernel	Art. 468-1 CTC	12.07.10.90.00
14	Reduced rate (goods)	Cotton seeds	Art. 468-1 CTC	12.07.29.00.00
15	Reduced rate (goods)	Oil palm fruit	Art. 468-1 CTC	12.07.99.99.00
16	Reduced rate (goods)	Flours and meals of oil seeds or oleaginous fruits, other than those of mustard	Art. 468-1 CTC	12.08
17	Reduced rate (goods)	Crude oil, whether or not degummed	Art. 468-1 CTC	15.07.10.00.00

ID	Type	Tax Expenditure	Legal Reference (Law/Identifier/Date)	
18	Reduced rate (goods)	Palm crude oil	Art. 468-1 CTC	15.11.10.00.00
19	Reduced rate (goods)	Sunflower crude oil	Art. 468-1 CTC	15.12.11.10.00
20	Reduced rate (goods)	Cotto crude oil	Art. 468-1 CTC	15.12.21.00.00
21	Reduced rate (goods)	Palm kernel or babassu crude oil	Art. 468-1 CTC	15.13.21.10.00
22	Reduced rate (goods)	Low erucic acid rape or colza crude oil	Art. 468-1 CTC	15.14.11.00.00
23	Reduced rate (goods)	Maize (corn) crude oil	Art. 468-1 CTC	15.15.21.00.00

ID	Type	Tax Expenditure	Legal Reference (Law/Identifier/Date)	
24	Reduced rate (goods)	Sausages and similar products, of meat, meat offal, blood or insects; food preparations based on these products.	Art. 468-1 CTC	16.01
25	Reduced rate (goods)	Other prepared or preserved meat, meat offal, blood or insects	Art. 468-1 CTC	16.02
26	Reduced rate (goods)	Cane or beet sugar and chemically pure sucrose, in solid form	Art. 468-1 CTC	17.01
27	Reduced rate (goods)	Molasses resulting from the extraction or refining of sugar.	Art. 468-1 CTC	17.03
28	Reduced rate (goods)	Chocolate and other food preparations containing cocoa	Art. 468-1 CTC	18.06.32.00.90
29	Reduced rate (goods)	Uncooked pasta, not stuffed or otherwise prepared containing eggs	Art. 468-1 CTC	19.02.11.00.00

ID	Type	Tax Expenditure	Legal Reference (Law/Identifier/Date)	
30	Reduced rate (goods)	Pasta, whether or not cooked or stuffed (with meat or other substances) or otherwise prepared, such as spaghetti, macaroni, noodles, lasagna, gnocchi, ravioli, cannelloni; couscous, whether or not prepared	Art. 468-1 CTC	19.02.19.00.00
31	Reduced rate (goods)	Bakery products made of sagú, yuca or achira.	Art. 468-1 CTC	19.05
32	Reduced rate (goods)	Extracts, essences and concentrates, of coffee, and preparations with a basis of these extracts, essences or concentrates or with a basis of coffee	Art. 468-1 CTC	21.01.11 .00
33	Reduced rate (goods)	Stevia and natural sweeteners	Art. 468-1 CTC	21.06.90.61.00
34	Reduced rate (goods)	Artificial sweeteners	Art. 468-1 CTC	21.06.90.69.00
35	Reduced rate (goods)	Flours, meals and pellets, of meat or meat offal, of fish or of crustaceans, molluscs or other aquatic invertebrates, unfit for human consumption; greaves	Art. 468-1 CTC	23.01

ID	Type	Tax Expenditure	Legal Reference (Law/Identifier/Date)	
36	Reduced rate (goods)	Bran, sharps and other residues, whether or not in the form of pellets, derived from the sifting, milling or other working of cereals or of leguminous plants.	Art. 468-1 CTC	23.02
37	Reduced rate (goods)	Residues of starch manufacture and similar residues, beet-pulp, bagasse and other waste of sugar manufacture, brewing or distilling dregs and waste, whether or not in the form of pellets.	Art. 468-1 CTC	23.03
38	Reduced rate (goods)	Oil-cake and other solid residues, whether or not ground or in the form of pellets, resulting from the extraction of soybean oil.	Art. 468-1 CTC	23.04
39	Reduced rate (goods)	Oil-cake and other solid residues, whether or not ground or in the form of pellets, resulting from the extraction of ground-nut oil	Art. 468-1 CTC	23.05
40	Reduced rate (goods)	Oil-cake and other solid residues, whether or not ground or in the form of pellets, resulting from the extraction of vegetable or microbial fats or oils, other than those of heading 23.04 or 23.05	Art. 468-1 CTC	23.06
41	Reduced rate (goods)	Vegetable materials and vegetable waste, vegetable residues and by-products, whether or not in the form of pellets, of a kind used in animal feeding, not elsewhere specified or included.	Art. 468-1 CTC	23.08

ID	Type	Tax Expenditure	Legal Reference (Law/Identifier/Date)	
42	Reduced rate (goods)	Preparations of a kind used in animal feeding.	Art. 468-1 CTC	23.09
43	Reduced rate (goods)	Wood in the rough, whether or not stripped of bark or sapwood, or roughly squared.	Art. 468-1 CTC	44.03
44	Reduced rate (goods)	Cotton, not carded or combed	Art. 468-1 CTC	52.01
45	Reduced rate (goods)	Containers for compressed or liquefied gas, of iron or steel	Art. 468-1 CTC	73.11.00.10.00
46	Reduced rate (goods)	Hand tools, the following : spades, shovels, mattocks, picks, hoes, forks and rakes; axes, bill hooks and similar hewing tools; secateurs and pruners of any kind; scythes, sickles, hay knives, hedge shears, timber wedges and other tools of a kind used in agriculture, horticulture or forestry.	Art. 468-1 CTC	82.01
47	Reduced rate (goods)	Knives and cutting blades, for machines or for mechanical appliances for agricultural, horticultural or forestry machines	Art. 468-1 CTC	82.08.40.00.00

ID	Type	Tax Expenditure	Legal Reference (Law/Identifier/Date)	
48	Reduced rate (goods)	Carburators and their parts (spare parts) components of the vehicular gas plan.	Art. 468-1 CTC	84.09.91.60.00
49	Reduced rate (goods)	Equipment for the conversion of the fuel supply system for motor vehicles to dual use (gas / gasoline) components of the vehicular gas plan.	Art. 468-1 CTC	84.09.91.91.00
50	Reduced rate (goods)	Repuestos para kits del plan de gas vehicular.	Art. 468-1 CTC	84.09.91.99.00
51	Reduced rate (goods)	Spare parts for kits of the vehicular gas plan.	Art. 468-1 CTC	84.14.80.22.00
52	Reduced rate (goods)	Compressor parts (spare parts) components of the vehicular gas plan.	Art. 468-1 CTC	84.14.90.10.00
53	Reduced rate (goods)	Dryers for agricultural products	Art. 468-1 CTC	84.19.31.00.00

ID	Type	Tax Expenditure	Legal Reference (Law/Identifier/Date)	
54	Reduced rate (goods)	Heat exchangers; pasteurizers	Art. 468-1 CTC	84.19.50.10.00
55	Reduced rate (goods)	Sprayers for agricultural use	Art. 468-1 CTC	84.24.82.90.00
56	Reduced rate (goods)	Front loader	Art. 468-1 CTC	84.29.51.00.00
57	Reduced rate (goods)	Agricultural, horticultural or forestry machinery for soil preparation or cultivation; lawn or sports-ground rollers	Art. 468-1 CTC	84.32
58	Reduced rate (goods)	Milking machines and dairy machinery	Art. 468-1 CTC	84.34
59	Reduced rate (goods)	Poultry incubators and brooders	Art. 468-1 CTC	84.36.21.00.00

ID	Type	Tax Expenditure	Legal Reference (Law/Identifier/Date)	
60	Reduced rate (goods)	Other machines and apparatus for poultry farming.	Art. 468-1 CTC	84.36.29
61	Reduced rate (goods)	Parts of machines or apparatus for poultry farming.	Art. 468-1 CTC	84.36.91.00.00
62	Reduced rate (goods)	Ace dehuller and coffee pulper	Art. 468-1 CTC	84.38.80.10.00
63	Reduced rate (goods)	Electric motors and generators (excluding generating sets).	Art. 468-1 CTC	85.01
64	Reduced rate (goods)	Electric accumulators, including separators therefor, whether or not rectangular (including square).	Art. 468-1 CTC	85.07
65	Reduced rate (goods)	Battery chargers for electric vehicles, hybrids and plug-in hybrids, electric motorcycles and electric bicycles, including those that are included in the vehicles, those of fast charging (electrolineras) and those of home recharging.	Art. 468-1 CTC	85.04

ID	Type	Tax Expenditure	Legal Reference (Law/Identifier/Date)	
66	Reduced rate (goods)	Electric charge inverters for use in electric, hybrid and plug-in hybrid vehicles.	Art. 468-1 CTC	85.04
67	Reduced rate (goods)	Electric, hybrid and plug-in hybrid vehicles for the transport of 10 or more people, including the driver.	Art. 468-1 CTC	87.02
68	Reduced rate (goods)	Electric, hybrid and plug-in hybrid vehicles designed primarily for the transport of people (except heading 87.02), including family-type vehicles ("break" or station wagon) and racing vehicles.	Art. 468-1 CTC	87.03
69	Reduced rate (goods)	Electric, hybrid and plug-in hybrid motor vehicles for the transport of goods.	Art. 468-1 CTC	87.04
70	Reduced rate (goods)	Electric, hybrid and plug-in hybrid motor vehicles for special uses except those designed mainly for the transport of people or goods.	Art. 468-1 CTC	87.05
71	Reduced rate (goods)	Chassis of electric motor vehicles of headings 87.02 and 87.03, only for public transport.	Art. 468-1 CTC	87.06

ID	Type	Tax Expenditure	Legal Reference (Law/Identifier/Date)	
72	Reduced rate (goods)	Bodies of electric motor vehicles of headings 87.02 and 87.03, including cabins, only for public transport.	Art. 468-1 CTC	87.07
73	Reduced rate (goods)	Electric motorcycles whose value exceeds 50 UVT (USD 270 approx.)	Art. 468-1 CTC	87.11
74	Reduced rate (goods)	Bicycles and Electric bicycles (including delivery tricycles) whose value exceeds 50 UVT.	Art. 468-1 CTC	87.12
75	Reduced rate (goods)	Ferries, freighters, barges and similar boats for the transport of people or goods.	Art. 468-1 CTC	89.01
76	Reduced rate (goods)	Tugs and pusher craft.	Art. 468-1 CTC	89.04
77	Reduced rate (goods)	Other vessels, including warships and lifeboats other than rowing boats.	Art. 468-1 CTC	89.06.90

ID	Type	Tax Expenditure	Legal Reference (Law/Identifier/Date)	
78	Reduced rate (goods)	Parts and accessories dispensers (spare parts), components of the vehicle gas plan.	Art. 468-1 CTC	90.25.90.00.00
79	Reduced rate (goods)	Control units for electric motors for use in electric, hybrid and plug-in hybrid vehicles	Art. 468-1 CTC	90.31
80	Reduced rate (goods)	Battery cooling and battery control units for use in electric, hybrid and plug-in hybrid vehicles.	Art. 468-1 CTC	90.32
81	Reduced rate (goods)	Gasoline and diesel	Art. 468-1 CTC	
1	Reduced rate (services)	The storage of agricultural products in general warehouses of deposit and the commissions directly related to negotiations of products of agricultural origin that are carried out through legally constituted bags of agricultural products	Art. 468-3 CTC	
2	Reduced rate (services)	Agricultural insurance	Art. 468-3 CTC	

ID	Type	Tax Expenditure	Legal Reference (Law/Identifier/Date)	
3	Reduced rate (services)	Prepaid and complementary medicine plans, surgery and hospitalization insurance policies, health services insurance policies and, in general, additional plans, in accordance with current regulations	Art. 468-3 CTC	
4	Reduced rate (services)	The surveillance, supervision, janitorial, cleaning and temporary employment services, provided by legal entities, as long as the aforementioned services are provided by people with physical or mental disabilities in degrees that allow adequate performance of the assigned tasks,	Art. 468-3 CTC	
5	Reduced rate (services)	Passenger air tickets, related services and the administrative fee associated with their marketing.	Art. 468-3 CTC	
1	Temporary (Exclusion)	Artisan crafts	Law 2068 of 2021	Temporary - 2021
2	Temporary (Exclusion)	Restaurants under franchise agreements	Law 2068 of 2021	Temporary - 2021
3	Temporary (Exclusion)	Import of goods subject to postal traffic under USD200	Law 2155 of 2021	Permanent

ID	Type	Tax Expenditure	Legal Reference (Law/Identifier/Date)	
1	Temporary (Exemption)	Importation and sale of supplies indispensable for the prevention and the provision of the medical services against COVID-19	Decree 438 of 2020, Decree 551 of 2021	Temporary - 2020 and 2021
2	Temporary (Exemption)	Hotel and tourism services	Law 2068 of 2021	Temporary - 2021
3	Temporary (Exemption)	VAT free days (clothing, appliances, toys, sports items, school supplies, goods and supplies destined to the agricultural sector)	Law 2155 of 2021	3 days in a year
4	Temporary (Exemption)	Mobile phone plans (voice calls and Internet) up to two UVTs during 4 months	Decree 540 of 2020	
5	Temporary (Exemption)	Import of cars for the transport of passengers or cargo	Decree 789 of 2020	until 31 December 2021
1	Temporary (Reduced rate)	Flight tickets		until December 2022

ID	Type	Tax Expenditure	Legal Reference (Law/Identifier/Date)	
2	Temporary (Reduced rate)	National air fuel Jet A1 and/or air fuel 100/130		
1	Temporary (Refund)	VAT paid by some sports organizations during some athletic events in 2021 and 2022	Law 2154 of 2021	2021 and 2022

Printed by Libri Plureos GmbH in Hamburg,
Germany

9 789264 706712